Counseling on Sexual Issues

A Handbook for Pastors and Other Helping Professionals

Andrew J. Weaver, John D. Preston, and Charlene A. Hosenfeld

THE
PILGRIM
PRESS
Cleveland

To my brother in Christ, David K. Switzer
— AJW

To the Ohana Family
— JDP

To my parents,
Lucille Livingston Hosenfeld and Charles I. Hosenfeld,
with love and gratitude
— CAH

The Pilgrim Press
700 Prospect Avenue
Cleveland, Ohio 44115-1100
thepilgrimpress.com

© 2005 by The Pilgrim Press

All rights reserved. Published 2005

Printed in the United States of America on acid-free paper

09 08 07 06 05   5 4 3 2 1

Library of Congress Cataloging-in-Publication Data
Weaver, Andrew J., 1947-
    Counseling on sexual issues : a handbook for pastors and other helping
professionals / Andrew J. Weaver, John D. Preston, and Charlene A. Hosenfeld.
        p.   cm.
    Includes index.
    ISBN 0-8298-1618-6 (pbk. : alk. paper)
    1. Sex counseling–Handbooks, manuals, etc. 2. Pastoral counseling–Handbooks,
manuals, etc. I. Preston, John, 1950- II. Hosenfeld, Charlene A., 1950- III. Title.
HQ60.5.W42 2005
253.5–dc22   2005053468

Contents

Contents

Part Three
SUMMARY

Foreword

Once again, Andrew Weaver and his colleagues have managed to produce what some scholars in the past have called the most difficult of projects, that of "intelligent vulgarization" — that is, converting or translating often complicated and even esoteric research or scholarly discourse into readable and useful information for the practitioner. That sort of endeavor is in itself a rather extraordinary activity, but in this instance it takes on an additional dimension of wonderment in that it is done on a topic of singular complexity and controversy: human sexuality.

Nor is this difficult topic oversimplified via journalistic generalizations that we often find in the popular media. Indeed, the authors support their very readable prose with comprehensive, relevant, and accessible references from a wide range of professional and academic journals in such fields as psychology, medicine, sociology, sexology, psychotherapy, etc. In other words, the *critical* reader — if he or she is so inclined — may take additional steps in the attempt to understand such topics as masturbation, infidelity, sexual abuse, sexual sadism, voyeurism, rape, homosexuality, pornography, pedophilia, genital herpes, erectile dysfunction, sexual harassment, abortion, etc.

Equally helpful are the realistic case studies used to illustrate the many sexual topics addressed — many of them demonstrating how a multitude of clinical knowledge gleaned from such fields as pastoral care, psychiatry, gerontology, medicine, and marriage and family therapy can truly assist the pastor in appreciating the massive implications of sexual experiences and behaviors as they are manifested in faith communities and beyond.

As research has demonstrated repeatedly, religious professionals — pastors, priests, rabbis, religious sisters, imams, clergy of all faiths and persuasions — have been, and remain, a first-line mental health resource in the United States. Recognizing this reality, the authors are eager to present solid information so that the religious professional can make enlightened decisions regarding referral or intervention. This is not, however, a manual that assumes that the only, or even the major, function of the religious professional in a congregational setting is that of being a referral agent feeding cases to mental health professionals (as important as that function is!), but, rather, that there are many instances when the religious professional, properly educated, trained, and willing, can be the primary person to "treat" the person who is experiencing a sexual problem. Better still, the authors detail specific ways in which an enlightened faith community can and ought to be a proper and effective milieu for the resolution of a variety of sexual issues.

What perhaps troubles me regarding the manual is that (1) it will not find its way into the hands of pastors and other religious professionals serving in a community setting but instead will end up on the shelves of specialists in pastoral counseling/psychotherapy, or that (2), if it does find its way into congregational life, too many clergy simply do not believe that their ministry can contribute to the delivery of competent, sensitive, effective treatment of many of the problems identified in this book. My own bias is the recognition of the great potential of faith communities as a bona fide healing milieu in the area of mental health must begin to be formed in seminary — to make the discipline of pastoral care equally essential and crucial in the preparation of religious professionals as are the fields of systematic theology, scripture studies, and homiletics.

This volume can contribute to creating that level of consciousness in the postmodern seminarian, at the same time serving as well as a quite useable manual for those pastors, priests, rabbis, imams, and other religious professionals who already believe that they can significantly contribute directly to the resolution of many of the mental health issues plaguing our world, including those designated as "sexual" in nature.

— ORLO C. STRUNK JR., PH.D.

Professor Emeritus of the Psychology of Religion
and Pastoral Psychology, Boston University;
Chair of the Editorial Committee and Managing Editor,
The Journal of Pastoral Care and Counseling;
Adjunct Professor (Counseling), Webster University

Acknowledgments

We are grateful to the Reverend Carolyn L. Stapleton for her exceptional editing and research skills, which added immeasurably to the quality and usefulness of the text. Thanks to Adrienne L. Strock and Michelle Housh for their help in preparing and editing the manuscript.

Let him kiss me with the kisses of his mouth!
For your love is better than wine,
your anointing oils are fragrant,
your name is perfume poured out;
therefore the maidens love you.
Draw me after you, let us make haste.

—Song of Solomon 1:1–4 NRSV

How to Use This Book

Counseling on Sexual Issues: A Handbook for Pastors and Other Helping Professionals is designed to be a text for those in training for pastoral ministry, as well as being a practical resource for women and men already serving in ministry. The volume addresses a variety of sexual and related issues (such as adult survivors of child sexual abuse, erectile dysfunction, genital herpes, HIV/AIDS, sexuality and illness, infertility, pedophilia, pornography, and sexual orientation) and the mental health difficulties that may be experienced as a result. Responding to individuals who have sexual concerns is among the most difficult and complex of situations that pastors face. Clergy need accurate and practical information on sexual matters that concern those who come to them seeking pastoral counsel. This volume furnishes such data.

Part 1 explains the vital role that clergy and the faith community serve in the care of persons who are struggling with sexual issues and related problems. This section spells out the need for special expertise by pastors and other religious professionals to recognize and address sexual concerns. The scientific evidence that nonpunitive, nurturing religious beliefs and practices serve a healing function for those struggling with emotional difficulties that may be related to these issues is presented.

The heart of the book is the case studies found in part 2, which use real-life situations and highlight practical implications for pastors working with those seeking counsel. The format incorporates relevant research and identifies the needs of persons faced with concerns related to human sexuality. The case studies are multidisciplinary in approach, integrating clinical knowledge in pastoral care, psychology, sexology, nursing, psychiatry, gerontology, sociology, medicine, social work, and marriage and family therapy, along with current scientific findings on the role of religion in mental and physical health. The volume recognizes that the difficulties which individuals and families face related to sexual issues do not stand in isolation from one another but are interrelated. For example, the chapter on adult survivors of child abuse also addresses psychological trauma, dissociation, shame, and depression.

The book is designed so that a reader can easily locate information on specific issues related to human sexuality for which individuals and families seek help. It is a practical, easy-to-use guide on how to assess problems and respond to them.

Each case provides an example of a person who has struggled with a specific concern and is in need of help. Included in each chapter is information about how a religious professional would assess the problem, what aspects of the situation are most important, how to identify the major issues, specific directions about what a pastor and congregation can do, when to refer for assistance from other professionals, and additional resources that can provide help. National organizations (often with toll-free numbers and Internet addresses) that supply information and support for individuals and families with these concerns are identified for each topic addressed. Cross-cultural aspects are discussed as well.

Part 3 of the book has a section on how and when to make a referral. Technical terms are defined in the glossary at the end of the volume, and there is a brief summary and conclusion.

The text is written for people of all faiths, with an appreciation for the richness of the intergenerational and multicultural diversity found in religious communities. The authors are people of faith with specialties in mental health.

Dr. Weaver is a clinical psychologist and ordained United Methodist minister who has served rural and urban parishes. He is the associate publisher of *Zion's Herald,* based in New York City. He has written over 140 scientific articles and book chapters and has coauthored 12 books. Dr. Preston is professor of psychology at Alliant International University in Sacramento, California, and an active layman in the United Methodist Church. He has written over 45 scientific articles and book chapters and has authored or coauthored 16 books. Dr. Hosenfeld is a Presbyterian laywoman who works as a staff psychologist at Hawaii State Hospital and has a private practice in Honolulu in which she has worked extensively with patients who have sexual and related issues.

PART ONE

Introduction

Clergy, Faith, and Sexual Issues

Religious community is important to a significant portion of the U.S. population. There are nearly 500,000 churches, temples, and mosques across the country with a presence in virtually every locale (Bradley et al., 1990). About 4 of 10 Americans attend a place of worship at least once a week, and approximately 6 of 10 do so at least once a month. Nearly 9 of 10 Americans say that they pray at least occasionally (Gallup and Lindsay, 1999). These behaviors and rates of religious involvement have remained fairly constant in the U.S. for the past 70 years (Gallup and Lindsay, 1999).

Given the prevalence of religion, it should not be surprising that clergy are front-line mental health counselors for millions of Americans (Weaver et al., 2002). The 353,000 Christian and Jewish clergy (4,000 rabbis, 49,000 Catholic priests, and 300,000 Protestant ministers, according to the U.S. Department of Labor, 1998) are among the most trusted professionals in society (Gallup and Lindsay, 1999). The U.S. Surgeon General's recent *Report on Mental Health* found that each year one of six adults and one of five children obtain mental health services from either a health care provider, a clergyperson, a social services agency, or a school (Satcher, 2000).

Of the many matters presented to clergy by persons seeking counseling, research shows that family and marital issues are the most common. Sixteen separate studies, conducted between 1979 and 2001, found that those seeking pastoral counsel predominantly bring concerns related to marriage and the family (Weaver, Koenig, and Larson, 1997), such as infidelity, sexual abuse, difficulties related to infertility, and sexual problems between marital partners (Francis et al., 2000; O'Kane and Millar, 2001; Wood, 1996). Researchers found that 85 percent of parish-based clergy indicate that family issues are the most frequent and difficult matters that they encounter (Wasman, Corradi, and Clemens, 1979). In a survey of 405 pastors in 10 geographical regions of the United States, Benner (1992) found that 84 percent of the clergy reported marriage and divorce as the most commonly presented problem categories. Frequent church attendees in the Midwestern United States are seven times more likely to seek clergy for help with marriage and family problems (86 percent) than to seek assistance from secular mental health specialists (12.5 percent), according to Privette and colleagues (1994).

Americans Are Sexually Active

A large study of the sexual behavior of men aged 20–39 showed that most American males are sexually active (Billy et al., 1993). The National Survey of Men revealed that 95 percent have had vaginal intercourse and 23 percent have had 20 or more vaginal sex partners in their lifetime. About one-fifth of never-married and formerly married males had had four or more partners over a recent 18-month period. Conservative Protestants had had the fewest number of vaginal sex partners in their lifetime, and men in the "no religion" category had had the most partners. In general, males who were not members of an organized faith, particularly a conservative one, tended to engage in riskier sexual practices. These findings are consistent with the understanding that membership in some social groups instills quite particular values about sexual behavior and may prohibit engaging in a variety of sexual practices.

Most American women report having a satisfactory sex life. A questionnaire was administered to 3,289 females, aged 18–73 years (Rosen et al., 1993). The majority of the sample (73.5 percent) was found to be sexually active, and 84.1 percent were married or involved in a committed relationship. A range of sexual behavior frequencies were found — 48.5 percent reported at least weekly vaginal intercourse, compared to 28.4 percent who were not having vaginal intercourse at the time of the study. Among the sexually active respondents, 49.6 percent reported having as much sexual activity with their partners as they wished, while 41.1 percent reported less than they wanted, and 9.2 percent reported more than desired. Most of the sample (68.6 percent) rated their overall sexual relationship as satisfactory. Age and relationship status were significant predictors of satisfaction, with older women and singles reporting a higher incidence of sexual problems.

People with Sexual Issues Seek Clergy Counsel

Although not the most frequent of marital problems presented to religious leaders, many individuals and couples do seek guidance for sexual issues. Twenty-one separate studies over two decades in diverse populations have found that clergy report being asked for counsel on such matters as sexual abuse, infidelity, sexual problems between marital partners, pornography, sex offenses, sex education, masturbation, sexually transmitted diseases, sexual identity (Abramczyk, 1981; Coyne-Beasley and Schoenbach, 2000; Francis et al., 2000; Ingram and Lowe, 1989; Lowe, 1986; Mannon and Crawford, 1996; O'Kane and Millar, 2001; Virkler, 1979; Wood, 1996; Wylie, 1984). Not surprisingly, pastors indicate that they feel less confident and prepared to address sexual issues in comparison to other types of problems about which they are consulted (Mannon and Crawford, 1996; Wylie, 1984; Virkler, 1979). Responding to individuals who have sexual concerns is one of the most difficult circumstances that clergy face today. The intensity of feelings, including a pastor's own, can make it hard to provide the guidance about sexuality that is sought. Clergy need solid, practical information on subjects that concern the people who come to them seeking pastoral counsel.

Unfortunately, research has found that there is inadequate sex education in most seminaries, despite the requests of students for more course offerings in the area (Conklin, 1997). Theological students today are older and more diverse in ethnicity, gender, and attitudes about sexuality than were prior generations. Interviews of 39 faculty teaching sex education in 25 accredited Protestant, Catholic, and Jewish seminaries indicated that the general perception was that sex education courses in theological schools lack the support needed to legitimize them as a necessary part of pastoral training. The researcher concluded that "sexual education should be structured around pastoral issues and grounded in ministry experience" (Conklin, 1997, p. 167). That is the fundamental premise of this book.

Fifty to 60 percent of Christian and Jewish clergy state that they want additional postseminary training on sexual topics (Ingram and Lowe, 1989; Lowe, 1986; Wylie, 1984). When pastors have been offered education on sexual and related issues, they have reported that it was helpful. African American clergy who received HIV/AIDS training indicated that they were more comfortable counseling persons with AIDS and much more active in educating their congregations on the subject than they were prior to the training (Crawford et al., 1992).

Faith Communities and Sexual Education

Although faith communities report they are open to and supportive of offering sex education for their young people (Kennedy and Whitlock,

1997), few actually do so. In a study of 637 African American churches in the northern United States, 4 percent (27 of 637) had programs addressing human sexuality and teen pregnancy, but only 1 percent addressed AIDS or other health-related issues (Rubin et al., 1994). In a promising survey of 34 African American clergypersons in North Carolina representing seven Christian traditions, the pastors ranked HIV/AIDS and sexuality transmitted disease (STD) education and sexual behavior among their greatest concerns and highest priorities for educating their youth (Coyne-Beasley and Schoenbach, 2000). About three-fourths of the clergy had talked about AIDS or drug and alcohol abuse prevention with adolescents in their churches, and they wanted additional training on sex education.

More than one million U.S. teenagers become pregnant each year, with eight of ten of these pregnancies being unintended (PPFA, 1993). The problem of unplanned adolescent pregnancy has resulted in a variety of prevention programs, some of which have been developed with the collaboration of faith communities. In an Illinois project involving teens and parents from nine churches, it was found that congregations could play an important and cost-effective role in sex education in the community (Isberner and Wright, 1988). The four-session team-taught course involved health educators, counselors, nurses, pastors, teachers, and parents. The program covered communication skills, personal responsibility, the Christian view of love and marriage, reproductive anatomy, contraception, and STD prevention. The course evaluation showed that the church members strongly agreed that religious communities can have an important role in helping parents enhance teens' responsible behavior and provide sex education and moral guidance.

Many People Have Sexual and Related Issues

The following five examples show the breadth and diversity of sex-related issues that millions of people bring to clergy and other professionals who work within faith communities.

Sexually Transmitted Diseases

STDs, including AIDS, are a particularly serious risk for sexually active teens and young adults. In the past twenty years, the prevalence and severity of STDs has increased steadily among American youth. Every hour someone under the age of 20 is infected with HIV (Griffin, 1996). Other STDs that sexually active teens are at risk of contracting include: chlamydia, trichomoniasis, human papilloma virus, genital herpes, hepatitis B and C, gonorrhea, and syphilis. It is estimated that

25 percent of adolescents will contract an STD by the time they grad-
uate from high school (Scott, 1996). Such statistics indicate that clergy
are likely to have youth and their families seek them for help related
to STDs, including AIDS. In the case of AIDS, pastors are called upon
to assist people who often have profound psychological distress from
dealing with chronic and deteriorating illness. Researchers have found
that a combination of spiritual practices and mental health treatment
increases the coping ability of persons who are living with HIV/AIDS
(Somlai et al., 1996).

Premature Sexual Behavior

Slightly more than half of American females and nearly two-thirds of
males have had intercourse by age 18 (Moore et al., 1996). A number
of negative consequences are related to teenage sexual activity and adolescent pregnancy. Early teen intercourse is statistically associated with
subsequently large numbers of and older sexual partners (Koyle et al.,
1989). Adolescents who are sexually active are more likely to be involved in delinquent behavior and the use of drugs and alcohol (Elliott
and Morse, 1989). Teenage parents are more likely than nonparents to
drop out of school, creating long-term educational and economic disad-
vantages for themselves. And a large number of adolescent pregnancies
end in abortion, which may lead to serious psychological consequences,
especially for young teens (White and DeBlassie, 1992).

Research has consistently shown the constraining effects of religious involvement on premature sexual behavior among adolescents
and young adults (Pluhar et al., 1998; Resnick et al., 1997). Lower
rates of intercourse, fewer sexual partners, and negative attitudes toward premarital sexual activity have been found in teens who regularly
attend church and believe religion is important in their lives than among
those who do not (Holder et al., 2000). It has been estimated that adolescents involved in religious communities may be 50 percent less likely
to engage in sexual intercourse than their nonreligious peers (Spilka et
al., 1985).

Sexual Assault

In the United States, sexual assault is the most rapidly growing violent
crime. There were 261,000 victims of rape, attempted rape, or sexual assault in the year 2000 alone (Rape, Abuse, and Incest National
Network, 2002). The National Women's Study (Resnick et al., 1993)
estimated that 12.1 million (12.7 percent) of adult American females
have experienced a completed rape at some point in their lives. Researchers found that very large numbers of women suffer from severe

emotional trauma in the aftermath of rape (Rothbaum et al., 1992). One of five persons who are victimized in a violent crime (such as rape, attempted rape, robbery, aggravated assault, simple assault) seeks the counsel of a clergyperson (Norris et al., 1990). This is the same number seeking help from all other mental health professionals or medical doctors combined (Norris et al., 1990). Unfortunately, many pastors appear to be unprepared to counsel females who have been sexually assaulted (Sheldon and Parent, 2002).

According to recent research at Boston University's School of Public Health, active faith can be an important element in healing and recovery. Using a national sample of 3,543 women victims, scientists found that frequent worship service attendance was a source of strength and comfort for rape survivors — buffering the negative impact of sexual assault on their mental health (Chang et al., 2001). In a study of predominately inner-city, ethnic minority females who had been sexually assaulted in the previous 9 to 24 months, it was found that religious activities were strongly associated with well-being. Increased spiritual involvement can help restore a sense of well-being in traumatized women (Kennedy et al., 1998).

Sexual Dysfunction

A common health concern is sexual dysfunction (APA, 2000), along with the emotional problems that accompany it, such as depression and anxiety. These dysfunctions are marked by disturbances in sexual desire, as well as psychological and physical changes associated with the sexual response cycle. The difficulties can include: lack of desire for sex, arousal problems (such as erectile difficulties in men, lack of lubrication in women), inability to achieve climax or ejaculation, anxiety about sexual performance, climaxing or ejaculating too rapidly, physical pain during intercourse, and not finding sex pleasurable (Laumann et al., 1999).

Sexual dysfunction is higher for women (43 percent) than men (31 percent) and is related to age. It is more likely among persons with poor physical and emotional health, and it is strongly associated with negative experiences in sexual relationships and lack of overall well-being. Research has found that victims of unwanted sexual contact exhibit long-term negative changes in sexual functioning (Laumann et al., 1999). Pastors who counsel couples need to be able to recognize the psychological effect that sexual dysfunction can have on marital relationships.

Infertility

Infertility is generally defined as the failure to conceive after one year of intercourse with no use of birth control. Estimates for infertility vary from 6.1 million American women and their partners — 10 percent of the reproductive age population (American Society for Reproductive Medicine, 1998) — to one in every 6 couples (Morrow et al., 1995). Infertility has been described as a "traumatic crisis" which has a "demoralizing effect" on individuals and couples (Whiteford and Gonzalez, 1995) that can result in psychological, marital, and sexual dysfunction.

Female infertility generally results from hormonal problems causing such conditions as irregular ovulation and structural problems (Gutman, 1985). In addition to other responses to the diagnosis, the stigma often attached to infertility can cause women to feel defective.

Male infertility generally results from problems with sperm production, maturation, motility, or a combination of these. Men can react to infertility in a variety of negative ways, such as feeling personally or sexually inadequate, depressed, hostile, or guilty. Males may also experience sexual dysfunction or relationship conflicts (Irvine and Cawood, 1996), as well as self-blame or coping through avoidance (Morrow et al., 1995). Clergy who counsel infertile couples must be able to recognize and address the psychological effect that infertility has on individuals and couples.

Sexual Misconduct Among Clergy

Sexual misconduct by clergy has become a national concern. In a study of Southern Baptist senior pastors working in six southeastern states, researchers found that high levels of stress were strongly associated with sexual misconduct with adult members of the congregation (Seat et al., 1993). Ministers with several sources of chronic stress were at the greatest risk. For example, clergy in the midst of personal crises (such as painful marriages or other emotional difficulties) are particularly vulnerable, especially if they are unable to reach out for counseling (Thoburn and Balswick, 1994; Francis and Turner, 1995). In addition, those with less confidence in their ability as counselors were more likely to engage in sexual misconduct than those with more confidence. Unfortunately, a full 80 percent of the ministers had been given no written guidelines aimed at preventing sexual misconduct (Seat et al., 1993).

The study of Southern Baptist pastors found that 5.8 percent indicated that they had engaged in sexual contact with a person currently affiliated with their congregation (Seat et al., 1993), which is slightly lower than the 6.5 percent found in a nationwide study of psychiatrists (Gartrell et al., 1987). Based on a 5.8 percent misconduct rate and the U.S. Department of Labor's 1998 figure of 353,000 clergypersons in this country, it could be extrapolated that more than 20,000 clergy have had sexual contact with at least one adult in their congregation. These rates are reinforced by a survey of psychologists which found that among therapists treating victims of sexual misconduct by prior counselors or therapists, clergy accounted for 11 percent of the cases in Wisconsin and 17 percent of the cases in Rhode Island (Wincze et al., 1996).

Given the harm caused to the religious community by the sexual misconduct of pastors, sexual ethics training, like that offered mental health professionals (Housman, 1999; Wiederman, 1999), should be given high priority in seminary and postseminary continuing education. Sexual ethics training is addressed in this volume.

Women Clergy and Counseling on Sexual Issues

According to United States Bureau of Labor statistics for 2000, the number of female clergy was 50,922, a significant increase from 16,408 in 1983 (Lyons, 2002). The fact that one in seven ordained persons in the U.S. is a woman is changing and expanding the range of problems presented to and addressed by clergy. As more females take pastoral leadership in religious communities, women in congregations are bringing increasing numbers of personal problems such as sexual issues to these female pastors (Wood, 1996). Sixty-three percent of Evangelical Lutheran clergywomen more frequently counsel females than males, and many of the problems brought are sexual issues, including adultery, sexual abuse, incest, sexual orientation, pornography, sex offenses, and unplanned and unwanted pregnancy (Wood, 1996).

Marked increases in the numbers of women as both clergy and mental health professionals offer new opportunities for these two groups, in which females were historically underrepresented, to work together. One-third of the 68,875 seminary students in Canada and the United States are now women, increasing from just 10 percent in 1972 (Bedell, 2000). At the same time, 61 percent of the members of the American Psychological Association are female (APA, 1995). Collaboration and training between women mental health professionals and clergy offer many opportunities for dealing with important issues that particularly affect females.

Summary

This book addresses a number of sexual issues of concern to clergy and to those who come to them for guidance. These are problems that religious professionals and pastors are called upon to respond to within churches and communities, often with inadequate information. Given the intensity of public debate over sexual issues, one can assume that there will be an increasing number of public and private occasions in which ministers, priests, rabbis, imams, and other religious professionals will have opportunities to offer knowledgeable and sensitive help. The need is real for clergy and other religious professionals to learn how to competently recognize sexual issues, identify when to make referrals to mental health clinicians, help persons find available community resources, and train members of their faith communities to provide emotional support to affected individuals and families.

References

Abramczyk, L. W. (1981). The counseling function of pastors: A study in practice and preparation. *Journal of Psychology and Theology*, 9, 257–265.

American Psychiatric Association. (2000). *Diagnostic and Statistical Manual of Mental Disorders* (4th ed. text revision). Washington, DC: American Psychiatric Association.

American Psychiatric Association. (1995). *Women in the American Psychological Association*. Washington, DC: American Psychological Association.

American Society for Reproductive Medicine. (1998). *Fact sheet: Infertility*. Retrieved November 26, 2002, from *www.americaninfertility.org/asrm/infertility.html*.

Bedell, K. B. (2000). *Yearbook of American and Canadian Churches*. Nashville: Abingdon Press.

Benner, D. G. (1992). *Strategic Pastoral Counseling: A Short-term Structure Model*. Grand Rapids, MI: Baker.

Billy, J. O. G., Tanfer, K., Grady, W. R., and Klepinger, D. H. (1993). The sexual behavior of men in the United States. *Family Planning Perspectives*, 25(2), 52–60.

Blue Cross and Blue Shield of Massachusetts. (2002). *Healthy me*. Retrieved December 10, 2002, from *www.ahealthyme.com*.

Bradley, M. B., Green, N. M., Jones, D. E., Lynn, M., and McNeil, L. (1990). *Churches and Church Membership in the United States, 1990*. Atlanta: Glenmary Research Center.

Chang, B. H., Skinner, K. M., and Boehmer, U. (2001). Religion and mental health among women veterans with sexual assault experience. *International Journal of Psychiatry in Medicine*, 31(1), 77–95.

Conklin, S. C. (1997). Sexuality education in seminaries and theological schools: Perceptions of faculty advocates regarding curriculum and approaches. *Journal of Psychology and Human Sexuality*, 9(3–4), 143–174.

Coyne-Beasley, T., and Schoenbach, V. J. (2000). The African-American church: A potential forum for adolescent comprehensive sexuality education. *Journal of Adolescent Health*, 26(4), 289–294.

Crawford, I., Allison, K. W., Robinson, W. L., Hughes, D., and Samaryk, M. (1992). Attitudes of African-American Baptist ministers towards AIDS. *Journal of Community Psychology*, 20(4), 304–308.

Elliott, D. S., and Morse, B. J. (1989). Delinquency and drug use as risk factors in teenage sexual activity. *Youth and Society*, 21(1), 32–57.

Francis, L. J., Robbins, M., and Kay, W. K. (2000). *Pastoral Care Today*. Farnham, Surrey: Waverly Abbey House.

Francis, P. C., and Turner, N. R. (1995). Sexual misconduct within the Christian church: Who are the perpetrators and those they victimize? *Counseling and Values*, 39, 218–227.

Gallup, G. H., and Lindsay, D. M. (1999). *Surveying the Religious Landscape: Trends in U.S. Beliefs*. Harrisburg, PA: Morehouse Publishing.

Gartrell, N., Herman, J., Olarte, S., Feldstein, M., and Localio, R. (1987). Reporting practices of psychiatrists who knew of sexual misconduct by colleagues. *American Journal of Orthopsychiatry*, 57(2), 287–295.

Griffin, C. B. (1996). "Living Health," *Blue Cross and Blue Shield of Massachusetts*, 3, 3.

Gutman, M. (1985). Fertility management: Infertility, delayed childbearing, and voluntary childlessness. In D. C. Goldberg (ed.), *Contemporary Marriage: Special Issues in Couples Therapy* (pp. 120–165). Homewood, IL: Dorsey.

Holder, D. W, Durant, R. H., Harris, T. L., Daniel, J. H., Obeidallah, D., and Goodman, E. (2000). The association between adolescent spirituality and voluntary sexual activity. *Society for Adolescent Medicine*, 26, 295–302.

Housman, L. M. (1999). The current state of sexual ethics training in clinical psychology: Issues of quantity, quality, and effectiveness. *Professional Psychology: Research and Practice*, 30(3), 302–311.

Ingram, B. L., and Lowe, D. (1989). Counseling activities and referral practices of rabbis. *Journal of Psychology and Judaism,* 13, 133–148.

Irvine, S., and Cawood, E. (1996). Male infertility and its effect on male sexuality. *Sexual and Marital Therapy,* 11(3), 280–283.

Isberner, F. R., and Wright, W. R. (1988). Sex education in Illinois churches: The octopus program. *Journal of Sex Education and Therapy,* 14(2), 29–33.

Kennedy, J. E., Davis, R. C., and Taylor, B. G. (1998). Changes in spirituality and well-being among victims of sexual assault. *Journal for the Scientific Study of Religion,* 37, 322–328.

Kennedy, P., and Whitlock, M. L. (1997). Therapeutic implications of conservative clergy views on sexuality: An empirical analysis. *Journal of Sex and Marital Therapy,* 23(2), 140–153.

Koyle, P., Jensen, L., Olsen, J., and Cundick, B. (1989). Comparison of sexual behaviors among adolescents having an early, middle and late first intercourse experience. *Youth and Society,* 20(4), 461–475.

Laumann, E. O., Paik, A., and Rosen, R. C. (1999). Sexual dysfunction in the United States: Prevalence and predictors. *American Medical Association,* 281(6), 537–544.

Lindner, E. W. (ed.). (2003). *Yearbook of American and Canadian Churches 2003.* Nashville: Abingdon Press.

Lowe, D. W. (1986). Counseling activities, and referral practices of ministers. *Journal of Psychology and Christianity,* 5, 22–29.

Lyons, L. (2002, May). *Church reform: Women in the clergy.* Gallup Tuesday Briefing, The Gallup Organization. Retrieved November 5, 2002, from *www.gallup.com/content/default.asp?ci=5950&pg=1.*

Mannon, J. D., and Crawford, R. L. (1996). Clergy confidence to counsel and their willingness to refer to mental health professionals. *Family Therapy,* 23(3), 213–231.

Moore, K. A., Miler, B. C., Sugland, B. W., Morrison, R. R., Glei, D. A., and Blumenthal, C. (1996). *Beginning too soon: Adolescent sexual behavior, pregnancy and parenthood.* Report prepared for the Office of the Assistant Secretary for Planning and Evaluation, U.S. Department of Health and Human Services.

Morrow, K. A., Thoreson, R. W., and Penney, L. L. (1995). Predictors of psychological distress among infertility clinic patients. *Journal of Consulting and Clinical Psychology,* 63(1), 163–167.

Norris, F. H., Kaniasty, K. Z., and Scheer, D. A. (1990). Use of mental health services among victims of crime: Frequency, correlates, and subsequent recovery. *Journal of Consulting and Clinical Psychology, 58*(5), 538–547.

O'Kane, S., and Millar, R. (2001). An investigation into the counseling-type work of Roman Catholic priests: A survey of one diocese in Northern Ireland. *British Journal of Guidance and Counseling, 29*(3), 323–335.

Planned Parenthood Federation of America. (1993). *Pregnancy and Childbearing among U.S. Teens.* New York: Planned Parenthood Federation of America.

Pluhar, E., Frongillo, E. A., Stycos, J. M., and Dempster-McClain, D. (1998). Understanding the relationship between religion and the sexual attitudes and behaviors of college students. *Journal of Sex Education and Therapy, 23,* 288–296.

Privette, G., Quackenbos, S., and Bundrick, C. M. (1994). Preferences for religious and nonreligious counseling and psychotherapy. *Psychological Reports, 75,* 539–546.

Rape, Abuse, and Incest National Network. (2002). *Facts about sexual assault.* Retrieved January 24, 2004, from *www.rainn.org/statistics .html*.

Resnick, H. R., Kilpatrick, D. G., Dansky, B. S., Saunders, B. E., and Best, C. B. (1993). Prevalence of civilian trauma and post-traumatic stress disorder in a representative national sample of women. *Journal of Consulting and Clinical Psychology, 61,* 984–991.

Resnick, M. D., Bearman, P. S., Blum, R. W., Bauman, K. E., Harris, K. M., Jones, J., Tabor, J., Beuhring, T., Sieving, R. E., Shew, M., Ireland, M., Bearinger, L. H., and Udry, J. R. (1997). Protecting adolescents from harm. *Journal of the American Medical Association, 278*(10), 823–832.

Rosen, R. C., Taylor, J. F., Leiblum, S. R., and Bachmann, G. A. (1993). Prevalence of sexual dysfunction in women: Results of a survey study of 329 women in an outpatient gynecological clinic. *Journal of Sex and Marital Therapy, 19*(3), 171–188.

Rothbaum, B. O., Foa, E. B., Riggs, D. S., Murdock, T., and Walsh, W. (1992). A prospective examination of post-traumatic stress disorder in rape victims. *Journal of Traumatic Stress, 5,* 455–475.

Rubin, R. H., Billingsley, A., and Caldwell, C. H. (1994). The role of the black church in working with black adolescents. *Adolescence, 29*(114), 251–266.

Satcher, D. (2000). Mental health: A report of the Surgeon General — executive summary. *Professional Psychology: Research and Practice*, 31(1), 13–15.

Scott, M. A. K. (1996). Reducing the risks: Adolescents and sexually transmitted diseases. *Nurse Practitioner Forum*, 7(1), 23–29.

Seat, J. T., Trent, J. T., and Kim, J. K. (1993). The prevalence and contributing factors of sexual misconduct among Southern Baptist pastors in six southern states. *Journal of Pastoral Care*, 47(4), 363–370.

Sheldon, J. P., and Parent, S. L. (2002). Clergy's attitudes and attributions of blame toward female rape victims. *Violence Against Women*, 8(2), 233–256.

Somlai, A. M., Kelly, J. A., Kalichman, S. C., Mulry, G., Sikkema, K. J., McAuliffe, T., Multhauf, K., and Davantes, B. (1996). An empirical investigation of the relationship between spirituality, coping and emotional distress in people living with HIV infection and AIDS. *Journal of Pastoral Care*, 50(2), 181–191.

Spilka, B., Hood, R. W., and Gorsuch, R. L. (1985). *The Psychology of Religion: An Empirical Approach*. Englewood Cliffs, NJ: Prentice-Hall.

Thoburn, J. W., and Balswick, J. O. (1994) An evaluation of infidelity among male Protestant clergy. *Journal of Pastoral Psychology*, 42(4), 285–294.

United States Department of Labor. (1998). *Occupational outlook handbook: United States Department of Labor*. Washington, DC: Bureau of Labor Statistics.

Virkler, H. A. (1979). Counseling demands, procedures, and preparation of parish ministers: A descriptive study. *Journal of Psychology and Theology*, 7, 271–280.

Wasman, M., Corradi, R. B., and Clemens, N.A. (1979). In-depth continuing education for clergy in mental health: Ten years of a large scale program. *Pastoral Psychology*, 27, 251–259.

Weaver, A. J., Koenig, H. G., and Larson, D. B. (1997). Marital and family therapists and the clergy: A need for clinical collaboration, training and research. *Journal of Marital and Family Therapy*, 23(1), 13–25.

Weaver, A. J., Revilla, L. A., and Koenig, H. G. (2002). *Counseling Families Across the Stages of Life: A Handbook for Pastors and Other Helping Professionals*. Nashville: Abingdon Press.

Weaver, A. J., Samford, J., Kline, A. E., Lucas, L. A., Larson, D. B., and Koenig, H. G. (1997). Clergy and psychologists working together?

A systematic analysis of research on clergy in eight major American Psychological Association journals: 1991–1994. *Professional Psychology: Research and Practice*, 28(5), 471–474.

Weinbender, M. L. M., and Rossignol, A. M. (1996). Lifestyle and risk of premature sexual activity in a high school population of Seventh-day Adventists: Valuegenesis. *Adolescence*, 31(122) 265–281.

White, S. D., and DeBlassie, R. (1992). Adolescent sexual behavior. *Adolescence*, 27(105), 183–191.

Whiteford, L. M., and Gonzalez, L. (1995). Stigma: The hidden burden of infertility. *Social Science and Medicine*, 40(1), 27–36.

Wiederman, M. W. (1999). Sexuality training for professional psychologists: A national survey of training directors of doctoral programs and predoctoral internships. *Professional Psychology: Research and Practice*, 30(3), 312–317.

Wincze, J. P., Richards, J., Parsons, J., and Bailey, S. (1996). A comparative survey of therapist sexual misconduct between an American state and an Australian state. *Professional Psychology: Research and Practice*, 27(3), 289–294.

Wood, N. S. (1996). An inquiry into pastoral counseling ministry done by women in the parish setting. *Journal of Pastoral Care*, 50(4), 340–348.

Wylie, W. E. (1984). Health counseling competencies needed by the minister. *Journal of Religion and Health*, 23, 237–249.

Understanding Human Sexuality: A Pastoral Perspective

For people of faith, human sexuality is a divine gift to be celebrated and respected. Sexuality is a basic component of personality — one of our most fundamental means of communicating and expressing love. It is a primary dimension of each person, a mysterious blend of spirit and body that shares in God's own creative life and love. Sexuality is also a relational power, not merely a capacity for performing specific acts. It calls us to personal as well as spiritual growth, drawing us out from self to interpersonal bonds and commitments. Sexuality includes the qualities of sensitivity, intimacy, compassion, and mutual support.

Unfortunately, sexual problems can take a significantly negative toll on a person's life and can be devastating for relationships. The direct effects on individuals with sexual dysfunction include worry, low self-esteem, and the loss of a potentially satisfying aspect of human experience. Additionally, there are difficulties in relationships; frequently sexual problems such as impotence or low sexual desire can be misinterpreted as a reflection of a lack of love or desire for closeness. Certainly, troubled relationships can lie at the heart of sexual problems (for example, marital problems have been found to be the most common cause of sexual arousal problems in the general population [Dunn et al., 1999]). However, many primary sexual dysfunctions have little to do with the quality of love and closeness in an intimate relationship.

An example is erectile dysfunction (ED), which may affect 50 percent of men between the ages of 40 and 70 (Laumann et al., 1999). The most common cause of ED is stress. It has been well established that specific stress hormones (such as norepinephrine and epinephrine) can directly interfere with a man's ability to achieve and maintain an erection even when there is ample sexual attraction and desire. When a male experiences significant life stresses over a period of time unrelated to his relationship or sexual performance (such as work stress), the rise in stress hormone levels can begin to affect his ability to have an erection. Once this happens, men frequently become quite worried about the erectile failure. The next time they have a romantic encounter, there is so much anxiety ("Will I be able to get an erection?") that it, in and of itself, results in elevated stress hormones causing the loss of an erection. It turns out that this anticipatory or performance anxiety is the number-one factor contributing to ongoing ED. To pursue this example further, if a man's wife worries that his lack of arousal is a sign of a relationship problem or a loss of his attraction for her, he may be even more anxious about having another failure experience. His response may be to avoid interactions that might lead to sex, which in turn can cause his wife's concerns to grow. This cascade of events can then devolve into a serious relationship problem. Often such scenarios are complicated by significant misunderstandings and lack of communication.

There are typically many people in a congregation who have some type of sexual problem, not just ED, and often these come to the attention of clergy.

Seeking Help

The past four decades have seen important advances in the understanding of human sexuality and the development of effective medical and psychological treatment interventions for sexual dysfunctions (Leiblum and Rosen, 2000). However, the vast majority of those experiencing sexual problems never seek treatment. The reason is obvious: people simply feel uncomfortable about openly discussing sexual matters. This whole subject is loaded — often fraught with feelings of guilt, shame, and embarrassment. In fact, researchers have found that among topics judged to be difficult to disclose, talking about sexual issues is considered to be the most risky (Barbach, 1982; Solano, 1981).

Where do those people turn who do seek help? Those who are best equipped to treat sexual problems are appropriately trained physicians and mental health professionals. However, in the United States, more people are inclined to turn to clergy for help during times of emotional crisis than to health care professionals. But there is a significant barrier that must be overcome. For many individuals, uneasiness about sexual issues is tied to experiences they have had in their families of origin and/or their faith community. This is especially so if sex has been talked about in a shaming or condemning manner and if this has been communicated in a religious context (for example, that certain sexual feelings or behaviors are sinful).

Additionally, believing that sexual urges or practices are sinful may be a manifestation of one's understanding of God as judging and condemning (versus loving and merciful). Often such beliefs about God are projected onto a pastor or rabbi, affecting a person's expectations (for example, anticipating that if issues like sexual desire or masturbation are raised, the spiritual leader will be critical and shaming). Undoubtedly, many individuals would like pastoral guidance or support, but are so worried about potential criticism that they never speak with clergy about such matters.

Others find the courage to bring their concerns to a religious leader — only to have their worst fears realized. In one case, a man's wife had been suffering for several years with advanced Alzheimer's disease and was severely demented (she no longer spoke and spent all day vacantly gazing out the window). This man had lost the woman he loved long ago. His confession to his priest was that in his loneliness he had begun to experience some sexual attraction to a woman in his church. The priest told him that he should be ashamed of his sinful feelings and should pray for forgiveness. Unfortunately, on returning home this man attempted suicide.

Sexuality is an element of human experience that is potentially a source of joy and a unique expression of love. However, it can be a hothouse for painful and destructive emotions that can tear marriages apart and cause substantial personal suffering. Here are the challenges:

- How can clergy communicate to parishioners that concerns about all areas of human experience (including sexuality) are permissible to bring to them?

- How can pastors reduce shame and guilt and develop an attitude of compassionate understanding that will help people feel safe enough to be open about their troubles?

- What are appropriate, loving, and caring pastoral responses to sexual concerns?

- How can clergy most effectively facilitate referrals to other professionals, if treatment is warranted?

These and other practical issues are the focus of subsequent chapters.

Defining "Normal" Sexual Functioning

There is controversy concerning what is "normal" sexual functioning and what constitutes deviance or dysfunction. This is underscored by the results of a study published in the *New England Journal of Medicine* (Frank et al., 1978). One hundred happily married couples were interviewed, and 80 percent reported that their sexual life was satisfying. Despite this, 40 percent of the men in the survey reported problems with impotency or ejaculatory problems and 63 percent of women reported low sex drive, sexual arousal problems, or inorgasmia (difficulty experiencing orgasms). Thus, what might be formally diagnosed as sexual dysfunction by standardized diagnostic criteria may be acceptable to some individuals. True dysfunction results in distress, and what is apt for some people is not for others.

The sex drive (desire) varies substantially among emotionally and physically healthy adults. Should both partners in a relationship have similar levels of sexual desire — even if it is low — there may be compatibility and no "dysfunction." However, if there is an imbalance in desire, relationship difficulties can and often do develop. These problems have hampered efforts of researchers to define what is normal versus what is dysfunctional, but more importantly it can lead to confusion and misunderstanding between sexual partners.

Cultural factors play an important role in defining "normality." In the Hebrew scriptures, Abraham was married to his sister, and in early Christianity there were sects that allowed polygamy — practices not accepted in our culture today. In the first century, Paul considered sexual abstinence to be a virtue and suggested that one's spiritual development could be enhanced by living celibately (Wincze and Carey, 2001, p. 3). Clearly, times change, and so do social customs.

In the medical and psychological literature, there is general agreement that healthy sexuality is characterized by normal biological functioning and by sexual interactions that occur in the context of love, trust, respect, and an absence of significant physical pain or emotional distress. Additionally, healthy sexuality is respectful of the willingness of both partners — that is, that both are voluntary participants and there is no coercion.

The definition of normality is also significantly influenced by the life experiences of the person(s) seeking guidance and by a pastor's own beliefs and knowledge about human sexuality. Thus, in the exploration of various problems in future chapters, it will be helpful to remember that a definition of what constitutes healthy sexuality is somewhat elusive and influenced by personal and cultural factors.

A Multitude of Causal Factors

It is important not to assume the most obvious causes of sexual problems. Biological and emotional factors underlying sexual functioning are numerous and complex. Specifics are addressed in subsequent chapters; highlighted here are some of the more important factors that must be considered when striving to understand the true nature of sexual problems.

Biomedical Factors

Many medical conditions commonly cause sexual changes or problems, including:

- Chronic pain conditions (such as arthritis)
- Endocrine disorders, such as diabetes
- Sex hormone changes (testosterone, estradiol/estrogen, prolactin)
- Female hormone changes accompanying menopause or post-hysterectomy
- Pelvic inflammatory disease
- Endometriosis
- Prostate disease
- Sexually transmitted diseases (STDs)
- Abuse of alcohol or other types of substances
- Psychiatric disorders (such as anxiety, post-traumatic stress disorder [PTSD], depression, bipolar disorder)
- Cardiac disease
- Dyspareunia: genital pain prior to, during, or after sexual intercourse
- Vaginismus: involuntary spasm of the muscles in the vagina that interferes with sexual intercourse

Emotional Factors

Sexual functioning is significantly affected by emotional distress. Sometimes this is related to traumatic or problematic sexual experiences (such as a history of childhood sexual abuse), although stresses completely unrelated to sexual concerns can also result in sexual dysfunction. Listed below are common psychological and emotional issues that can underlie sexual problems:

- Significant relationship difficulties (see below)
- Childhood sexual abuse

- A history of being raped or sexually assaulted
- Anticipatory or performance anxiety
- Guilt or anxiety concerning sex
- Depression or bipolar illness
- Anxiety disorders (such as panic disorder or PTSD)
- Significant life stresses (such as financial worries, health concerns, job problems, bereavement)
- Sometimes sexual obsessions (for example, online pornography) are a form of what mental health professionals call "acting out." This is behavior that serves to distract one from some form of emotional pain, such as a deep and painful sense of loneliness, feelings of failure and low self-esteem, or unmourned losses.

Relationship Factors

Various problems in intimate relationships may be critical factors in the emergence of sexual dysfunctions. First, there is a basic assumption that several conditions must exist for sexual attraction and adequate functioning to occur:

- Healthy and non–guilt laden attitudes about sex
- An accurate understanding about human sexuality (for example, knowing that most females need direct clitoral stimulation to experience an orgasm). Misinformation about the rudiments of sexual functioning often lies at the root of sexual dysfunctions.
- Some degree of physical attraction
- A relationship that provides an atmosphere of safety, love, and respect

Factors that are common sources of relationship-based sexual problems include:

- Sexual desire mismatches (for example, one partner has an inherently low sex drive and the other a high one)
- Sexual aversion (sex is experienced as disgusting, frightening, or is associated with significant guilt, shame, or embarrassment)
- Sexual interactions in the context of a healthy, loving relationship that trigger intense feelings/memories regarding past sexual trauma (such as rape or childhood sexual abuse), resulting in anxiety, and sexual inhibition

- When there has been a sexual difficulty (for example, ED) that is responded to by a partner in ways that belittle or humiliate, this can lead to significant uneasiness and performance anxiety which will exacerbate a problem. Even in the absence of humiliation by a partner, a man experiencing ED may need a lot of compassionate reassurance.

- The partner(s) have strong religious proscriptions regarding sexual behavior that lead to shame-laden and inhibited sexuality

- Partners have significantly different spiritual/religious views regarding sexuality

- Guilt over an extramarital affair or past infidelity

- Using sex to manipulate the partner, for example, as a way to dominate, use, or punish

- Negative body image (feeling unattractive or ashamed of one's body)

- Fears of vulnerability or rejection

- Lack of attraction

- Failures of one or both partners to clearly communicate regarding sexual matters (such as what feels good or what feels uncomfortable)

- Serious relationship problems (such as frequent fights, domestic violence, lack of nonsexual intimacy, emotional distance or withholding, significant substance abuse)

Balanced and Helpful Pastoral Responses

A categorical, right-wrong/good-bad approach to understanding human sexuality is simply not appropriate, due to the enormously complex nature of sexual problems. Such judgments, especially if communicated to those seeking guidance, usually are counterproductive. Each individual who begins to open up to discuss such personal matters as sexual problems in all likelihood has had to gather a great deal of courage to present these concerns to a spiritual leader. Criticizing or not understanding the unique and personal nature of each individual's situation puts that person at high risk for engendering strong negative feelings (such as shame), leading the individual to withdraw and close the door on their suffering. However, a compassionate attitude that communicates, "I am not here to judge, but simply to try to understand and help," has the best chance of assisting a person who has turned to a pastor at a time of personal distress and need.

In order to be able to provide an appropriate atmosphere for discussing sexual issues, three basic preparations are required of clergy:

- Be ready to hear about things that might be shocking or embarrassing for many persons. To be heard without a negative reaction, in itself, can be profoundly healing.

- Know the territory; become familiar with the variety of sexual problems and dysfunctions, how they are defined, and what treatments are available, so that appropriate referrals can be made.

- Importantly, come to terms with your beliefs and attitudes about sex and sexual practices. This final point deserves further elaboration.

Sexual issues are difficult for most people to talk about in an open manner. This is even true for many well-trained physicians, nurses, and mental health professionals. It is important for clergy to get clear about their own beliefs and anxieties regarding sexuality before offering guidance to others.

When parishioners begin to discuss sexual issues (often done in a very tenuous way), it may be helpful to say something like, "One of the hardest things to openly talk about is sexuality. Since it is an important aspect of one's life, I am willing to discuss any concerns you have about sexuality. I will do my best to listen and understand what is troubling you without being judgmental."

Finally, Wincze and Carey (2001, pp. 70–77) advise that it is important to anticipate that many of those seeking counseling will:

- Be embarrassed and have trouble discussing sexual matters

- Have hidden stories that may not immediately come to light or of which their partner is ignorant (such as extramarital affairs, an experience of having been raped, obsession with online pornography, homosexual feelings)

- Be misinformed about basic human sexual functioning

- Be in a very disturbed relationship for which the sexual dysfunction may be just one outward sign

References Barbach, L. G. (1982). *For Each Other: Sharing Sexual Intimacy.* Garden City, NY: Doubleday.

Dunn, K. M., Croft, P. R., and Hackett, G. I. (1999). Association of sexual problems with social, psychological and physical problems in men and women: A cross sectional population survey. *Journal of Epidemiology and Community Health*, 53, 144–148.

Frank, E., Anderson, C., and Rubinstein, D. (1978). Frequency of sexual dysfunction in "normal" couples. *New England Journal of Medicine*, 299, 111–115.

Laumann, E. O., Paik, A., and Rosen, R. C. (1999). Sexual dysfunction in the United States: Prevalence and predictors. *Journal of the American Medical Association*, 281, 537–544.

Leiblum, S. R., and Rosen, R. C. (eds.) (2000). *Principles and Practice of Sex Therapy* (3rd ed.). New York: Guilford Press.

Solano, C. H. (1981). Sex differences and the Taylor-Altman self-disclosure stimuli. *Journal of Social Psychology*, 115, 287–288.

Wincze, J. P., and Carey, M. P. (2001). *Sexual Dysfunction: A Guide for Assessment and Treatment*. New York: Guilford Press.

PART TWO
Case Studies

Abortion

"She was scared and ashamed"

A s Megan waited in Rev. King's office, she wondered how she was going to tell him she was pregnant. She was scared and ashamed. The longer she sat, the more unbelievable her situation seemed to her. She had never faced anything so daunting in her 18 years.

Rev. King was delighted to see Megan, whom he had known all her life. He was pleased that she would stop to visit him while home on her first semester break from college. However, he noticed that the usually ebullient young woman was quiet and looked tired and drawn.

Though she had told no one else, she haltingly explained that two weeks ago she found out that she was pregnant. As she recounted the painful story, she sobbed with shame and embarrassment. Megan told him she had often sat next to Jason, a junior, in class and that they always talked and joked with each other. She thought he was a nice, fun-loving guy, and she was a bit attracted to his wildness. When he asked her to go with him to his fraternity's party, she was flattered that this attractive, older guy was interested in her and accepted the invitation.

The party turned out to be just Jason, his three roommates, and their dates drinking at his apartment. Although everyone else was getting drunk, Megan had only one beer. Jason got very inebriated, and he manipulated her into going into his bedroom alone with him. She felt trapped since the other three couples were disappearing into other rooms. She was self-conscious, but did not want to seem entirely out-of-place with these older, more experienced students. Reluctantly, she went to Jason's room — but she had no intention of having sex. When Jason began to get physical with her, she asked him to stop, but he would not. She did not yell or fight him, but she told him again and again to stop. He held her arms above her head. He was strong and drunk, and he easily forced himself on her sexually. She was horrified and felt entirely powerless. Afterward, he fell asleep. She was shocked

Rape

by what had happened — and ashamed that she had been so "stupid" about his expectations and about the reality of the situation. As she grabbed her clothes and hurriedly stepped out into the night, she felt a darkness settle over her life.

She crept back into her dorm so as not to have to face anyone. She went to the bathroom and showered for a half hour. Megan talked to no one about what had occurred. When she saw Jason again, he acted like nothing had happened; she was not even sure he remembered. She blamed herself.

The semester ended and she returned home for winter break. She did not sleep well and was constantly thinking about what happened. She was tired, irritable, and cried alone every day. Her parents noticed that she was quieter than usual, but most of the time she was successful at staying out of their sight. They thought she was busy with old friends, while she was in fact avoiding everyone as best she could.

"I don't know what to do. I don't have a boyfriend. My parents will be so disappointed in me. Med school is out the window, and my life is over." Megan sobbed quietly for a moment. Then, glancing at Rev. King, she said, "I'm thinking about having an abortion."

Pastoral Care Assessment

Rev. King knew this young woman and realized the potentially devastating effect the situation could have on her. She had been dealing with her feelings by herself, without support from anyone. She was not sleeping well, was eating little, and had withdrawn from her friends and family. Her expressions of confusion, hopelessness, and self-blame alerted the pastor to Megan's need for help, and the nature of the situation dictated that assistance be available immediately.

The pastor realized what Megan had not — that she had in fact been raped. He knew that though she did not view it as rape at this time, Megan needed to understand her experience in this context in order to heal emotionally and to make informed decisions about her actions and future.

Relevant History

Megan's ties to her church were strong. She was as comfortable at the church as she was shopping at the mall with her friends. Baptisms, confirmations, choir rehearsals, Sunday school, church picnics, Girl Scout meetings in the church basement, weddings, and church camp in the summers — these had been woven into the fabric of her life as long as she could remember. Her world had always been safe, secure, nurturing, and happy, untouched by abuse, financial problems, drugs, alcohol, family breakups, or serious illness. She had grown into an intelligent, well-adjusted young woman. Megan had been popular in her small, rural high school and had earned good grades. Her career goal since ninth grade had been to become a doctor like her father. Her motivation was not a big salary or material things, but rather to be of service to others. Megan's dream was to become a pediatrician. She had heard of doctors who donated time to treat children in countries where basic medical care was lacking, and she thought that would be fulfilling work. She had begun college at the large state university two hours from her home only five months ago.

Megan had a steady boyfriend for almost two years when she was in high school, but had not been serious about anyone since their break-up a year ago. She had always planned to remain a virgin until she found her life partner.

Date rape

Approximately 13,000 women have abortions each year after becoming pregnant due to rape or incest (Alan Guttmacher Institute [AGI], 2002). Estimates of sexual abuse are inexact because of the difficulty in collecting data and the many unreported cases. Estimates vary, but range from 15 to 33 percent of all U.S. females having experienced some form of sexual abuse (Collins and Marsh, 1998; Feldt, 2002). The U.S. Department of Justice's National Crime Victimization Survey (2001) found that 66 percent of sexual assaults were committed by friends, acquaintances, or family members of the victim (Rape, Abuse, and Incest National Network, 2003).

The Centers for Disease Control statistics for 1995 indicated that 7.8 percent of all U.S. women's first experience of intercourse was "rape" or "not voluntary." For girls whose first intercourse occurred under age 15, the percentage was 22.1 (Centers for Disease Control [CDC], 2003).

Studies have estimated that between 5 and 15 percent of high school and college women have been victims of date rape (Finkelson and Oswalt, 1995; Schubot, 2001; Smith, White, and Holland, 2003). A study of female high school students in South Dakota in 1993, 1995, and 1997 found the prevalence of date rape to be 11.8 to 14.9 percent, and this is likely an underestimation (Schubot, 2001). Another study found that of a random sample of 200 women at one college, five percent had been date raped — and that none of them had reported the rape to authorities because of self-blame or embarrassment (Finkelson and Oswalt, 1995).

A U.S. Department of Justice report based on a study of 4,445 college females indicated that during the academic year of the survey,

1.7 percent of the women were victims of a completed rape, and 1.1 percent were victims of an attempted rape. Nearly 90 percent knew the offender, most of whom were classmates, friends, ex-boyfriends, or acquaintances. Most of the rapes on campus (almost 60 percent) occurred in the woman's residence, 31 percent occurred in other living quarters on campus, and 10 percent occurred at fraternities. For about half of the completed rapes, the females did not perceive the incident as rape (Fisher et al., 2000).

Many instances of date rape may not be premeditated, but some are, and reports of drug-facilitated date rapes have become common. These are most likely to occur at bars, nightclubs, and rave parties. Such rapes occur after the victim unknowingly ingests fast-acting drugs slipped into a drink. These sedative-type drugs (approximately 20 different kinds) cause disinhibition, passivity, muscle relaxation, loss of will to resist, and amnesia; their effects are increased when they are combined with alcohol (Schwartz et al., 2000). Alcohol alone has been shown to impair both male and female college students' perceptions. In a study involving college students' reactions to a potential date rape story, those who had been drinking viewed the woman as being more sexually aroused than those who had not been imbibing. The man in the story who was pressuring the woman to have sex despite her repeatedly saying "no" was viewed as behaving most appropriately by those who had been drinking (Abbey et al., 2002).

Abortion Statistics

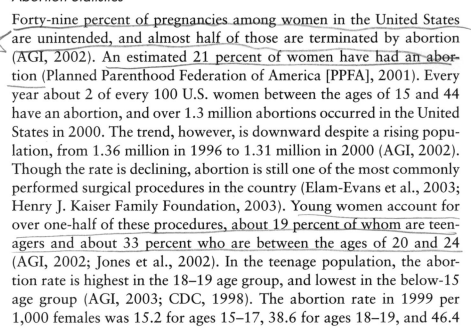

Forty-nine percent of pregnancies among women in the United States are unintended, and almost half of those are terminated by abortion (AGI, 2002). An estimated 21 percent of women have had an abortion (Planned Parenthood Federation of America [PPFA], 2001). Every year about 2 of every 100 U.S. women between the ages of 15 and 44 have an abortion, and over 1.3 million abortions occurred in the United States in 2000. The trend, however, is downward despite a rising population, from 1.36 million in 1996 to 1.31 million in 2000 (AGI, 2002). Though the rate is declining, abortion is still one of the most commonly performed surgical procedures in the country (Elam-Evans et al., 2003; Henry J. Kaiser Family Foundation, 2003). Young women account for over one-half of these procedures, about 19 percent of whom are teenagers and about 33 percent who are between the ages of 20 and 24 (AGI, 2002; Jones et al., 2002). In the teenage population, the abortion rate is highest in the 18–19 age group, and lowest in the below-15 age group (AGI, 2003; CDC, 1998). The abortion rate in 1999 per 1,000 females was 15.2 for ages 15–17, 38.6 for ages 18–19, and 46.4

for ages 20–24 (AGI, 2003). Though the abortion debate continues between pro-life and pro-choice advocates, both sides agree that abortion is not a good thing and agree that empowering women to avoid unplanned and unwanted pregnancies through education and family planning services would significantly reduce the number of abortions (Gillespie, 2004).

Abortion Risks

Abortions are considered to be low-risk surgical procedures (AGI, 2002; American College of Obstetricians and Gynecologists [ACOG], 2001) with less than 1 percent of all abortion patients suffering a major medical complication. The risk of death is one in 500,000 at eight or fewer weeks, increasing to one in 27,000 at 16–20 weeks. For comparison, the risk of death from childbirth is about 11 times higher than the risk from abortion (AGI, 2002). The risks and complications related to abortion increase as the length of pregnancy increases (ACOG, 2001; AGI, 2002). Most abortions (88 percent) occur during the first 12 weeks of a pregnancy. Many women who delay the procedure until after the fifteenth week do so because of difficulties in affording or locating abortion services. Teenagers are more likely than older women to have abortions at later stages of pregnancy, increasing their medical risks (AGI, 2002).

Emotional Effects

Emotional responses to having an abortion might include feelings of guilt, regret, loss, and/or anger. Although some women who have abortions suffer severe emotional trauma that has been called "post-abortion trauma" or "post-abortion syndrome," neither the American Psychological Association nor the American Psychiatric Association recognizes these disorders (PPFA, 2001). Studies have shown no evidence of widespread psychological trauma associated with having an abortion (Adler et al., 1992; Dagg, 1991; Russo and Zierk, 1992; Stotland, 1992), regardless of a woman's race or religion (Russo and Dabul, 1997). Research shows that a woman's emotional well-being prior to an abortion is the best predictor of her post-abortion emotional well-being (Russo and Dabul, 1997).

Rev. King had a strong emotional response to Megan's situation, but his intention was to stay in the role of compassionate pastor. Over the years in counseling parishioners, he had had ample opportunity to examine and ponder the diverse opinions regarding abortion. He knew it was not a black-and-white issue. He had come to believe that though

Response to Vignette

abortion is never a preferred outcome for a pregnancy, at times the complexities of life made it an unfortunate necessity. Megan's situation exemplified many of these complexities.

His initial response to her was to offer a nonjudgmental ear — to listen as she sorted through her options aloud. They met several times in a two-week period, and he continued to offer compassion and support. He talked to her about their church's position on abortion, while at the same time offering her a broad spiritual and historical perspective.

Rev. King talked with her about the involuntary nature of the sexual intercourse, and opened her eyes to the fact that she had been raped. He referred her to a psychologist to help her process her feelings and options. He strongly encouraged her to seek counseling so she could eliminate her feelings of guilt and shame and get help to regain her vital spirit and active life.

He also talked with her about options other than abortion. They discussed adoption and the possibility of her keeping and raising the baby. She shared her love for children and her future personal and career plans. Many tears flowed during Megan's conversations with her pastor. In the end, she was clearer about her options and felt much less guilty and ashamed about what had happened to her. Significantly, she maintained her spiritual connection to her church and her faith. When she left Rev. King's office on her last day home, she told him she was fairly certain what her decision was going to be, and that she would be in touch.

Rev. King, despite personal misgivings about the option of abortion, felt good about having been able to maintain a nonjudgmental and compassionate stance toward Megan. He prayed for this young, bright parishioner to make the decision that was right for her.

Treatment within the Faith Community

Strong and diverse opinions about abortion abound in our society and in religious communities. Clergy are influenced in their responses by the doctrine of their own faith. A survey of mainline Protestant (American Baptist Church, Christian Church–Disciples of Christ, Evangelical Lutheran Church in America, Presbyterian Church U.S.A., Reformed Church in America, United Methodist Church, and Unitarian Universalist Association) clergy found ideological and attitudinal differences between clergymen and clergywomen — with women being more liberal. Of all the social and political issues on the survey, the biggest gender gap was on the issue of abortion. Clergywomen were less likely than were clergymen to agree to the statement, "We need a constitutional amendment prohibiting all abortions unless to save the mother's life or in cases of rape or incest." However, the ratings of clergymen and clergywomen in the survey indicated that on average both were in favor of a woman having the right to have an abortion, although clergywomen were much stronger in their support (Deckman et al., 2003).

Although religions worldwide are often assumed to prohibit abortion, the truth in fact is much more complex. The current Catholic antiabortion position dates from Pope Pius XI in 1930; prior to that, though abortion was generally opposed, the voice of the Catholic church was not unanimous. Today the Catholics for a Free Choice organization reflects divergence from the official position (Religious Coalition for Reproductive Choice [RCRC], 2003). Many theories over the centuries have supported the option of abortion in certain situations, and Catholics have a history of deviating from official doctrine when personal or social needs preclude following it. This appears to be the case in regard to prohibitions against contraceptive use. Predominately Catholic countries in Latin America and Europe have birth rates that are at or near population replacement rates — an unlikely result if all Catholics were following church instructions (Maguire, 2001). In the United States, Catholic women have abortions at the same rate as the population as a whole (RCRC, 2003).

Other religions have equally complex positions and practices. Although Hindu writings are strongly against abortion, in India where 80 percent of the people are Hindus, people can and do have abortions. Since 1971 abortion has been legal in India. Buddhism, like Hinduism, generally prohibits abortion — but there are exceptions related to the life and health of the mother. Judaism permits abortion as a health procedure and considers the fetus not to be "ensouled" during the first 40 days after conception. The major Islamic schools of law permit abortions during the first four months of pregnancy, though generally only for very serious physical health reasons (Maguire, 2001).

The American Friends Service Committee stated in 1970 and 1989 its support for a "woman's right to follow her own conscience concerning child-bearing, abortion and sterilization." The United Methodist Church's Social Principles state "we recognize tragic conflicts of life with life that may justify abortion, and in such cases support the legal option of abortion under proper medical procedures." The Episcopal Church's statement of 1994 reads "[i]n those cases where an abortion is being considered, members of this Church are urged to seek the dictates of their consciences in prayer, to seek the advice and counsel of members of the Christian community...." It further states that any legislation regarding abortion "must take special care to see that individual conscience is respected and that the responsibility of individuals to reach informed decisions in this matter is acknowledged and honored...." The Presbyterian Church (U.S.A.) in 1992 reaffirmed a woman's right to an abortion. In 1988, the American Baptist Churches, U.S.A., recognized a division "as to the proper witness of the church to the state regarding abortion..." and so "acknowledge the freedom of each individual to advocate for a public policy on abortion that reflects his or her beliefs." The official statements of many religious organizations speak of the difficulties, complications, life situations, and social issues related to abortion. None are "pro-abortion," but many recognize extenuating circumstances that make abortion a far less than ideal solution, but nonetheless at times a reasonable one (RCRC, 2003).

Faith communities are not of one mind or voice on the issue of abortion. It therefore behooves clergy to educate themselves on the history, traditions, current thinking, and stated positions of various religions to provide an educated and balanced perspective from which to counsel congregants.

Indications for Referral   Unintended pregnancy can be an extremely stressful situation and can result in feelings such as confusion, self-blame, guilt, embarrassment, anger, grief, anxiety, and sadness. Deciding to give birth to and raise or give up for adoption a child from an unintended pregnancy can also trigger many of the same emotions. Research indicates the most severe psychological issues occur prior to rather than after an abortion, so consideration should be given to making a referral for counseling at that time. This should be done immediately, due to the time constraints on making a decision.

A woman is most likely to benefit from psychological services if she is experiencing hopelessness, helplessness, suicidal ideation, and/or other symptoms of depression or anxiety. If she does not have a support network of friends or family, she might benefit from the ongoing support of a therapist who could be a sounding board, provide feedback and information, and make referrals to appropriate agencies. Clergy who have a strong agenda either to support or forbid abortions should refer a pregnant woman to a supportive, neutral therapist or counselor to help her cope with the complexities of the issues surrounding unintended pregnancy, abortion, adoption, and childbearing/childrearing. Care should be taken to avoid referrals to counseling centers that are specifically pro-life or pro-choice (or given various other labels by proponents on either side of the debate) because they have agendas to either steer a woman away from or toward an abortion as an option.

If rape and/or incest are factors, a referral should definitely be made to someone who is well-trained in working with women who have been victimized. These are complex issues with many psychological ramifications and should be handled as such.

Depression and anxiety are more likely to occur before rather than after an abortion (Adler and David, 1990; Runkle, 1998). A mental health professional can assist a pregnant woman in addressing these issues, as well as assisting her in exploring her options and in decision making. A therapist can also help her plan for her future, no matter what decision she makes. Depression rates for women who have had abortions have been shown to be no higher after time than for women who never had an abortion or who give birth to a child of an unintended pregnancy (PPFA, 2001). In a California Wellness Foundation lecture in 1997, Major (as cited in Runkle, 1998) identified some risk factors for postabortion depression: a history of mental health problems, low self-esteem, lack of support, poor relationship with male partner, inner conflict about the decision, high stress levels related to other life issues, pressure from others to decide in a specific way, and exposure to antiabortion picketing. Since many of these are experienced by women prior to an abortion, efforts should be made to detect and treat postabortion depression. Medical or genetic indications for an abortion also increase the likelihood of serious postabortion psychological disturbances (Lazarus, 1985).

Treatment by Mental Health Specialist

Quality mental health professionals do not have an agenda related to a client's decision. Some agenda-driven clinics, though, attempt to pressure women into having or not having an abortion. Tactics such as films of aborted fetuses, or graphic, judgmental language about abortion are used (National Abortion Federation, 1999; Runkle, 1998). This can confuse a woman in her decision making and can perpetuate self-blame; it is not a responsible or helpful approach.

Education about all the options available and about research in the field is part of a therapeutic response. Cognitive therapy focuses on helping a woman identify her beliefs and attitudes, examine these, and decide if they are reasonable and accurate. Ideas that the patient determines to be unreasonable or inaccurate are then the focus of change. This form of psychotherapy is especially beneficial for a woman who has self-denigrating ("I'm stupid"; "I'm always making a mess of things") and self-blaming ("It's my fault") thoughts or feelings. However, it can be a valuable therapeutic approach for any woman experiencing the emotional turmoil resulting from an unwanted pregnancy and can help her examine her values and beliefs about life; this in turn can help her make informed decisions. Supportive therapy can also be invaluable at a time in a woman's life when she is emotionally distraught and in the process of making life-altering decisions.

Cross-Cultural Issues   Overall, the highest U.S. abortion rates per 1,000 are for women who are 19–29 years old, unmarried, African American or Hispanic, and poor. In 2000 the abortion rate for females between the ages of 15 and 44 was 21 in 1,000. About 41 percent of those women were European American, 32 percent were African American, 6 percent were Asian/Pacific Islander, and slightly less than 1 percent were Native American. Though the largest percentage (and therefore the highest numbers) of abortions are obtained by European American females, they actually have the lowest rate (13 in 1,000) because they have the largest population size in the United States. African Americans have the highest rate (49), and Hispanics (33) and Asians (31) fall in between. Overall the age group with the highest rate (47) is 20–24 years, and the lowest rate (4) is for women aged 40 and over. Almost one of every five females who has an abortion is a teenager, with the highest teenage rate being in the 18- to 19-year-age group (Jones et al., 2002).

Abortion rates decreased by 11 percent from 1994 to 2000, with the greatest declines among 15- to 17-year-olds, women with the highest incomes, those with college degrees, and those with no religious affiliation. Rates of decline for African American and Hispanic adolescents were less than those for European American teens. The rates for poor females overall increased from 1994 to 2000 (Jones et al., 2002).

In a study of 721 women who had abortions, 86 percent reported having a religion, and 43 percent reported attending church at least once a month (Russo and Dabul, 1997). In a survey completed in 2000–2001 of a representative sample of 10,000 females who had obtained abortions, 17 percent were married, 16 percent had been previously married, and 67 percent had never married. With regard to religious affiliation, 43 percent identify themselves as Protestants, 27 percent as Catholics, 8 percent as "other," and 22 percent as having no religious affiliation. Thirteen percent identified themselves as "born-again" or evangelical (three-fourths of these identified as Protestant); these women are included in the previous categories (Jones et al., 2002).

Statistics on adoption are limited, since no single source exists for collection of this information (National Adoption Information Clearinghouse, 2003). The Centers for Disease Control and Prevention's National Center for Health Statistics, however, reports that slightly less than 1 percent of babies born to never-married women were given up for adoption. Never-married African American females have been consistently less likely than never-married European American women to relinquish their babies for adoption (CDC, 2002).

Resources

Alan Guttmacher Institute; 120 Wall Street, 21st Floor, New York, NY 10005; (212)248-1111; *www.agi-usa.org*; *www.guttmacher.org*; a nonprofit organization focused on sexual and reproductive health research, policy analysis, and public education. It publishes journals and reports on these topics.

American Adoption Congress; 1025 Connecticut Avenue, NW, Suite 1012, Washington, DC 20036; (202)483-3399; see their Web site at *www.americanadoptioncongress.org*; a voluntary, nonprofit organization focused on adoption reform, education, and advocacy. The Web site provides book recommendations and links to adoption-related Web sites. The organization holds regional and international conferences and produces a quarterly publication related to adoption reform.

Centers for Disease Control and Prevention, *www.cdc.gov*, an agency of the U.S. Department of Health and Human Services, provides information and reports about abortion and adoption with links to related Web sites.

Concerned United Birthparents; 2000 Walker Street, Des Moines, IA 50317; (800)822-2777; (515)263-9558; *www.cubirthparents.org*; a national, nonprofit organization with a focus on issues related to birthparents. The organization offers support and education to birthparents, adoptees, adoptive parents, and professionals.

Medem; 649 Mission Street, 2nd Floor, San Francisco, CA 94105; (415)644-3800; *www.medem.com*; provides an online physician-patient communications network to facilitate access to information.

MedlinePlus Health Information, an online service of the U.S. National Library of Medicine and the National Institutes of Health, provides an extensive list of links to reputable sources for adoption-related information (*www.nlm.nih.gov/medlineplus/adoption.html*) as well as abortion-related information (*www.nlm.nih.gov/medlineplus/abortion.html*), which includes a medical encyclopedia and dictionary. Information is available in English and Spanish.

National Abortion Federation; 1755 Massachusetts Avenue, NW, Suite 600, Washington, DC 20036; Hotline (800)772-9100 in English and Spanish; (202)667-5881; *www.prochoice.org/naf*; a professional association of abortion providers (clinics, women's health centers, physicians, researchers, clinicians, and educators) in the Unites States and Canada. It provides information about abortion, fact sheets available for downloading, a history of legal issues (*Roe v. Wade*), information about abortion clinic violence, and a list of publications. Its brochure, *Making Your Choice: A Woman's Guide to Medical Abortion*, is available in Chinese, Croatian, English, Russian, Spanish, and Vietnamese.

National Adoption Information Clearinghouse; 330 C Street, SW, Washington, DC 20447; (703)352-3488; (888)251-0075; *naic.acf.hhs .gov/index.cfm*; a comprehensive resource on all aspects of adoption. The Clearinghouse is a government agency under the U.S. Department of Health and Human Services Administration for Children and Families. The Web site provides a national adoption directory, information for and about adoptive parents, birth parents, and adopted persons; questions and detailed answers regarding decision making, types of adoption, and arranging adoption; as well as information on adoption-related legal issues, statistics, conferences, publications, professionals, and databases. It provides detailed information on how to find reliable adoption information Web sites.

Planned Parenthood Federation of America; 434 West Thirty-third Street, New York, NY 10001; (212)541-7800; (800)230-PLAN; *www.plannedparenthood.org*; was founded in 1916 as the first birth control clinic in the Unites States and is a voluntary reproductive health care organization that provides information on birth control, pregnancy, parenting, and sexually transmitted diseases. Its Web site has a fact sheet on abortion, including the cited references and a quiz to help recognize the warning signs of date rape.

Rape, Abuse and Incest National Network; 635-B Pennsylvania Avenue, SE, Washington, DC 20003; (202)544-1034; (800)656-4673; *www.rainn.org*; is the largest anti–sexual assault organization in the United States. It provides brochures, reports, and statistics on rape and sexual assault, and information about counseling resources.

Religious Coalition for Reproductive Choice; 1025 Vermont Avenue, NW, Suite 1130, Washington, DC 20005; (202)628-7700; *www.rcrc.org*; a national interfaith alliance of religiously and theologically diverse groups dedicated to preserving reproductive choice as part of religious liberty and finding solutions to unintended pregnancy, the spread of HIV/AIDS, inadequate health care, and the reduction in reproductive health care services. Its Web site provides a list of the alliance's member organizations and provides excerpts from these organizations' official statements.

Teenwire.com, a Web site of Planned Parenthood Federation of America that provides sexuality and relationship information for teens in English and Spanish.

Helpful Books

Behind Every Choice Is a Story (Gloria Feldt with Carol Trickett Jennings, Denton: University of North Texas Press, 2002).

The Healing Choice: Your Guide to Emotional Recovery after Abortion (Candace De Puy and Dana Dovitch, New York: Fireside/Simon and Schuster, 1997).

In Good Conscience: A Practical, Emotional, and Spiritual Guide to Deciding Whether to Have an Abortion (Anna Runkle, San Francisco: Jossey-Bass, 1998).

The Open Adoption Experience: A Complete Guide for Adoptive and Birth Families — From Making the Decision through the Child's Growing Years (Lois Ruskai Melina and Sharon Kaplan, New York: HarperCollins, 1993).

Our Bodies Ourselves: For the New Century (Boston Women's Health Book Collective, New York: Touchstone, 1998).

Sacred Choices: The Right to Contraception and Abortion in Ten World Religions (Daniel C. Maguire, Minneapolis: Fortress Press, 2001).

References

Abbey, A., Buck, P. O., Zawacki, T., and Saenz, C. (2002). Alcohol's effect on perceptions of a potential date rape. *Journal of Studies on Alcohol*, 64, 669–677.

Adler, N., and David, H. P. (1990). Psychological responses after abortion. *Science*, 248, 41–44.

Adler, N., David, H. P., Major, B. N., Roth, S. H., Russo, N. F., and Wyatt, G. E. (1992). Psychological factors in abortion. *American Psychologist*, 47, 1194–1204S.

Alan Guttmacher Institute. (2002). *Facts in brief: Induced abortions.* Retrieved January 22, 2004, from *www.guttmacher.org*.

Alan Guttmacher Institute. (2003). *U.S. teenage pregnancy statistics with comparative statistics for women aged 20–24.* Retrieved January 15, 2004, from *www.guttmacher.org/pubs/teen_stats.html*.

American College of Obstetricians and Gynecologists. (2001). *Induced abortion.* Available from *www.medem.com/medlb/article*.

American College of Obstetricians and Gynecologists. (2002). *Pregnancy choices: Raising baby, adoption and abortion.* Available from *www.medem.com /medlb/article.*

Centers for Disease Control and Prevention. (2002). *Adoption, adoption seeking, and relinquishment for adoption in the United States* (Advance Data 306). CDC/National Center for Health Statistics. Retrieved January 22, 2004, from *www.cdc.gov/nchs/products/pubs/pubd/ad/301-310/ad306.htm.*

Centers for Disease Control and Prevention. (2003). *Fertility, family planning, and women's health: New data from 1995 national survey of family growth* (Series 23, No. 19), CDC/National Center for Health Statistics. Retrieved January 22, 2004, from *www.cdc.gov/nchs/data/series/sr_23/sr23_019.pdf.*

Centers for Disease Control and Prevention. (1998). *State-specific pregnancy rates among adolescents — United States, 1992–1995* (Morbidity and Mortality Weekly Report, 47, No. 24). Available from *www.cdc.gov.*

Collins, B., and Marsh, K. (1998). *Healing for Adult Survivors of Childhood Sexual Abuse.* Duluth, MN: Whole Person Associates.

Dagg, P. K. (1991). The psychological sequelae of therapeutic abortion — denied and completed. *American Journal of Psychiatry*, 148, 578–585. Abstract retrieved January 18, 2004, from EBSCO/CINAHL database.

Deckman, M. M., Crawford, S. E. S., Olson, L. R., and Green, J. C. (2003). Clergy and the politics of gender. *Journal for the Scientific Study of Religion*, 42, 621–632.

Elam-Evans, L. D., Strauss, L. T., Herndon, J., Parker, W. Y., Bowens, S. V., Zane, S., and Berg, C. J. (2003). Abortion surveillance — United States, 2000. *Morbidity and Mortality Weekly Report*, 52 (Issue SS), 1–32.

Feldt, G. (2002). *Behind every choice is a story.* Denton: University of North Texas Press.

Finkelson, L., and Oswalt, R. (1995). College date rape: Incidence and reporting [Abstract]. *Psychological Reports*, 77, 526.

Fisher, B. S., Cullen, F. T., and Turner, M. G. (2000). *The sexual victimization of college women.* (NCJ 182369). Washington, DC: U.S. Department of Justice, Office of Justice Programs, National Institute of Justice. Retrieved January 24, 2004, from *www.rainn.org/statisticsarc.html#college.*

Gillespie, D. (2004). Making abortion rare and safe. *The Lancet*, 363, 74.

Henry J. Kaiser Family Foundation. (2003). *Fact sheet: Abortion in the U.S.* Retrieved January 22, 2004, from *www.kff.org/womenshealth/326902-index.cfm.*

Jones, R. K., Darroch, J. E., and Henshaw, S. K. (2002). Patterns in the socioeconomic characteristics of women obtaining abortions in 2000–2001. *Perspectives on Sexual and Reproductive Health*, (34), 226–235.

Lazarus, A. (1985). Psychiatric sequelae of legalized first trimester abortion. *Journal of Psychosomatic Obstetrics and Gynecology*, 4, 140–150.

Maguire, D. C. (2001). *Sacred Choices: The Right to Contraception and Abortion in Ten World Religions.* Minneapolis: Fortress Press.

MedlinePlus Health Information. *Adoption.* Retrieved January 22, 2004, from *www.nlm.nih.gov/medlineplus/adoption.html.*

National Abortion Federation. (1999). *Post abortion issues.* Available from *www.prochoice.org.Facts/Factsheets/FS8.htm.*

National Adoption Information Clearinghouse. (2003). *Adoption statistics — A brief overview of the data.* Washington, DC: U.S. Department of Health and Human Services, Administration for Children and Families. Retrieved January 22, 2004, from *naic.acf.hhs.gov/pubs/s_over.cfm.*

Planned Parenthood Federation of America (2001). *The emotional effects of induced abortion.* Retrieved January 15, 2004, from *www.plannedparenthood.org/library/facts/emoteff_010600.html.*

Rape, Abuse, and Incest National Network. (2003). *Facts about sexual assault.* Retrieved January 24, 2004, from *www.rainn.org/statistics.html.*

Religious Coalition for Reproductive Choice. (2003). *Religious organizations support reproductive choice.* Retrieved January 20, 2004, from *www.rcrc.org.*

Runkle, A. (1998). *In good conscience: A practical, emotional, and spiritual guide to deciding whether to have an abortion.* San Francisco: Jossey-Bass.

Russo, N. F., and Dabul, A. J. (1997). The relationship of abortion to well-being: Do race and religion make a difference? *Professional Psychology: Research and Practice*, 28, 23–31.

Russo, N. F., and Zierk, K. L. (1992). Abortion, childbearing, and women's well-being. *Professional Psychology: Research and Practice*, 23, 269–280.

Schubot, D. B. (2001). Date rape prevalence among female high school students in a rural Midwestern state during 1993, 1995, and 1997.

Journal of Interpersonal Violence, 16, 291–296. Abstract retrieved January 18, 2004, from EBSCO/CINAHL database.

Schwartz, R. H., Milteer, R., and LeBeau, M. A. (2000). Drug-facilitated sexual assault ("date rape"). *Southern Medical Journal*, 93, 558–561.

Smith, P. H., White, J. W., and Holland, L. J. (2003). A longitudinal perspective on dating violence among adolescent and college-age women. *American Journal of Public Health*, 9, 1104–1109.

Stotland, N. L. (1992). Commentary: The myth of the abortion trauma syndrome. *Journal of the American Medical Association*, 268, 2078–2079.

Adult Survivors of Child Sexual Abuse

"She felt ashamed of her body"

Twenty-seven-year-old Beth sought the help of parish nurse Linda Wyatt because of her anxiety about a scheduled hospital visit. Beth has a history of back pain and has been treating herself because she hates to go to the doctor. She says she often feels ridiculed and ashamed when she sees physicians because she is obese. She was recently referred for an MRI, but she panicked as she lay on her back inside the dark tunnel of the machine and left the hospital before the exam was complete. She told Linda that she was afraid of keeping her second hospital appointment for fear that the doctors would think she was childish for leaving the MRI.

Beth is an incest survivor. In her late teens she was hospitalized for a suicide attempt when she suddenly remembered her abuse. Occasionally she has nightmares about being forced to go to the hospital. She has been doing well recently with the support of her friends at church and her weekly survivors group. Beth has not had any medical care for years because of the flashbacks and panic attacks that she experienced during previous visits. When she does get medical treatment she often experiences disconnectedness from her body. She also feels ashamed of her body and guilt for being overweight.

The parish nurse was able to help Beth by evaluating her back pain and discussing methods of pain relief, while encouraging her to pursue additional medical evaluations — including the completion of the MRI. After consulting with Father Ciarrocchi, the parish priest, Linda Wyatt arranged for the MRI technician to meet with Beth to explain the procedure and to discuss ways that the technician could help her feel more comfortable during the test. The parish nurse taught Beth some breathing exercises to alleviate her anxiety and encouraged her to bring a friend to the examination. Father Ciarrocchi called Chaplain Judith Wu at the hospital and arranged for her to meet with Beth to offer her spiritual and emotional support. Chaplain Wu had great pastoral and interpersonal skills and was able to help Beth feel more at ease with hospital staff.

Pastoral Care Assessment

Child sexual abuse survivors, like Beth, have a difficult road ahead of them. Not only have they survived the horror and confusion of the abuse, but they also must learn to endure and cope with its lasting negative effects, which can range from occasional bad feelings to acute emotional distress (Browne and Finkelhor, 1986). Depression, self-destructive behavior or suicide attempts, anxiety, post-traumatic stress disorder (PTSD), and panic attacks are the most commonly identified psychological problems that survivors of sexual abuse face (Polusny and Follette, 1995).

Many of the symptoms seen in victims are thought to be related to the dynamics of surviving abuse. In order to psychologically survive (especially if the perpetrator is a trusted adult), the child takes the blame for the experience, believing that something negative about themselves caused it and viewing themselves as "bad." Therefore, shame, guilt, and low self-esteem are common, as well as anger, fear, and a lack of trust (Herman, 1992).

Denial and dissociation, used to cope with the abuse at the time, may last for many years (Herman, 1992). Dissociation is the act of escaping a stressful or harmful situation by allowing the mind to leave the present horrible reality. The intense pain of sexual abuse creates a situation where the victim, in order to cope, tries to dissociate from her or his body. It can be described as a type of daydreaming or a need to find a place for the mind to hide while being sexually violated.

Survivors of abuse are also thought to be at higher risk for having certain medical problems and complaints. A victim's physical health and well-being may be affected by his or her history of abuse (Law, 1993). Many survivors suffer from insomnia, gastrointestinal problems, obesity, chronic pain, headache, and somatization, and they can be frequent users of medical care services.

Relevant History

Sexually abused children have more symptoms of emotional distress than nonabused children (Kendall-Tackett et al., 1993). Fears, PTSD, behavior problems, sexualized behaviors, and poor self-esteem occur most often, but no single symptom characterizes the majority of sexually abused children. Penetration, the duration and frequency of the abuse, the degree of force, the relationship of the perpetrator to the child, and maternal support affect the degree of distress. Child sexual abuse is also associated with greater vulnerability to revictimization in adulthood. Such experiences may have a cumulative effect on the emotional well-being of an individual (Meásmah-Moore et al., 2000).

Diagnostic Criteria

Child sexual abuse occurs when a child is used for the sexual gratification of an older adolescent or adult. It involves the abuse of power that an adult has over a child. In a national study, Finkelhor and colleagues (1990) found that 27 percent of women and 16 percent of men had experienced sexual abuse as children. The long-term psychological damage of childhood sexual abuse can be very harmful (Herman, 1992). Researchers have also pointed out that many survivors suffer from other psychological and physical abuse and neglect. Their problems in adulthood are related to sexual abuse in addition to these other kinds of abuse and neglect (Hobfoll, 2002).

Difficulties in social and interpersonal functioning, fear and distrust of others, low self-esteem, and feelings of hostility are common in child sexual abuse survivors (Browne and Finkelhor, 1986). Additionally they may have sexual adjustment problems, substance abuse problems, and eating disorders (Polusny and Follette, 1995). Approximately one-third of students seeking counseling in one university counseling center reported having been sexually abused as children (Stinson and Hendrick, 1992). Sexual abuse occurs in all communities regardless of race, religion, cultural heritage, or social or economic status.

Incest is a particularly cruel form of child sexual abuse. It occurs within the family, initiated by a parent, stepparent, sibling, or other relative. Unlike stranger or acquaintance abuse, incest is the violation of an ongoing bond of trust between a child and a caretaker. In incest, a person whom the child trusts and depends on for care, nurturance, and support takes advantage of that relationship (Bass and Davis 1994). Force is often not necessary; rather, the child's dependency is used against her or him. No child is emotionally prepared to cope with incest, and it is unfortunately often accompanied by a host of other family problems (such as distorted family relationships, a high degree of conflict and rigidity, secrecy, enmeshment, poverty, and substance abuse).

Response to Vignette

The parish nurse and chaplain understood that medical exams are very problematic for many survivors of sexual abuse because they elicit feelings of submission or forced containment. A gynecologic examination is especially difficult for many because it not only involves contact with the genitalia, but it also may replicate a sense of submission to a relative stranger that involves a lack of control. These and other medical exams may trigger flashbacks where a survivor reexperiences the sexual abuse as if it were occurring at that moment. It is usually accompanied by visual images or flashes of images of the abuse. Flashbacks are often triggered by an event, action, or sometimes even a smell that is reminiscent of the sexual abuse or the abuser, and they can be especially frightening experiences.

Survivors can also feel shame, anxiety, anger, and sadness. These emotions are exacerbated by medical personnel who are controlling or who demean individuals for their distress. Chaplain Wu was very helpful to Beth by being sensitive and responsive to her concerns and fears and assisting other staff in understanding the issues.

It is crucial that Beth have control in the situation and be an active participant in the examination by letting the medical personnel know when she is uncomfortable. Beth may need time to consider having an exam or may need several attempts before she feels enough control and trust. She may also need to stop the process if she feels uncomfortable and complete it at another time. Negotiation with the person concerning even the smallest decisions helps to build a sense of trust, safety, and control. If the survivor has a regular and trusted psychotherapist, some collaboration in preparation for the test may be useful.

Treatment within the Faith Community

Researchers surveyed over 5,400 Midwestern women at several major universities about childhood sexual abuse, religion, and mental health (Doxey et al., 1997). The primary purpose of the study was to investigate the role of religion in ameliorating the effects of childhood sexual abuse in adulthood. There were 653 women who reported being sexually abused while growing up. Childhood sexual abuse was associated with less emotional maturity, lower self-esteem, more instability in relationships with partners, higher levels of depression, and lower levels of religious involvement. In this study the worst mental health outcomes were among abused women with no religion and the best were nonabused women who were religious. The authors of the study suggested that "religion may extend to women an ability to pray and communicate with a God, a seemingly natural means of therapy and healing. There may be less guilt associated with the experience of prayer through both receiving forgiveness and the ability to forgive the perpetrator. They may also find support by being a member of a religious organization or church that helps them cope" (Doxey et al., 1997, p. 186).

Evidence suggests that some women do not seem to suffer as traumatically as others. These women have found ways to cope and thrive in spite of the traumatic experience of child sexual abuse. Valentine and Feinauer (1993) interviewed 22 women in a high-risk group for low self-esteem, depression, shame, and other long-term interpersonal difficulties due to their experience of childhood sexual abuse. Unlike many of their contemporaries, however, they have been able to have relationships, stable careers, and healthy personalities. The resiliency themes derived from these interviews included the ability to find emotional support outside the family, self-regard or the ability to think well of oneself, spirituality and rejection of self-blame, and an inner-directed mind-set. The researchers stated, "Active participation in a church group was often a 'critical turning point' in their lives as well as influential in their perceptions of themselves as worthy and valuable individuals" (Valentine and Feinauer, 1993, p. 222).

Indications for Referral

A referral to a mental health specialist is essential for adequate treatment of the psychological trauma inflicted by sexual abuse/incest. The referral should be to someone who has training and experience in working with incest survivors. Keep in mind that women who have been sexually assaulted will often only accept treatment from a female.

Multiple personality disorder, a fairly rare and the most severe form of dissociation, can occur among survivors of child sexual abuse. When the abuse is very severe, dissociation or "splitting" can become the only means of escape. In splitting, alternate personalities develop to help an individual survive the abuse. In one study of 185 people in treatment for multiple personality, almost all of them had experienced sexual abuse in childhood (Holmstrom, 1988). A person suffering from multiple personality disorder must be referred to a highly experienced and knowledgeable clinician.

Treatment by Mental Health Specialist

A therapist can help survivors sort out their emotions and thinking. Treatment helps to put the memories into a context that acknowledges the trauma and normalizes the symptoms associated with sexual abuse, develops alternative coping strategies, and provides a safe environment where the person can heal from the pain. Maltz (1991) has noted that sexual disorder issues often are a part of therapy for survivors of child sexual abuse.

A support group for survivors of child abuse can also be very helpful in reducing the distress experienced (Morgan and Cummings, 1999). Childhood sexual abuse trauma occurs within relationships, and healing is very difficult in isolation. Within healing relationships with other victims, adult survivors can realize that they are not alone in their struggles. In a group, a survivor can talk to others who have been through the same experiences and can learn how to comfort others as well as accepting comfort and support. They also learn that the perpetrators are the only people responsible for the abuse and that expressing their anger about the abuse is part of the healing process.

Cross-Cultural Issues   Native Americans have been seen as having particular risk for child abuse. This may be related to the high use of alcohol and the overall low economic level in many Native American communities (Robin et al., 1997). Researchers studied the impact of child abuse on 160 adult Native American women's emotional well-being (i.e., depressive mood and anger) and AIDS. Child physical/emotional abuse was found to have a greater effect on the increase of depressive mood, anger, and risk of AIDS than did child sexual abuse (Hobfoll, 2002). In addition, women who were physically/emotionally abused as children had more than five times greater odds of having a sexually transmitted disease in their lifetimes than did women who experienced only marginal or no physical/emotional abuse. Moreover, consistent with the communal culture of Native Americans, social support was found to contribute more to resilience in these women than other factors tested.

Resources   Adults Molested as Children United; P.O. Box 952, San Jose, CA 95108; (408)453-7616.

FaithTrust Institute; 2400 North Forty-fifth Street, Suite 10, Seattle, WA 98103; (877)860-2255; *www.faithinstitute.org*. The center offers training, consultation, videos, and publications to clergy, laity, seminary faculty, and students.

Incest Survivors Anonymous; P.O. Box 17245, Long Beach, CA 90807; (310)428-5599; is an international association based on the 12-step approach. Women, men, and teens meet to share experiences, strength, and hope in order to recover peace of mind. Send a self-addressed stamped envelope for information if you are a survivor.

Incest Survivors Resource Network International; P.O. Box 7375, Las Cruces, NM 88006; (505)521-4260.

Interfaith Sexual Trauma Institute; St. John's Abbey and University, Collegeville, MN 56321; (320)363-3931; *www.csbsju.edu/isti*.

National Coalition Against Sexual Assault; 125 North Enola Drive, Enola, PA 17025; (717)232-7460; is a membership organization committed to the prevention of sexual violence through intervention, education, and public policy.

National Committee to Prevent Child Abuse; P.O. 2866, Chicago, IL 60690; (800)55-NCPCA; *www.childabuse.org*; will provide information on child abuse and prevention.

National Council on Child Abuse and Family Violence; 1155 Connecticut Avenue, NW, Suite 400, Washington, DC 20036; (800)222-2000.

National Organization for Victim Assistance; 1757 Park Road, NW, Washington, DC 20010; (800) TRY-NOVA; online at *www.trynova.org*. This group, founded in 1975, provides support, referrals, and advocacy for victims of violent crime and disasters.

Rape, Abuse and Incest National Network; 635-B Pennsylvania Avenue, SE, Washington, DC 20002; (800)656-4673; *www.rainn.org*.

Survivors Connections; 52 Lyndon Road, Cranston, RI 02905; fax: (401)941-2335; *members.cox.net/survivorconnections*; is a grassroots activist organization for survivors of sexual assault.

Survivors of Incest Anonymous; World Service Office, P.O. Box 190, Benson, MD 21018; (410)893–3322; *www.siawso.org*.

Survivors Network of Those Abused by Priests; P.O. Box 438679, Chicago, IL 60643; (312)483-1059; *www.snapnetwork.org*. This is an international group founded in 1990 to support men and women who were sexually abused by Roman Catholic leaders. It provides extensive phone networking, information, and support groups.

VOICES IN ACTION, Inc.; P.O. Box 148309, Chicago, IL 60614; (800)7-VOICE-8; *www.voices-action.org*.

Helpful Books

Allies in Healing: When the Person You Love Was Sexually Abused as a Child (Laura Davis, New York: Harper, 1991).

Beginning to Heal: A First Book for Survivors of Child Sexual Abuse (Ellen Bass and Laura Davis, New York: Harper, 1994).

The Courage to Heal (Ellen Bass and Laura Davis, New York: Harper Perennial Library, 1994).

Incest and Sexuality: A Guide to Understanding and Healing (Wendy Maltz and Beverly Holman, New York: Lexington Books, 1991).

Outgrowing the Pain Together: A Book for Spouses and Partners of Adults Abused As Children (Eliana Gil, New York: Dell Trade Publishing, 1992).

Partners in Recovery: Lovers and Survivors: A Partner's Guide to Living and Loving a Sexual Abuse Survivor (Yvette S. DeBeixedon, San Francisco: Robert D. Reed, 1995).

Perilous Rivalry: When Siblings Become Abusive (Vernon R. Wiehe and Teresa Herring, Lanham, MD: Lexington Books, 1991).

Secret Survivors: Uncovering Incest and Its Aftereffects in Women (E. Sue Blume, New York: Ballantine Books, 1998).

Sexual Abuse Prevention: A Course of Study for Teenagers (Rebecca Voelkel-Haugen and Marie M. Fortune, Cleveland: United Church Press, 1996).

The Sexual Healing Journey: A Guide for Survivors of Sexual Abuse (Wendy Maltz, New York: Harper, 1992).

Sibling Abuse: Hidden Physical, Emotional, and Sexual Trauma (Vernon R. Wiehe, Thousand Oaks, CA: Sage Publications, 1997).

Violence in the Family: A Workshop Curriculum for Clergy and Other Helpers (Marie M. Fortune, Cleveland: United Church Press, 1991).

References

Alexander, P. C., and Schaeffer, C. M. (1994). A typology of incestuous families based on cluster analysis. *Journal of Family Psychology*, 8(4), 458–470.

Bass, E., and Davis, L. (1994). *The Courage to Heal: A Guide for Women Survivors of Child Sexual Abuse*. New York: Harper and Row.

Browne, A., and Finkelhor, D. (1986). The impact of child sexual abuse: A review of the research. *Psychological Bulletin*, 99, 66–77.

Doxey, C., Jensen, L., and Jensen, J. (1997). The influence of religion on victims of childhood sexual abuse. *International Journal for the Psychology of Religion*, 7(3), 179–186.

Finkelhor, D., Hotaling, G., Lewis, I. A., and Smith, C. (1990). Sexual abuse in a national survey of adult men and women: Prevalence, characteristics, and risk factors. *Child Abuse and Neglect*, 14, 19–28.

Herman, J. (1992). *Trauma and Recovery*. New York: Basic Books.

Hobfoll, S. E. (2002). The impact of perceived child physical and sexual abuse history on Native American women's psychological well-being and AIDS risk. *Journal of Consulting and Clinical Psychology*, 70(1), 252–257.

Holmstrom, C. (1988). Counseling survivors of sexual abuse. *Canadian Journal of Psychiatric Nursing*, 29(4), 6–8.

Kendall-Tackett, K. A., Williams, L. M., and Finkelhor, D. (1993). The impact of sexual abuse on children: A review and synthesis of recent empirical studies. *Psychological Bulletin*, 113(1), 164–180.

Law, A. (1993). Does a history of sexual abuse in childhood play a role in women's health problems? A review. *Journal of Women and Health*, 2(2), 165–72.

Maltz, W. (1991). *The Sexual Healing Journey*. New York: Harper-Collins.

Meásmah-Moore, T. L., Long, P. J., and Siegfried, N. J. (2000). The revictimization of child sexual abuse survivors: An examination of the adjustment of college women with child sexual abuse, adult sexual assault, and adult physical abuse. *Child Maltreatment*, 5(1), 18–27.

Morgan, T., and Cummings, A. L. (1999). Impact of sexual abuse on children: A review and synthesis of recent empirical studies. *Journal of Consulting and Clinical Psychology*, 67(1), 28–36.

Polusny, M. A., and Follette, V. M. (1995). Long-term correlates of child sexual abuse: Theory and review of the empirical literature. *Applied and Preventive Psychology*, 4, 143–166.

Robin, R. W., Chester, B., Rasmussen, J. K., Jaranson, J. M., and Goldman, D. (1997). Prevalence, characteristics, and impact of childhood sexual abuse in a southwestern American Indian tribe. *Child Abuse and Neglect*, 21, 769–787.

Stinson, M. H., and Hendrick, S. S. (1992). Reported childhood sexual abuse in university counseling center clients. *Journal of Counseling Psychology*, 39, 370–374.

Valentine, L., and Feinauer, L. L. (1993). Resilience factors associated with female survivors of childhood sexual abuse. *American Journal of Family Therapy*, 21(3), 216–224.

Cybersex — Pornography Addiction

"It's almost like he's cheating on me"

Doris Miller was clearly distressed as she sat in her pastor's study. Rev. Barbara Harris listened carefully to the parishioner whom she had known for several years. Doris was almost in tears when she said, "Pastor, this is hard to talk about. Steve is constantly online viewing pornography. I hate knowing that my husband would rather masturbate than make love to me. I've begged him not to do it, but he says it's the only thing that satisfies him. If anything sexual happens between us, I'm always the one to start it. I'm disgusted that he's turned on by those women more than his own wife — it's almost like he's cheating on me."

Pastoral Care Assessment   Research on the partners of sexual addicts examined how Internet sexual activity affected them (Schneider, 2000). Participants in the study reported their mate's online sexual involvement always included viewing pornography. Additionally, they exchanged sexually explicit letters, e-mails, and chats; placed advertisements to meet potential sexual partners; and had online affairs that often led to telephone or live encounters and illegal behavior (such as viewing child pornography).

The effect of their partners' cybersex activity on these women is often characterized by feelings of betrayal, fear, anger, mistrust, diminished self-esteem (especially in terms of unattractiveness and personal inadequacy), and degradation. Many females report a decrease in sexual intimacy with their mate, resulting from feelings that they were objectified during intercourse or that their partners were no longer emotionally involved in lovemaking (Schneider, 2000). Another commonly reported response is that the women were unable to compete with the young, attractive models in the pornography — a perception that led them to confusion, doubts about their physical desirability, and reduced feelings of intimacy. Many females who discover a partner's pornography use are traumatized because it confronts them with a world that they find bewildering and incomprehensible (Bridges et al., 2002).

Pornography is created mainly for the male consumer and is readily **Relevant** available on the Internet. It is estimated that the online sex industry **History** is worth over 1 billion dollars a year (Kornblum, 1999). Americans spend more money annually on all forms of pornography than on movie tickets and the performing arts combined (American Porn, 2001).

The Internet provides easy access to vast amounts of information, as **Diagnostic** well as the ability to have rapid and brief contacts with others. In 1997 **Criteria** it was estimated that more than 15 million users went online each day and spent an average of 9.8 hours a week visiting some of the more than 200 million available sites. New Web pages are being added at the rate of 300,000 each week (Computerworld, 1998). For most individuals, the availability of this tool and the means of accessing information enhance their lives. At the same time, this form of communication can create problems for those who are susceptible to intense sexualized interactions. Researchers found a strong association between time spent online for sexual pursuits and negative effects on one's life (Cooper et al., 1999).

Sex is the number-one searched topic on the Internet (Cooper, 1998). It was estimated that during the month of April 1998, the five most frequently accessed sexually oriented adult Web sites had roughly 9 million visitors, which represents 15 percent of the 57 million Americans using the Internet (Goldberg, 1998). As people spend increasing amounts of time in cyberspace, mental health professionals are questioning how this technology affects interpersonal relations (Kandell, 1998) and have noticed Internet-related problems, especially with pornography and other forms of cybersex.

Professionals who work in this field are persuaded that sexually compulsive behavior has reached epidemic levels in the United States (Cooper et al., 1999). Researchers surveyed over 9,100 adults who had used the Internet for sexual pursuits at least once. The 8 percent who were heavy users reported high numbers of personal problems typically associated with addictive behaviors (Cooper et al., 1999). The number of individuals who have sexual compulsivity problems is difficult to estimate. People with these issues often are fearful of the reactions of others, feel ashamed, and are likely to hide the frequency and details of their behavior. The Internet further complicates this by facilitating anonymity and enabling sexual activities to be pursued in an isolated and solitary fashion.

"Internet addiction" implies a psychological dependence that is marked by an increasing investment of time and money, unpleasant feelings when off-line, increasing tolerance to the effects of being online, and denial of the problem (Kandell, 1998). Depression has been found to be an important factor in the development of pathological Internet use (Young and Rogers, 1998), and it may be that excessive use is related to psychological difficulties associated with social isolation (Leiblum, 1997).

Response to Vignette

After talking with Rev. Miller, Doris decided to confront Steve about his behavior. She told him that he must seek counseling or she could not continue to live with him. Her husband reluctantly consented to see a psychologist for an evaluation. During the session Steve disclosed that his attraction to Internet pornography had been recreational curiosity until he lost his job 6 months ago. Prior to his unemployment, he did not have symptoms of sexual compulsion. Around the time he was laid off, he began going online to fill the hours when he was alone. As Steve became more stressed about being out of work, he became increasingly involved with Internet porn. As his online cybersex continued, he would periodically decide he wanted to stop, but unfortunately, he returned.

Steve had developed a cycle of behavior in which he experienced shame and depression, and then used the Internet for sexual gratification, followed by the shame and depression being temporarily blocked. With each cycle came more feelings of shame, loss of control, and decreased self-esteem, which fueled a downward spiral. He began to loathe himself and realized that outside assistance might be necessary, although his shame kept him from seeking the help he wanted until Doris confronted him. Steve was using cybersex pornography as an escape to distract himself from his negative feelings about his job loss.

Treatment within the Faith Community

The potential of the Internet to disseminate large amounts of pornographic material within an unregulated marketplace with a huge, international audience should be of great concern to the faith community. In 1997, Mehta and Plaza analyzed 150 randomly selected images from 17 Internet newsgroups and found that the most prevalent themes were close-ups of genitalia (43 percent); images with an erect penis (35 percent); fetishes, including lingerie and high-heeled shoes (33 percent); and masturbation (21 percent). In the study, they also examined themes illega_ under Canada's Criminal Code and discovered that 15 percent of their sample involved images with children. Their findings showed that images involving minors were usually nude poses or, in rare instances, simulated sexual activity with children or young-looking models. Other illegal and/or taboo subjects were bestiality (10 percent), urination (3 percent), group sex (11 percent), and bondage/discipline (10 percent).

Seems odd to group all this together

Without comprehensive sex education programs in faith communities and schools the de facto sex education for our children and adolescents becomes television, movies, videos, and increasingly Web sites. The Internet, in particular, ensures the ready availability of all conceivable forms of sexual material. Advocacy for the curtailment of such access for minors should be a priority for religious communities. Children who are naturally curious about sexual matters are confronted with a flood of crude and aberrant information by the multibillion-dollar sex entertainment industry, which includes major corporations such as AT&T and GM (American Porn, 2001).

Young children do not have the cognitive and emotional development to assimilate such material. Exposing them to the harshest aspects of sexuality cannot but have an injurious influence. Experts are concerned that such exposure will develop sexual callousness in youngsters, which can negatively influence and distort their concepts of sexuality (Zillmann, 2000).

In a number of studies, violent sexually explicit materials were found to cause arousal in males. After watching such films, many of the subjects became less sympathetic toward female rape victims and showed greater belief in myths, such as viewing rape victims as responsible for their assaults (Malamuth, 1993).

Indications for Referral

Rev. Harris understood that the responsible practice of ministry requires her to be prepared to recognize the emotional needs of persons in distress, as well as to make effective referrals to specialized professionals. The pastor had developed a working relationship with several mental health clinicians who had a comprehensive knowledge of the services available in the community and worked with her as a colleague. She was acquainted with both psychologists and psychiatrists who specialized in treating individuals with addictions. Rev. Harris understood that most sexual problems do not occur in a vacuum and that relationship issues are often involved. She knew a marriage and family therapist who could help Steve and Doris address underlying issues in their relationship that might be related to their current difficulties.

Treatment by Mental Health Specialist

A full psychological evaluation that includes a history of sexual development should be completed for individuals who are sexually compulsive. It will identify other conditions such as depression, anxiety, obsessive-compulsive behavior, and substance abuse that are often associated with this problem (Black, 1998). How and when to deal with such matters must be a part of the overall treatment plan. A mental health professional will look for any indication that a client's current situation is related to a history of hypersexuality, paraphilias, identity confusion, intimacy issues, or childhood sexual trauma. This information can help to determine the type of cybersex addiction that is involved. It sometimes may be the case that sexual acting-out problems have occurred prior to online sexual compulsion. For others like Steve, the Internet has acted as a catalyst for the manifestation of an addiction. Not acknowledging a problem is common in persons with sexual compulsion and is often caused by denial and feelings of shame and embarrassment.

Cross-Cultural Issues

In a Swedish study of 650 high schools, 94 percent of the boys and 74 percent of the girls had seen a pornographic film (Hammarén and Johansson, 2001). An association between watching pornography and having had anal intercourse was found in that research. In a second study, 1,000 young women visiting a family planning clinic in Stockholm were given a questionnaire asking about their sexual behavior and whether or not they had viewed pornography (Rogala and Tydén, 2003). Four of five had seen pornography, and one-third of these believed that it had affected their sexual activity. As many as 47 percent had experienced anal intercourse, and the majority considered it a negative experience. Since the use of condoms was low when having anal intercourse (40 percent), the consequences for the spread of sexually transmitted diseases was a concern.

Resources

Augustine Fellowship; Sex and Love Addicts Anonymous, P.O. Box 338, Norwood, MA 02062-0338; (781)255-8825; *www.slaafws.org*; is a 12-step fellowship which offers treatment and information about sexual addiction.

National Coalition for the Protection of Children and Families; 800 Compton Road, Suite 9224, Cincinnati, OH 45231; (513)521-6227; *www.nationalcoalition.org*; is dedicated to helping people live lives free from the influences of pornography and the sexualized messages of the culture. Founded in 1983, it is an alliance of representatives from businesses, foundations, citizen action groups, and religious organizations working to educate the public about the effects of our sex-saturated society on communities, individuals, children, and families. It also helps concerned citizens effect change within their communities and provides assistance to those whose lives have been negatively affected.

National Council on Sexual Addiction and Compulsivity; P.O. Box 725544, Atlanta, GA 31139; (770)541-9912; *www.ncsac.org*; offers articles, a member directory, contacts, and treatment information.

National Law Center for Children and Families; 3819 Plaza Drive, Fairfax, VA 22030-2512; (703)691-4626; *www.nationallawcenter.org*; is a nonprofit organization working to enforce the laws against pornography. Its mission is focused on the protection of children and families from its harmful effect by assisting law enforcement and improving the laws.

Open-mind, *www.open-mind.org*, is a site intended to help those seeking recovery from various addictions (including sex) and their family and friends to find support, resources, links, and information about recovery groups ranging from 12-step to "alternative" programs, as well as e-mail and discussion groups, treatment facilities, and various recovery-related, self-help, and mental health sites.

Parents Television Council; 707 Wilshire Boulevard #2075, Los Angeles, CA 90017; (800)882-6868 or (213)629-9255; *www.parentstv.org*; was established in 1995 as a nonpartisan group to restore television to its roots as a socially responsible entertainment medium.

Sex Addicts Anonymous; ISO of SAA, P.O. Box 70949, Houston, TX 77270; (800)477-8191; *www.sexaa.org*; is a fellowship where addicts can share experiences, strength, and hope with each other to overcome sexual addiction and help others recover.

SexHelp, *www.sexhelp.com*, offers an Internet sex screening test as well as information about sexual addiction, 12-step group resources, online chat groups, articles, links, and information about treatment services.

Sexual Addiction Recovery Resources; P.O. Box 18972, Boulder, CO 80308-1972; *www.sarr.org*; offers an extensive list of links to resources on sexual addiction.

Sexual Compulsives Anonymous; P.O. Box 1585, Old Chelsea Station, New York, NY 10011; (800)977-4325; *www.sca-recovery.org*; is a fellowship of men and women who share their experiences, strength, and hope with each other to try to solve their common problems and help others to recover from sexual compulsion.

Sexual Recovery Institute; 914 South Robertson Boulevard, Suite 103, Los Angeles, CA 90035; (310)360-0130; *www.sexualrecovery.com*;

provides information, articles, links, an online course, treatment services, monitored bulletin board service, and online chat groups about sexual addiction.

Helpful Books   *Cybersex Exposed: Simple Fantasy or Obsession?* (Jennifer P. Schneider and Robert Weiss, Center City, MN: Hazelden Information and Educational Services, 2001).

Cybersex Unhooked: A Workbook for Breaking Free of Compulsive Online Sexual Behavior (David L. Delmonico, Joseph Moriarty, and Elizabeth Griffin, Prescott, AZ: Hohm Press, 2001).

In the Shadows of the Net: Breaking Free of Compulsive Online Sexual Behavior (Patrick J. Carnes, Elizabeth Griffin, David Delmonico, and Joseph M. Moriarty, Center City, MD: Hazelden Information and Educational Services, 2001).

Obscene Profits: The Entrepreneurs of Pornography in the Cyber Age (Frederick S. Lane, New York: Taylor and Francis, 2001).

Out of the Shadows: Understanding Sexual Addiction (Patrick J. Carnes, Center City, MN: Hazelden Information and Educational Services, 2001).

Pornography and Sexual Representation: A Reference Guide (Joseph W. Slade, Westport, CT: Greenwood Press, 2001).

Rising Above Pornography (Rebecca Lomas, Albuquerque: Athena Press, 2002).

References   American Porn. (2001). Interview with Cardinal William Keeler. *American Porn*. Retrieved on April 13, 2003, from *www.pbs.org/wgbh/pages/frontline*.

Black, D. B. (1998). Compulsive sexual behavior: A review. *Journal of Practical Psychiatry and Behavioral Health*, 4, 219–229.

Bridges, A. J., Bergner, R. M., and Hesson-McInnis, M. (2002). Romantic partners' use of pornography: Its significance for women. *Journal of Sex and Marital Therapy*, 29, 1–14.

Computerworld. (1998). *Commerce by numbers: Internet population*. Retrieved on April 29, 2003, from *www.computerworld.com/home/Emmerce.nsf/All/pop*.

Cooper, A. (1998). Sexuality and the Internet: Surfing into the new millennium. *CyberPsychology and Behavior*, 1, 181–187.

Cooper, A., Scherer, C. R., Boies, S. C., and Gordon, B. L. (1999). Sexuality on the Internet: From sexual exploration to pathological expression. *Professional Psychology, Research and Practice*, 30(2), 154–164.

Freeman-Longo, R. E., and Blanchard, G. T. (1998). *Sexual Abuse in America: Epidemic of the 21st Century.* Brandon, VT: Safer Society Press.

Goldberg, A. (1998). *Monthly Users Report on Adult Sexually Oriented Sites for April 1998.* Washington, DC: Relevant Knowledge.

Hammarén, N., and Johansson, T. (2001). *Youth and Sexuality in Transition.* Skovde, Sweden: University of Skovde Press.

Kandell, J. J. (1998). Internet addiction on campus: The vulnerability of college students. *CyberPsychology and Behavior,* 1, 11–17.

King, S. A. (1999). Internet gambling and pornography: Illustrative examples of the psychological consequences of communication anarchy. *CyberPsychology and Behavior,* 2(3), 175–193.

Kornblum, J. (1999, February 14). "Slate" lesson: Sex sells on net, news doesn't. *USA Today,* 6B.

Leiblum, S. R. (1997). Sex and the net: Clinical implications. *Journal of Sex Education and Therapy,* 22, 21–28.

Malamuth, N. M. (1993). Pornography's impact on male adolescents. *Adolescent Medicine,* 4(3), 563–576.

Mehta, M. D., and Plaza, D. E. (1997). Pornography in cyberspace: An exploration of what's in Usenet. In S. Kiesler, ed. *Culture of the Internet.* Mahwah, NJ: Lawrence Earlbaum Associates.

Rogala, C., and Tydén, T. (2003). Does pornography influence young women's sexual behavior? *Women's Health Issues,* 13, 39–43.

Schneider, J. (2000). Effects of cyberspace addiction on the family: Results of a survey. *Sexual Addiction and Compulsivity,* 7, 31–58.

Strasburger, V. C., and Donnerstein, E. (1999). Children, adolescents, and the media: Issues and solutions. *Pediatrics,* 103, 129–139.

Young, K. S., and Rogers, R. C. (1998). The relationship between depression and Internet addiction. *CyberPsychology and Behavior,* 1, 25–28.

Zillmann, D. (2000). Influence of unrestrained access to erotica on adolescents' and young adults' dispositions toward sexuality. *Journal of Adolescent Health,* 27S, 41–45.

Erectile Dysfunction

"It was a side effect of his surgery"

Pastor Howell has been friends with James Sano, age 60, and his wife, Anne, for years. It was natural that James and Anne went to their pastor three months ago for counsel and emotional support after James was diagnosed with prostate cancer. Rev. Howell visited James after he underwent a necessary removal of his prostate to save his life. Since the surgery, James told him he has suffered from erectile dysfunction (ED). The doctors told James that while medical advances such as nerve-sparing surgery have occurred for treatment of ED, it continues to be the most common side effect of early treatment for prostate cancer.

Pastoral Care Assessment   Every three minutes, a new case of prostate cancer is diagnosed in the United States. Every 15 minutes, a man dies from it. Prostate cancer is the most common cancer in men in the United States, with 75 percent of diagnoses made in men over age 65 (American Cancer Society, 2002). The majority of newly diagnosed patients have an early-stage disease that is treated with radical prostatectomy (removal of part or all of the prostate gland), a procedure associated with high cure rates. Unfortunately, it has potentially disruptive side effects. Most notably, this surgery causes ED for most men, even those who undergo nerve-sparing procedures (Perez et al., 1997).

While sexual functioning declines with age, sexuality remains a significant aspect of a man's life well into his later years. Most males, even as they grow older, maintain a sense of themselves as sexual beings. It is natural that men who have ED after treatment for prostate cancer would experience a feeling of deep loss and a significant change in the quality of their lives. Regardless of the cause, ED can have a negative impact on self-esteem and interpersonal relationships. The good news is that there are several methods for relieving ED.

In the United States an estimated 650,000 men have ED as a result of surgery, including prostatectomies, colostomies, and cystectomies (Kaplan and Sadock, 1998). Two million men have the disorder because they suffer from diabetes mellitus; 300,000 because of other endocrine diseases; 1.5 million as a result of vascular disease; 180,000 because of multiple sclerosis; and another 400,000 because of traumas and fractures causing pelvic fractures or spinal cord injuries (Kaplan and Sadock, 1998).

ED, which is commonly known as impotence, is the inability to achieve or maintain an erection sufficient for sexual intercourse (APA, 2000). There are two types of ED: primary and secondary. Primary ED occurs when a man has never been able to engage in sexual intercourse. Secondary ED is more common, occurring when a man who once had the ability to have an erection and engage in sexual intercourse has lost it (APA, 2000).

An estimated 30 million men in the United States experience chronic ED, although as few as 5 percent seek treatment. It may affect 50 percent of men between the ages of 40 and 70 (Laumann et al., 1999). Transient loss of or inadequate erection affects men of all ages. ED has many causes, most of which are treatable, and it is not an inevitable consequence of aging (Kaplan and Sadock, 1998).

ED can be the result of organic factors, psychological factors, or both. Organic causes of erectile problems are related to blood flow to the penis, which is necessary to have a rigid and erect penis. At the time of erection, blood flows into the cavernous and spongy bodies of the penis. As blood pressure rises, there is an increase in blood inflow and erection (Kaplan and Sadock, 1998).

Organic causes can be divided into five parts: neurological (diabetes, pelvic or spinal cord trauma, pelvic surgery), vascular (pelvic surgery or trauma, abnormal thickening and loss of elasticity in the arterial walls), postsurgical (prostatectomy, removal of part or all of the prostate gland or radical cystectomy, the surgical removal of a cyst or urinary bladder), drugs (alcohol, tranquilizers, some antidepressants), and hormonal (low serum testosterone level, high serum estrogen level) (Kaplan and Sadock, 1998).

Diabetics, smokers, and men with low testosterone are most prone to have defects in several of the biological systems needed for erection (Shabsigh and Anastasiadis, 2003). Smoking causes ED by producing a buildup of fatty deposits in delicate blood vessels, which blocks the blood supply to the penis. The drug nicotine can also damage certain valve mechanisms involved in the trapping of blood in the penis.

Older men most often suffer from ED (Feldman et al., 1994). Chronic medical illnesses are more common with age. As men grow older they need greater genital stimulation to achieve adequate erection. ED, however, is not universal in aging men; having an available sex partner is related to continuing potency, as is a history of consistent sexual activity. Among the psychological causes of ED are depression, anxiety, relationship problems, and stress (APA, 2000).

Response to Vignette

In his 30 years in ministry, Rev. Howell had counseled many men who had had prostate cancer. Jim was fortunate that the disease was caught early, and it appeared not to have spread beyond the prostate. The pastor was aware that the new "nerve saving" procedures gave James a greater chance to recover from the surgery with fewer side effects, including ED, than was the case only a few years ago. James had made all the positive lifestyle changes that might be beneficial. He stopped smoking, avoided drinking alcohol, adopted a healthier diet, exercised regularly, and made sure he had quality sleep (Shabsigh and Anastasiadis, 2003). It was also helpful that Anne and James had a solid relationship with good communication. James's physician put him on the medication sildenafil citrate (Viagra) after several months as he began to fully heal from the surgery. The treatment proved to be successful as he began to regain the capacity to have an erection.

In 1998, the treatment of ED was substantially improved by the Federal Drug Administration's approval of Viagra. Unlike other therapies for ED, it does not produce erections in the absence of sexual stimulation. Rather, it enhances the flow of blood to the penis, thereby trapping blood in the penis when a man is sexually aroused. In clinical trials, Viagra has proved effective most of the time in men with ED from a variety of causes (Young et al., 2002).

Several trials have investigated how well it works following prostate treatment. A recent study of 549 men published by the American Cancer Society found that Viagra improved the sex life of 49 percent of patients who had undergone radical prostatectomy or radiotherapy (Schover et al., 2002). Men who underwent radical prostatectomy found that Viagra worked best when both nerves were left intact. Viagra does not seem to be effective early in the recovery phase but increases in efficacy as the nerves recover from injury during surgery (McCullough, 2001).

In general, the most common side effects from Viagra have been headaches, flushing, and heartburn (Shabsigh and Anastasiadis, 2003). It should not be taken by men who take nitrates (such as nitroglycerin for angina), and it must be used with caution by men with other cardiovascular conditions and by those taking medications to lower blood pressure. Viagra should never be used without first consulting a medical doctor.

Intracavernosal injection therapy is also an effective treatment for many men. Three common drugs used for this technique are Papaverine, Alprostadil, and Phentolamine. Alprostadil can also be inserted in the penis in pellet form via the urethra. These medications facilitate erection by relaxing the smooth muscle tissues in the penis. However, unless patients are given proper education and encouragement, discontinuation rates are high (Shabsigh and Anastasiadis, 2003).

Rev. Howell had a working relationship with a psychologist who specialized in sex therapy. The pastor suggested they see her for a few sessions. The couple found that it was helpful for them to share their feelings and listen to the psychologist's practical suggestions. For example, James and Anne found that sex in the morning when an erection is more likely was a useful tip. They avoided sex when James was stressed or tired. Anne was more vigorous in her stimulation of his penis, before and at intervals during intercourse as needed. They also tried to use sexual positions in which vaginal tension increased for heightened penile stimulation. They spent more time on sexual activities other than intercourse. For instance, rather than relying on intercourse alone, as was customary when they were younger, it was helpful for both Anne and James to achieve orgasm via other techniques (such as manual stimulation). They found that they enjoyed new sexual activities outside of their usual repertoire, such as taking turns at giving or receiving sexual pleasure. The psychologist also encouraged Anne and James to experience sexual pleasure after erectile difficulty occurred. Encouragement often serves to reduce both the partner's frustration and performance pressure. Not uncommonly, such a response resulted in a pleasurable experience for Anne and James.

Prostate cancer is the male equivalent of breast cancer — although it receives a great deal less attention, the death rates are similar. There are 190,000 new cases of prostate cancer each year, making it the most commonly diagnosed carcinoma in the United States among men. More than 30,000 American males lose their lives to it each year, and one in six will have the disease (National Prostate Cancer Coalition, 2003). If a close relative has prostate cancer, a man's risk of the disease more than doubles.

If symptoms occur, they may include difficulty starting urination, reduced force of the stream of urine, frequently urinating small amounts,

Treatment within the Faith Community

urinating often during the night, painful urination, and bone pain. However, often there are no symptoms, which is why screening is so important (National Prostate Cancer Coalition, 2003).

Faith communities can play an essential role in screening for cancer. Research has found that the participation of clergy and key lay members in church-based cancer control programs improves access to and participation in screening, particularly by African and Hispanic Americans (Davis et al., 1994). A recent study published in the *American Journal of Public Health* found that church-based telephone counseling in ethnic minority communities in Los Angeles significantly increased the regular use of mammography (Duan et al., 2000). Such faith-based programs can have great impact in promoting regular cancer screening. Their support and implementation by religious communities will help ensure congregations that are healthy in both body and soul.

Indications for Referral

Clergypersons should find at least one mental health professional whom they trust and to whom they can refer someone who needs counseling for sexual issues. Clergy are not trained in sex therapy and should not go beyond their expertise when addressing pastoral care questions. However, pastors and other religious professionals need to be informed about health issues that often affect those they serve. For clergy to give parishioners accurate information about a topic like ED can provide guidance, lower the stigma attached to the topic, decrease the isolation, and facilitate a referral to a specialist.

Treatment by Mental Health Specialist

Difficulty in achieving or sustaining an erection is the most common sexual disorder in men seeking help in sex therapy clinics (Spector and Carey, 1990). Psychological and interpersonal factors have also frequently been associated with the disorder. There are several medical and surgical approaches to treating ED. These include surgical prostheses or penile implants, intracavernosal injection of vasoactive drugs, constriction rings and vacuum pump devices, as well as medications such as sildenafil citrate (Viagra), yohimbine (Yocon), and apomorphine (Uprima).

In order to appropriately treat ED, determining the actual cause of the problem is the first priority. Current research suggests that the man should undergo a comprehensive evaluation by both a medical specialist and a psychologist (Ackerman and Carey, 1995). It is recommended that this evaluation include a physical examination, psychosocial evaluation, and specific laboratory studies as needed. Many treatments for ED include both a medical and a psychological intervention. Psychological treatments are used not only for the dysfunction, but also to help the individual (and the couple) deal with the sensitivity of the subject (Ackerman and Carey, 1995).

Experts have emphasized the importance of cognitive or psycho-educational interventions for erectile disorder (Rosen et al., 1994). Males with chronic erectile difficulties typically have distorted thinking about the nature of sexual arousal, sexual skills, and their partners' expectations regarding sexual satisfaction. These inaccurate beliefs are potentially important foci for treatment. Rosen and colleagues (1994) have developed a cognitive-interpersonal therapy model that includes elements of cognitive restructuring, performance anxiety reduction, couples communication training, and relapse prevention planning.

Cross-Cultural Issues

A recent study in California examined the usefulness of Viagra in a group of 246 African American and 197 Hispanic American men with ED who were randomly selected to take Viagra or a placebo (Young et al., 2002). After 6 weeks, a significantly larger proportion of Viagra-treated patients reported better erections and improved ability to have sexual intercourse compared with the placebo-treated group. These results indicate that the usefulness of Viagra is maintained across these ethnic groups.

Resources

Cancer Care; 275 Seventh Avenue, New York, NY 10001; (800)813-HOPE; (212)712-8080; *www.cancercare.org*; is a national non-profit organization whose mission is to provide free professional help to people with all cancers through counseling, education, information, referral, and direct financial assistance.

Chronic Prostatitis/CPPS Discussion Forum, *www.chronicprostatitis .com*, provides support, information, and information forums for persons affected by chronic prostatitis, male chronic pelvic pain syndrome, or male interstitial cystitis.

Impotents World Association (Impotents Anonymous/I-Anon); P.O. Box 410, Bowie, MD 20718; (800)669-1603; 12-step fellowship for impotent men and their partners providing support and information. Newsletter included with affiliate membership. Physician reference list, videotapes and audiocassettes, and chapter development guidelines are available. Enclose a self-addressed stamped envelope when writing.

Malecare; 125 Second Avenue, Room 13, New York, NY 10003; (212)673-4920; *www.supportgroup.org*; an all-volunteer organization with support groups led by professionals who are themselves fighting cancer or are close relatives of cancer patients. Free weekly prostate cancer support groups in various cities. Also has support groups for gay men with prostate cancer.

Man to Man; American Cancer Society, P.O. Box 102454, Atlanta, GA 30368; (800) ACS-2345; *www.cancer.org/docroot/ESN/content/ ESN_3_1X_Man_to_Man_36.asp?sitearea=SHR;* helps men to cope with prostate cancer by providing community-based education, support, information, referrals, and support group meetings for patients and their family members. It also provides community education about prostate cancer, encouraging men and health care professionals to actively consider screening for prostate cancer appropriate to each man's age and risk for the disease. Call for information on local groups.

National Cancer Institute, Cancer Information Service; (800)422-6237 [(800)4-CANCER]; *www.nci.nih.gov;* coordinates the National Cancer Program, which conducts and supports research, training, health information dissemination, and other programs with respect to the cause, diagnosis, prevention, and treatment of cancer, rehabilitation from cancer, and the continuing care of cancer patients and the families of cancer patients.

National Prostate Cancer Coalition; 1154 Fifteenth Street, NW, Washington, DC 20005; (202)463-9455; *www.pcacoalition.org;* is an advocacy organization dedicated to ending the devastating impact of prostate cancer on men, families, and society. It increases awareness by educating the public about the disease, conducting free screenings for prostate cancer to at-risk communities, and engaging citizens and associations in an effort to build advocacy networks to encourage increases in funding for research on prostate cancer.

Us Too International; 930 North York Road, Suite 50, Hinsdale, IL 60521-2993; (800)808-7866; *www.ustoo.com;* is an international organization with more than 500 affiliated groups founded in 1990. It offers mutual support, information and education for persons with prostate problems (including cancer), their families, and friends.

Helpful Books *100 Questions and Answers about Erectile Dysfunction* (Pamela M. Ellsworth and Bob Stanley, Sudbury, NM: Jones and Bartlett, 2002).

Back to Great Sex: Overcome E.D. and Reclaim Lost Intimacy (Ridwan Shabsigh and Louis Ignarro, New York: Kensington Publishing, 2002).

Dr. Patrick Walsh's Guide to Surviving Prostate Cancer (Patrick C. Walsh and Janet Farrar Worthington, New York: Warner Books, 2002).

Erectile Dysfunction: Integrating Couple Therapy, Sex Therapy, and Medical Treatment (Gerald R. Weeks and Nancy Gambescia, New York: W. W. Norton, 2000).

His Prostate and Me: A Couple Deals with Prostate Cancer (Desiree Lyon Howe, Yakima, WA: Winedale Publishing, 2002).

Man to Man: Surviving Prostate Cancer (Michael Korda, New York: Knopf, 1997).

A Patient's Guide to Male Sexual Dysfunction (1st ed.) (Tom F. Lue, Newtown, PA: Handbooks in Health Care, 2000).

References

Ackerman, M. D., and Carey, M. P. (1995). Psychology's role in the assessment of erectile dysfunction: Historical precedents, current knowledge, and methods. *Journal of Consulting and Clinical Psychology*, 63, 862–876.

American Cancer Society. (2002). *Cancer Facts and Figures*. Atlanta: American Cancer Society.

American Psychiatric Association. (2000). *Diagnostic and Statistical Manual of Mental Disorders* (4th Ed. Text Revision). Washington, DC: American Psychiatric Association.

Bokhour, B. G., Clark, J. A., Silliman, R. A, and Talcott, J. A. (2001). Sexuality after treatment for early prostate cancer: Exploring the meanings of "erectile dysfunction." *Journal of Geriatric Internal Medicine*, 16, 649–655.

Davis, D. T., Bustances, A., Brown, C. P., Wolde-Tsadik, G., Savage, E. W., Cheng, X., and Howland, L. (1994). The urban church and cancer control: A source of social influence in minority communities. *Public Health Reports*, 109(4), 500–508.

Duan, N., Fox, S. A., Derose, K. P., and Carson, S. (2000). Maintaining mammography adherence through telephone counseling in a church based trial. *American Journal of Public Health*, 90(9), 1468–1471.

Feldman, H. A., Goldstein, I., Hatzichristou, G., Krane, R. J., and McKinlay, J. B. (1994). Impotence and its medical and psychosocial correlates: Results of the Massachusetts male aging study. *Journal of Urology*, 151, 54–61.

Kaplan, H. I., and Sadock, B. J. (1998). *Synopsis of Psychiatry: Behavioral Sciences/Clinical Psychiatry* (8th ed.). Baltimore: Williams and Wilkins.

Laumann, E. O., Paik, A., and Rosen, R. C. (1999). Sexual dysfunction in the United States: Prevalence and predictors. *Journal of the American Medical Association*, 281, 537–544.

McCullough, A. R. (2001). Prevention and management of erectile dysfunction following radical prostatectomy. *Urolology Clinic of North America*, 28(3), 613–627.

National Prostate Cancer Coalition. (2003). *Treatment Information.* Retrieved on June 3, 2003, from *www.pcacoalition.org/treatment_ info/.*

Perez, M. A., Meyerowitz, B. E., Lieskovsky, G., Skinner, D. G., Reynolds, B., and Skinner, E. C. (1997). Quality of life and sexuality following radical prostatectomy in patients with prostate cancer who use or do not use erectile aids. *Urology*, 50, 740–746.

Rosen, R. C., Leiblum, S. R., and Spector, I. (1994). Psychologically based treatment for male erectile disorder: A cognitive-interpersonal model. *Journal of Sex and Marital Therapy*, 20, 67–85.

Schover, L. R., Fouladi, R. T., Warneke, C. L., Neese, L., Klein, E. A., Zippe, C., and Kupelian, P. A. (2002). The use of treatments for erectile dysfunction among survivors of prostate carcinoma. *Cancer*, 95(11), 2397–2407.

Shabsigh, R., and Anastasiadis, A. G. (2003). Erectile dysfunction. *Annual Review of Medicine*, 54, 153–168.

Spector, I. P., and Carey, M. P. (1990). Incidence and prevalence of the sexual dysfunctions: A critical review of the empirical literature. *Archives of Sexual Behavior*, 19, 389–408.

Young, J. M., Bennett, C., Gilhooly, P., Wessells, H., and Ramos, D. E. (2002). Efficacy and safety of sildenafil citrate (Viagra) in black and Hispanic American men. *Urology*, 60(2 Suppl 2), 39–48.

Genital Herpes

"She was totally shocked"

Both Joyce and Mark Miller were lifelong members of the church and had been married there in a beautiful wedding. At twenty-four they were on top of the world and actively pursuing exciting careers. Joyce went to see her pastor, Rev. Donna Fernandez, a few months after her marriage. She told Rev. Fernandez that the preceding month she had come down with what she thought was a yeast infection. She experienced itching in her genital area and a painful, burning sensation while urinating. She wasn't too concerned — until the next day when her temperature rose to 103 degrees and she developed flu-like symptoms.

Joyce soon discovered sores on her genitals and went to see her gynecologist. She was surprised and dismayed when the doctor tested her for the herpes virus. "I was totally shocked. I never fooled around before my marriage, so how could I have contracted herpes?" The physician told her to return in a week for the test results. Two days later, Joyce felt so sick that she could barely walk and was in such pain that she had to sit in a bathtub filled with warm water in order to urinate. When she returned to her doctor, she discovered that she had tested positive for genital herpes. Her physician prescribed a common antiviral drug treatment. Still puzzled as to how she had become infected, she asked her husband if there was any chance that he had herpes. He denied the possibility, but agreed to be tested. When his results were positive, there was considerable anger, guilt, and stress in their relationship.

Pastoral Care Assessment

Genital herpes is a sexually transmitted disease (STD). About one in five adults in the United States has the virus. Since the late 1970s, the number of people with genital herpes has grown 30 percent (Armstrong et al., 2001) with the largest increase occurring in young teens. As many as 9 of 10 persons with the disease are unaware of it because they have very mild or no symptoms (Armstrong et al., 2001). The virus can travel the nerve pathways in the body and hide away, sleeping in nerve roots for long periods of time. Since anyone who is sexually active can contract genital herpes, it is important to learn to recognize the symptoms and get treatment as soon as possible. There are several blood tests that can give accurate results for the virus (Gillbert et al., 2002).

Genital herpes is not fatal for adults, but it can cause considerable distress among its sufferers. Depression, isolation, anger, guilt, self-criticism, loss of interest in sex or intimacy, self-imposed secrecy, and internal conflict all are commonly associated with the virus (Cummings, 1999). Given the social stigma of STDs, these reactions are not surprising. For many persons the anxiety and stress connected with a diagnosis of genital herpes may be worse than the actual symptoms. It is important to emphasize that it is a simple viral infection and not something about which to feel guilty or embarrassed. Individuals do not necessarily get genital herpes because they have had multiple sexual partners. It is possible to catch the disease even in a monogamous, long-term relationship, because a person can unknowingly have the virus for years without an outbreak (National Institute of Allergy and Infectious Diseases, 2003). Clergy and other religious professionals who are informed about herpes are in a position to give those suffering with it accurate information and emotional support that can facilitate psychological adjustment.

Relevant History   Women are at higher risk of contracting herpes than men, possibly due to a larger mucosal surface area exposed during sexual intercourse. The use of barrier protection, such as a condom, has been found to significantly reduce the transmission of the virus to females if used more than 25 percent of the time (Ooi and Dayan, 2002).

Diagnostic Criteria   Genital herpes is caused by the herpes simplex virus (HSV), which is in the family of viruses that also cause chicken pox and shingles. There are two types of herpes simplex: herpes simplex type 1 (HSV-1) and herpes simplex type 2 (HSV-2). HSV-1 causes a mild recurrent skin condition which can result in oral herpes ("cold sores" or "fever blisters" in the mouth or facial area), while HSV-2 causes genital herpes (similar symptoms in the genital region). However, outbreaks of HSV-2 can vary greatly from person to person (Ooi and Dayan, 2002).

Symptoms can last for 3 to 4 weeks, but they usually heal within 2 to 12 days. They may include sores, blisters, bumps, a rash, itching, burning, or tingling in the genital area. Like Joyce, some people have flu-like symptoms (headache, fever, swollen glands in the lymph nodes near the groin). Painful urination and a discharge (vaginal or penile) are possible, but uncommon, signs of genital herpes. The first outbreak may be the most extreme episode a person will have, and the average number of recurrences is four to five per year. Many individuals have outbreaks that heal quickly, cause no pain, or occur without being noticed (National Institute of Allergy and Infectious Diseases, 2003).

HSV is transmitted through direct skin-to-skin contact when a contagious area comes into contact with mucous membrane, primarily the mouth and genitals. Most skin on the body is too thick for the virus to enter. If a person with HSV-2 has sex, it is possible for his or her partner to become infected. Herpes is most often transmitted when there are no symptoms present. There are several days throughout the year, called asymptomatic reactivation or asymptomatic shedding, when a person can be contagious without having any symptoms (Ooi and Dayan, 2002).

There are no documented cases of a person getting genital herpes from an inanimate object such as a toilet seat, bathtub, or towel. HSV is a fragile virus and does not live long on surfaces. Although there is no cure for genital herpes there are antiviral medications in pill and ointment form approved by the Food and Drug Administration that are available for its treatment. These prescriptions may shorten the length of first episodes and reduce the severity and frequency of recurrent outbreaks (Gillbert et al., 2002).

In rare instances an infant can contract the virus from its mother. Twenty to 25 percent of pregnant women have genital herpes, and less than 0.1 percent of babies contract the disease. A mother passes her antibodies to the child during pregnancy, so women who acquire HSV-2 before becoming pregnant have a low risk of passing the virus to their babies. However, a mother who contracts genital herpes during the third trimester of pregnancy is at risk of passing it to the child because she has not had time to build up antibodies to HSV-2 (Rudnick and Hoekzema, 2002). Most women with genital herpes have normal vaginal deliveries. However, if a mother is symptomatic at the time of delivery, a Caesarean section is recommended.

If a baby contracts herpes during delivery, the symptoms tend to show within two to three weeks after birth. HSV-2 can be life-threatening to an infant. Half of the babies infected with the virus either die or suffer damage to their nerves. A child born with herpes can develop serious problems that may affect the brain, skin, or eyes. If babies born with the virus are treated immediately, their chances of being healthy are increased (Rudnick and Hoekzema, 2002). It is very important to avoid contracting herpes during pregnancy. Using condoms and not having sex while symptoms are present significantly reduces the risk of transmission.

Response to Vignette

Rev. Fernandez had the pastoral care and counseling skills to help the couple with the news that they were both infected with HSV-2. She was able to help them talk though their feelings of guilt, pain, and anger. The pastor researched the virus and was able to reassure them that the available medical treatments were effective and that the medications reduce the recurrence of symptoms for many. She was able to help both partners become more knowledgeable about herpes and help them put perspective on the experience.

Their pastor also assisted them in working on the process of forgiveness. Mark needed help to forgive himself for giving herpes to his wife, and Joyce needed to work on forgiving him for passing on the virus. They prayed together for God's help, and over time their faith enabled them both to forgive. The couple grew emotionally and spiritually from the experience and deepened their relationship with the help of God and Rev. Fernandez.

Several studies have shown that forgiveness is an important factor in successful marriage (Weaver and Furlong, 2000). Couples report that faith facilitates decision making, minimizes conflicts, and increases tolerance (Robinson, 1994). Couples who had been married for more than 20 years indicated that the capacity to seek and grant forgiveness had been essential to marital longevity and satisfaction (Fenell, 1993).

Treatment within the Faith Community

Researchers have found that individuals with genital herpes who are in support groups designed for their needs had less depression, loneliness, tension, anxiety, and mood disturbance than those without similar experience (Longo et al., 1988). Such groups can provide encouragement by allowing members to share their experiences, as well as facilitating the exchange of information. Members may also find that the groups are helpful in exposing them to new ways of thinking, overcoming denial, and enabling them to resolve ethical dilemmas.

Individuals with herpes often report feeling unlovable and untouchable. Support from faith communities who are accepting of those with this chronic and stigmatized medical condition can have great positive value. Congregations can also be of significant assistance by providing meeting space, as well as encouragement for those forming support groups. Additionally, faith communities can play an important role in addressing the stigma that is associated with herpes and other STDs through educational programs for teens and adults. Clergy can offer assistance by helping persons with HSV-2 to find resources and support.

There are some counseling situations that do not require a referral to a mental health specialist. Rev. Fernandez had the necessary skills to help Joyce and Mark address their crisis. However, some individuals become seriously depressed when they face the diagnosis of genital herpes or other STDs, especially those who feel a lot of anger about acquiring the infection (Dibble and Swanson, 2002). These persons will need a referral to a mental health professional.

Indications for Referral

Herpes-infected individuals who experience a major depression as a result of the psychological impact of the illness need to see a mental health clinician who is experienced in treating depression and knowledgeable about HSV-2. Symptoms of a major depression can include depressed mood, inability to enjoy things, difficulty sleeping, changes in patterns of eating and sleeping, problems in concentration and decision making, feelings of guilt, hopelessness, and decreased self-esteem (APA, 2000). A number of medications have been found to be effective in treating depression. Some of the newest antidepressants, called selective serotonin reuptake inhibitors (SSRIs), act in the brain on a chemical messenger called serotonin. SSRIs tend to have fewer side effects than older antidepressants and work best in conjunction with psychological counseling (Preston and Johnson, 1997).

Treatment by Mental Health Specialist

Researchers in Ohio examined the relationship between sexual behavior and HSV-2 among 96 African American college women (Lewis et al., 1999). Of the 96 females, 29 tested positive for HSV-2. The results of this study revealed that a history of STDs was predictive of genital herpes. Surprisingly, the number of lifetime partners, however, was not related to the disease. Four of the 13 students who reported only one lifetime partner were infected. These findings indicate that for young African American college women, the risk of getting genital herpes is high even with only one lifetime partner. Behavioral strategies focused on decreasing the number of sexual partners are not likely to be sufficient in preventing the spread of HSV-2 among young African American females. The development and use of alternative approaches to prevent the spread of HSV-2 among young African Americans should be considered.

Cross-Cultural Issues

American College of Obstetricians and Gynecologists; 409 Twelfth Street, SW, P.O. Box 96920, Washington, DC 20090; (202)863-2518; *www.acog.org*; serves as a strong advocate for quality health care for women, promotes patient education, and stimulates patient understanding of and involvement in medical care, and increases

Resources

awareness among its members and the public of the changing issues facing women's health care.

American Social Health Association, National Herpes Resource Center and Hotline; P.O. Box 13827, Research Triangle Park, NC 27709-9940; (919)361-8488; *www.ashastd.org/hrc/index.html*; is a trusted, nongovernmental resource that has advocated on behalf of patients to help improve public health outcomes since 1914. It provides facts, support, and resources to answer questions, find referrals, join HELP groups, and get access to in-depth information about sexually transmitted diseases.

Centers for Disease Control and Prevention (CDC); 1600 Clifton Road, Atlanta, GA 30333; (888)232-3228; *www.cdc.gov*; is recognized as the lead federal agency for protecting the health and safety of people — at home and abroad, providing credible information to enhance health decisions, and promoting health through strong partnerships. CDC serves as the national focus for developing and applying disease prevention and control, environmental health, and health promotion and education activities designed to improve the health of the people of the United States.

Division of STD Prevention, Centers for Disease Control and Prevention; (800)227-8922; *www.cdc.gov/nchstp/dstd/dstdp.html*; provides information, a 24-hour hotline, links to resources, national leadership through research, policy development, and support of effective services to prevent sexually transmitted diseases and their complications, such as enhanced HIV transmission, infertility, adverse outcomes of pregnancy, and reproductive tract cancer. It assists in training health departments, health care providers, and nongovernmental organizations.

National Institute of Allergy and Infectious Diseases, U.S. Department of Health and Human Services; 200 Independence Avenue, SW, Washington, DC 20201; (202)619-0257; (877)696-6775; *www.niaid.nih.gov/factsheets/stdherp.htm*; provides information, links, policy information, and financial guidance about diagnosis, treatment, and prevention of a wide range of diseases and other health issues.

National STD and AIDS Hotline, (800)227-8922 or (800)342-2437, provides 24-hour toll-free information on sexually transmitted diseases (STDs) to the general public. Health communication specialists are trained to convey accurate, basic information and referrals to free or low-cost clinics nationwide. Free educational literature about a wide variety of sexually transmitted diseases and prevention methods are also available. Specialists also answer questions about transmission, prevention, and treatment for diseases such as gonorrhea, Chlamydia, HPV/genital warts, herpes, HIV, and others.

Helpful Books

Genital Herpes (Hunter H. Handsfield, New York: McGraw-Hill, 2001).

The Official Patient's SourceBook on Genital Herpes (James N. Parker and Phillip M. Parker, San Diego: ICON Health Publications, 2002).

Understanding Herpes (Lawrence Raymond Stanberry and Regan Causey Tuder, Jackson: University of Mississippi Press, 1998).

References

American Psychiatric Association. (2000). *Diagnostic and Statistical Manual of Mental Disorders* (4th ed., text revision). Washington, DC: American Psychiatric Association.

Armstrong, G. L., Schillinger, J., Markowitz, L., Nahmias, A. J., Johnson, R. E., and McQuillan, G. M. (2001). Incidence of herpes simplex virus type 2 infection in the United States. *American Journal of Epidemiology*, 153(9), 912–920.

Cummings, A. L. (1999). Experiential interventions for clients with genital herpes. *Canadian Journal of Counseling*, 33(2), 142–156.

Dibble, S. L., and Swanson, J. M. (2002). Gender differences for the predictors of depression in young adults with genital herpes. *Public Health Nursing*, 17(3), 187–194.

Fenell, D. L. (1993). Characteristics of long-term first marriages. *Journal of Mental Health Counseling*, 15(4), 446–460.

Gillbert, L. K., Schultz, S. L., and Ebel, C. (2002). Education and counseling for genital herpes: Perspectives from patients. *Herpes*, 9(3), 78–82.

Lewis, L. M., Bernstein, D. I., Rosenthal, S. L., and Stanberry, L. R. (1999). Seroprevalence of herpes simplex virus-type 2 in African American college women. *Journal of the National Medical Association*, 91(4), 210–212.

Longo, D. J., Glum, G. A., and Yaeger, N. J. (1988). Psychosocial treatment for recurrent genital herpes. *Journal of Consulting and Clinical Psychology*, 56(1), 61–66.

National Institute of Allergy and Infectious Diseases. (2003). Health matters: What is genital herpes? *National Institutes of Health, U.S. Department of Health and Human Services*, retrieved June 10, 2003, from *www.niaid.nih.gov/factsheets/stdherp.htm*.

Ooi, C., and Dayan, U. (2002). Genital herpes: An approach for general practitioners in Australia. *Australian Family Physician*, 31(9), 825–830.

Preston, J., and Johnson, J. (1997). *Clinical Psychopharmacology Made Ridiculously Simple*. Miami: MedMaster.

Robinson, L. C. (1994). Religious orientation in enduring marriage: An exploratory study. *Review of Religious Research*, 35, 207–218.

Rudnick, C. M., and Hoekzema, G. S. (2002). Neonatal herpes simplex virus infections. *American Family Physician*, 65(6), 1138–1142.

Weaver, A. J., and Furlong, M. (eds.) (2000). *Reflections on Forgiveness and Spiritual Growth*. Nashville: Abingdon Press.

OTHER STDs

Sexually transmitted diseases (STDs), once called venereal diseases, are among the most common infectious diseases in the United States. In spite of all the publicity surrounding AIDS, STDs are on the increase. According to the National Institutes of Health, more than 20 STDs have been identified, most of which have no noticeable symptoms and can be diagnosed only through testing. Unfortunately, routine screening is not widespread, and both social stigma and lack of public awareness about STDs frequently limit needed testing. Every year, there are approximately 15 million new STD cases, some of which are curable. The estimated number of people living in the United States with an incurable STD is over 65 million. Two-thirds of all STDs occur in persons 25 years of age or younger. One in four new STD infections occurs in teenagers.

STDs, other than HIV, cost more than $8 billion each year to diagnose and treat both the disease and their complications.

Acquired Immunodeficiency Syndrome (AIDS) (see case 6)

AIDS is caused by the human immunodeficiency virus (HIV), which destroys the body's capacity to fight infections. There are an estimated 600,000 cases of AIDS diagnosed in the United States and 40,000 to 80,000 new HIV infections reported each year (Centers for Disease Control, 2003). Persons who have AIDS are very susceptible to other diseases. Transmission of the virus primarily occurs during sexual activity or by sharing needles used to inject intravenous drugs. Pregnant women with AIDS can transmit the virus to their babies.

Chlamydial Infections

These infections are the most common of all STDs, with an estimated 4 million new cases each year. Many people with chlamydial infection have few or no symptoms. Pelvic inflammatory disease (PID), a serious complication of the infection, has emerged as a major cause of infertility among women. Once diagnosed, chlamydial infections are treatable with antibiotics.

Cancroid

Cancroid is a highly contagious, though curable, STD, caused by the bacteria Haemophilus Ducreyi. It causes ulcers, usually of the genitals. Swollen, painful lymph glands or inguinal buboes in the groin area are often associated with cancroid. Left untreated, cancroid can facilitate the transmission of HIV. This STD is very common in Africa and is becoming more common in the United States. A person is considered to be infectious when ulcers are present. However, there has been no reported disease in infants born to women with active cancroid at time of delivery. Cancroid can be treated with antibiotics. Successful treatment cures the infection, resolves symptoms, and prevents transmission.

Genital Herpes (see this chapter)

An estimated 23 percent of adult Americans suffer from this infection, with half a million new cases each year. The major signs of herpes are painful blisters or open sores in the genital area. The sores disappear in 2 or 3 weeks, but the virus remains in the body and the lesions may recur occasionally. Genital herpes symptoms can be helped with antiviral medication, but the virus remains in the body and there is no cure. Women who acquire genital herpes during pregnancy can transmit the virus to the baby, which can have serious health risks to the child if left untreated.

Genital Warts

Genital warts are caused by the human papillomavirus (HPV). The warts first appear as hard, painless bumps in the genital area. Genital warts are spread by sexual contact with an infected partner and are very contagious. An estimated 1 million new cases are diagnosed in the United States each year. Scientists believe that HPV may also cause several types of genital cancer. The warts are treated with a topical substance or by freezing.

Gonorrhea

Gonorrhea, also known as "the clap," is a curable infection caused by bacteria. It targets the cells of the mucous membranes, including the surfaces of the urethra, vagina, cervix, fallopian tubes, anus, and rectum; the lining of the eyelid; and the throat. Gonorrhea is passed during oral, anal, or vaginal sex. Gonorrhea is not spread by shaking hands or on toilet seats. There are about 1.5 million cases in the United States each year. The early symptoms of gonorrhea often are mild, and most women have no symptoms of the disease. If symptoms develop, they usually appear within 2 to 10 days after sexual contact with an infected partner. The common signs of gonorrhea are discharge from the vagina or penis or painful/burning urination. It can be treated with antibiotics. The most common complication for women is infertility.

Hepatitis B

This is an inflammation of the liver caused by the virus Hepatitis B (HBV). In the severe form, it is a serious threat to health and can sometimes lead to liver failure and death. HBV is most commonly passed on to a sexual partner during intercourse, especially during anal sex, though it can also be contracted by sharing needles used to inject intravenous drugs. It is estimated that 70,000 persons in the United States become infected annually. At present, there are no specific treatments for the acute symptoms of this virus. Hepatitis B is 100 times more infectious than HIV.

Syphilis

This infection has been on the increase in many cities in the United States in recent years. An estimated 100,000 cases occur annually. Syphilis is an STD caused by a bacterium. The initial sign is a painless open sore in the genital area that generally appears within 2 to 6 weeks after sexual contact. If untreated, the disease can damage the central nervous system and cause death. Penicillin is commonly used to treat syphilis.

Trichomoniasis

Trichomoniasis, sometimes referred to as "trich," is a common STD that affects 2 to 3 million Americans each year. It is caused by a parasite and often occurs without symptoms. If symptoms occur, they are in the form of genital discharge. This is treatable with medication.

HIV/AIDS

"She felt overwhelmed by the diagnosis"

Mrs. Thomas was a longtime parishioner of the First African Methodist Episcopal Church where Rev. Claire Jefferson served as pastor. Mrs. Thomas and her husband had raised their granddaughter, Latisha, since she was 12 years old when her parents were killed in a car crash. Latisha, who is somewhat overweight and has low self-confidence, struggled with depression after the death of her parents. Rev. Jefferson counseled the family and had been a great deal of help to them over the years. Twenty-year-old Latisha had been living on her own for two years and working as an administrative assistant when she suddenly told Mrs. Thomas that she had tested positive for HIV (the human immunodeficiency virus). Devastated and confused, Mrs. Thomas went to see the pastor the next day. Latisha had contracted the disease by having sex with a man she met on the Internet. When Rev. Jefferson made a pastoral visit to see Latisha, the young woman was feeling overwhelmed, depressed, isolated, and frightened.

Latisha is clearly in the midst of a crisis after being confronted with **Pastoral Care** a traumatic diagnosis. In addition to education, Latisha needs support **Assessment** and counseling to get her through this initial stressful period. A careful assessment should be made to determine her level of depression and possible suicidal potential. Depressive symptoms are commonly reported as a response to a diagnosis of serious health problems (Wells et al., 1988), so it is important to be able to recognize and diagnose it. A major depression is present when there have been two weeks or more of feeling sad, gloomy, depressed, irritable, or experiencing a loss of interest, motivation, or enjoyment in usual activities (APA, 2000). Along with a depressed mood or loss of interest, a person may experience fatigue or loss of energy; lethargy or increased restlessness (agitation); extreme change (gain or loss) in appetite or weight; difficulty sleeping or sleeping too much; loss of social or sexual interest; feelings of worthlessness or excessive guilt; difficulty concentrating; feeling that life is not worth living, wanting to die, or feeling suicidal. If an individual has thought about suicide and has a means or plan, emergency mental health treatment is needed.

Latisha's feeling overwhelmed by her situation is normal and to be expected. People often face a deep grief while accepting a severe diagnosis. Unfortunately, though her relationships should be the key resource for helping her cope, HIV infection can have devastating effects on interpersonal relationships, including isolation, rejection, and overall loss of social support (Aguilera, 1994). An HIV diagnosis often brings with it multiple psychological effects including depression, anxiety, loss of hope about the future, and issues of death and dying (Fleishman and Fogel, 1994). Support systems should be put in place to help Latisha cope with the various challenges she will face. She needs concrete information, emotional support, and empowerment so that she can approach her illness in a positive and proactive manner. Straightforward counseling that gives her credit for being capable, responsible, and intelligent will be the most helpful. People often feel angry and guilty during periods of grief, without knowing that this is normal. When Latisha expresses her fears and concerns, Rev. Jefferson can help her with emotional/spiritual support.

Relevant History Recent data from the HIV Epidemiological Research Study reported that females with HIV and chronic depressive symptoms had a significantly greater decline in immune system indicators over several years than women with limited or no depressive symptoms (Ickovics et al., 2001). Women in this study with chronic depressive symptoms were twice as likely to die as those with no depressive symptoms. Given the high risk for chronic stress and subsequent risk for depressive symptoms among African American females with HIV, treating depression may be critical to survival.

The Internet tends to be a fairly quick, easy, and anonymous way to meet people. This high accessibility to other singles accelerates the pace of dating and sex, which may lead people to the dangerous practice of having multiple sex partners. Seeking partners via the Internet was found to be a fairly common practice in a sample of 856 persons seeking HIV testing and counseling in Colorado (McFarlane et al., 2000). Among the clients surveyed, most were men (69.2 percent) and heterosexual (65.3 percent). Of those, 135 (15.8 percent) had sought partners on the Internet, and 88 (65.2 percent) of these reported having sex with a partner initially met via the Internet. Of those with Internet partners, 34 (38.7 percent) had four or more such partners. This research supports the case that those who seek partners using the Internet appear to be more likely to have multiple sexual partners, which puts them at a greater risk of contracting HIV.

Diagnostic Criteria

AIDS (acquired immune deficiency syndrome) is caused by HIV, which selectively attacks T-helper/inducer cells and other cells (Centers for Disease Control, 2003). AIDS destroys the body's capacity to fight infections, making a person very susceptible to other diseases. AIDS can affect almost any system in the body. Common signs of AIDS include fever, night sweats, persistent fatigue, weight loss, diarrhea, dry cough, and dementia. Transmission of the virus primarily occurs during sexual activity and by sharing needles used to inject intravenous drugs. A pregnant woman with AIDS can transmit the virus to her fetus. HIV is not spread through everyday activities or casual contact (Centers for Disease Control, 2003). A person cannot be infected from drinking fountains, handshakes, hugs, sneezes, swimming pools, sweat, tears, or being around an infected person. Studies of thousands of households where AIDS patients have lived and been cared for have found no instances of transmission from the sharing of kitchen, laundry, or bathroom facilities (Centers for Disease Control, 2003).

AIDS was first described in 1981 in the USA and since then has become a worldwide pandemic. The HIV/AIDS epidemic in the United States continues to expand, with over 600,000 cases of AIDS diagnosed and 40,000 to 80,000 new HIV infections reported each year (Centers for Disease Control, 2003). Although the HIV/AIDS epidemic in the United States began more than two decades ago, primarily as a disease of gay and bisexual men, it has expanded to an increasing number of communities, with African Americans now disproportionately affected. AIDS mortality rates remain nearly 10 times higher among African Americans than European Americans (Centers for Disease Control, 1999), and the discrepancy is particularly notable in women. Approximately 1 in 160 African American females are believed to be infected with HIV, compared to 1 in 3,000 European American women (Centers for Disease Control, 1999). Among Americans 25 to 44 years old, AIDS accounts for one in three deaths among African American men and one in five deaths in African American women. The majority of women infected with HIV are of childbearing age, and many are of low income status (Centers for Disease Control, 1999).

Although there is currently no cure for HIV, many improvements have been made in the management of the disease since the discovery of highly active antiretroviral therapeutic agents in 1996 (Centers for Disease Control, 2003). Complex combinations of pharmaceuticals, called "drug cocktails," can now significantly reduce viral load and stabilize T-cell counts in some people with HIV. The advent of these new therapies has substantially lowered death rates associated with HIV. These innovations in treatment have highlighted the importance of early detection of the infection. Without an effective preventive vaccine in the foreseeable future, risk-reduction interventions targeted to the highest risk populations offer the greatest hope for curtailing the spread of HIV (Centers for Disease Control, 2003).

Response to Vignette

Rev. Jefferson can best use her lengthy pastoral relationship by providing an environment that will reduce Latisha's anxiety long enough to develop a plan of action. The plan should include acquiring education, as well as medical and emotional support. Referral information must be offered to Latisha so she can easily access persons and agencies that specialize in the treatment of HIV and depression. Since people often have misconceptions about HIV that add to the distress, providing her with factual information may be reassuring. It is important that the pastor be available to Latisha's family — since many people have little knowledge about HIV and AIDS, accurate information may help to address many fears and concerns. Family members may experience grief, guilt, blame, stigma, and isolation. People often feel angry and guilty during periods of grief, and they may also harbor irrational fears which can interfere with their ability to provide adequate care. By discussing the topic in an open and nonjudgmental manner, Rev. Jefferson will serve as a positive role model for dealing with the disease and its emotional consequences.

Some people, when diagnosed with HIV or when faced with a family member's diagnosis, adopt denial and avoidance coping strategies that can interfere with their utilization of health and psychological services (Chesney and Folkman, 1994). It will be important to discuss this tendency with Latisha and to try to motivate her to seek needed services promptly. It is necessary to explain that ignoring HIV will leave her feeling isolated and depressed and may keep her from getting the medical attention that will alleviate symptoms and help her to live longer. Once the acute anxiety and depression is stabilized, Latisha will need assistance with other issues, including those that many people are uncomfortable discussing, such as sexuality, long-term illness, and feelings about death. Clergy are in a unique position to help.

Churches and mosques are the largest social, informational, spiritual, and educational institutions in African American communities and have enormous influence on the social norms. African American religious communities and their leaders possess the potential to educate constituents to prevent the spread of HIV and provide models of compassion for dealing with people affected by HIV. Those living with HIV/AIDS may experience stigmatizing and discriminatory situations that can demoralize them and threaten their social and professional lives (Herek, 1999).

Treatment within the Faith Community

Churches in the African American community have historically been a strong voice against prejudices of every kind. They have also offered a wide array of support services for members and the larger community. The African American church has assisted with basic needs (food, shelter, clothing), childcare, elder care, health care, and transportation, as well as providing emotional, social, and spiritual support (Taylor and Chatters, 1986; Young et al., 2003). Churches have also served as agencies for health education and disease prevention programs (Duan et al., 2000; Kumanyika and Charleston, 1992). However, the stigma related to HIV/AIDS complicates the church's role in providing advocacy and support for those coping with its health challenge, and critics say that the African American faith community has not been in the forefront in addressing the epidemic (Flunder, 2001).

A chronic illness like AIDS places unique stressors on a person's mental health. Research examining people living with chronic illness has repeatedly found that religious commitment improves one's ability to cope with the problems related to long-term illness (Pargament, 1997) and is an effective support mechanism, often involving a search for spiritual meaning. Faith communities provide important social networks as well as facilitating personal adjustment. Congregations also offer an array of support resources such as economic assistance and pastoral care.

Somlai and colleagues (1996) found that individuals living with HIV/AIDS were more likely to participate in prayer and other formal religious activities than noninfected persons. Long-term survival for those with HIV/AIDS has been found to be strongly associated with both frequency of prayer and a positive mental attitude. In addition, persons with a strong religious commitment who have HIV/AIDS show less distress, have more hope, experience more social support, and are involved in helping others to a greater extent (Ironson et al., 2002). Religious behavior (such as worship attendance, prayer, spiritual discussion, reading religious materials) was found to be strongly associated with higher T-helper-inducer cell counts among homosexual men (Woods et al., 1999).

Given that people are living longer with current therapeutic strategies for HIV infection, quality of life has emerged as an important consideration. Research has shown that psychological well-being, social support systems, effective coping strategies, and spiritual well-being are important predictors of life quality in this group (Douailhy and Singh, 2001). Pargament and colleagues (1990) found that the best predictors of positive outcome for those with HIV/AIDS were the experience of God as a supportive partner, involvement in religious rituals, the search for spiritual and personal support through religion, and belief in a just, loving God. Jenkins (1995) found that African Americans with HIV, in comparison to European Americans with the disease, indicated a greater preference for a coping style involving religion.

Indications for Referral

Latisha will need to be referred to a mental health professional if she meets the criteria of a major depression or continues to feel overwhelmed. A serious risk in depression is suicide, because 15 percent of depressed persons take their lives (Preston, 2001). Unfortunately, many individuals suffering from depression never receive professional mental health treatment, contributing to chronic mental health deterioration and the risk of suicide. If at any point a person's difficulties are beyond a pastor's level of training or experience, a referral should be made immediately.

Treatment by Mental Health Specialist

A combination of medication and cognitive-behavioral therapy is the standard treatment for depression, and these treatments together have a success rate of 80 to 90 percent. Some of the newer antidepressants, called selective serotonin reuptake inhibitors (SSRIs), act in the brain on a chemical messenger called serotonin. SSRIs tend to have fewer side effects than older antidepressants (Preston et al., 2001). Medications for depression can be likened to a cast on a broken arm — a temporary support that promotes healing.

In cognitive-behavioral therapy, there is an attempt to change depression-producing beliefs and attitudes to healthier, more realistic ones. Behaviors that produce pleasure and fulfillment are also encouraged. Many depressed persons define their lives in global terms like "everything is going wrong" or "nothing is working out." Depressed individuals tend to conclude the worst, dwell on negative details, and devalue the positive. Cognitive-behavioral therapy seeks to stop or modify these pessimistic "automatic thoughts" that persons use to define themselves, their environment, and the future. If these beliefs go unrecognized and unchallenged, such distorted thinking may result in serious depression. Usually treatment involves self-monitoring of mood and activities, sometimes in the form of keeping a daily log.

Cross-Cultural Issues

Hispanic women constitute 17 percent of new AIDS cases among females. The most common means of exposure for Hispanic females is heterosexual contact (43 percent), followed by intravenous drug use (23 percent) (Centers for Disease Control, 2001). In the Commonwealth of Puerto Rico, the proportion of AIDS cases accounted for by women increased from 11 percent in 1986 to 25 percent in 1998 (Puerto Rico Health Department, 1998). Today, HIV infection is the third leading cause of death among Hispanic women between the ages of 25 and 44 in the United States (including Puerto Rico). When testing 142 Puerto Rican American females with HIV/AIDS in New York City for depression, researchers found high rates, with 2 of 3 scoring above the clinical depression range.

Resources

Advocates for Youth; 1025 Vermont Avenue, NE, Suite 200, Washington DC 20005; (202)347-5700; *www.advocatesforyouth.org*; provides information on STDs for youth and parents.

AIDS Advocacy in African American Churches Project; 611 Pennsylvania, SE, Suite 359, Washington, DC 20003; (202)546-8587.

AIDS National Interfaith Network; 1400 I Street, NW, Suite 1220, Washington, DC 20005; (202)842-0010; *www.thebody.com/anin/aninpage.html*; is a network of nearly 2,000 ministries working with faith-based AIDS networks to support community-based AIDS ministries and to educate AIDS service organizations, the religious community, and the general public about AIDS ministries. It provides support, care, and assistance to individuals with HIV/AIDS through programs including networking/collaboration, referral activities, public education, and federal AIDS policy advocacy.

American Social Health Association; P.O. Box 13827, Research Triangle Park, NC 27709; (800)783-9877; *www.ashastd.org*; has free and confidential information from their Web site about STDs and STD hotlines.

Ark of Refuge: HIV/AIDS Ministry; 1025 Howard Street, San Francisco, CA 94103; (415)861-1060; *www.arkofrefuge.org*; provides facts about HIV/AIDS, technical assistance, resources, housing information, and youth services to people of color, low-income people, women, and the homeless with HIV.

Balm in Gilead; 130 West Forty-second Street, Suite 450, New York, NY 10036; (212)730-7381; *www.balmingilead.org/home.asp*; is a national organization that provides leadership, technical support, and training to churches and organizations, and develops HIV/AIDS educational resources specifically for use by black congregations. The organization has a national network throughout the United States for collaboration on educational projects within the black church.

Centers for Disease Control, National Prevention Information Network; P.O. Box 6003, Rockville, MD 20849-6003; (800)458-5231; *www.cdcnpin.org*; is a resource guide to assist religious communities in developing HIV prevention programs. The guide lists religious publications, educational materials, national religious organizations that provide technical assistance, and Web sites that provide additional resources and information.

Critical Path AIDS Project; 2062 Lombard Street, Philadelphia, PA 19146; (215)545-2212; *www.critpath.org*; provides 24-hour online access to HIV information and local resources for the Philadelphia metropolitan area.

HIV/AIDS Ministries Network; Health and Welfare Ministries, United Methodist General Board of Global Ministries, 475 Riverside Drive, Room 350, New York, NY 10115; (212)870-3909; *gbgm-umc.org/health/aids*; is a network of United Methodists and others who care about the global HIV/AIDS pandemic and those whose lives have been touched. Its projects include Healthy Homes, Healthy Families and the AIDS Orphans Trust.

HIV Positive.com; 588 Broadway, Suite 810, New York, NY 10012; (810)878-8588; *www.hivpositive.com*; provides services, resources, data/fact sheets, financial support information, housing information, services to help persons find doctors, news about HIV/AIDS, and medication information.

Minority HIV/AIDS Initiative; Office of Minority Health Resource Center, EDN, P.O. Box 37337, Washington, DC 20013-7337; (800)444-6472; *www.omhrc.gov/OMH/AIDS/aidshome_new.htm*; provides funds to community-based organizations, faith communities, research institutions, minority-serving colleges and universities, health care organizations, state and local health departments, and correctional institutions to help them address the HIV/AIDS epidemic within the minority populations they serve.

National Association of People with AIDS; 1413 K Street, NW, Suite 7, Washington, DC 20005; (202)898-0414; *www.napwa.org*; is a national network of persons with AIDS founded in 1986 as a voice for health, social, and political concerns.

National Black Leadership Commission on AIDS; 105 East Twenty-second Street, Suite 711, New York, NY 10010; (212)614-0023; *www.nblca.org*; is a national organization that provides assistance to groups (such as the black church) through community development, technical assistance, and the formulation of public policy related to HIV/AIDS.

National Catholic AIDS Network; P.O. Box 422984, San Francisco, CA 94142; (707)874-3031; *www.ncan.org*; assists the church in recognizing the pain and challenges inherent in the HIV/AIDS pandemic and in living out the gospel mandate by offering compassionate support, education, referrals, and technical assistance.

Sexuality Information and Education Council of the United States; 130 West Forty-second Street, Suite 350, New York, NY 10036; (212)819-9776; *www.siecus.org*; has fact sheets on STDs.

Union of American Hebrew Congregations — Central Conference of American Rabbis Committee on AIDS; 2027 Massachusetts Avenue, NW, Washington, DC 20036; (202)232-4343; provides referrals to local congregations.

Helpful Books

And the Band Played On: Politics, People, and the AIDS Epidemic (Randy Shilts, New York: St. Martin's Press, 1999).

The Church with AIDS: Renewal in the Midst of Crisis (Letty M. Russell, Randall C. Bailey, and Anne P. Scheibner, Louisville: Westminster John Knox, 1990).

The Continuing Challenge of AIDS: Clergy Responses to Patients, Friends, and Families (Robert E. Beckley and Jerome R. Koch, Westport, CT: Greenwood Publishing Group, 2002).

A Guide to HIV/AIDS Education in Religious Settings (New York Department of Health, Distribution Center, Rensselaer, NY, 1999).

HIV/AIDS: Practical, Medical, and Spiritual Guidelines for Daily Living When You're HIV-Positive (Mark Jenkins, Center City, MN: Hazelden Information and Educational Services, 2000).

Living Well with HIV and AIDS (Allen L. Gifford, Diana Laurent, Kate Lorig, Virginia González, Palo Alto, CA: Bull Publishing, 2000).

The Samaritan's Imperative: Compassionate Ministry to People Living with AIDS (Michael J. Christensen, Nashville: Abingdon Press, 1994).

References   Aguilera, D. C. (1994). *Crisis Intervention: Theory and Methodology.* St. Louis: Mosby-Year Book.

American Psychiatric Association. (2000). *Diagnostic and Statistical Manual of Mental Disorders* (4th ed., text revision). Washington, DC: American Psychiatric Association.

Centers for Disease Control and Prevention. (2003). *National center for HIV, STD and TB prevention, divisions of HIV/AIDS prevention.* Retrieved on May 5, 2003, from *www.cdc.gov/hiv/pubs/facts.htm #Role.*

Centers for Disease Control and Prevention. (2001). *HIV/AIDS surveillance report* (Volume 13, Part 1). Atlanta: Centers for Disease Control and Prevention.

Centers for Disease Control and Prevention. (1999). *HIV/AIDS surveillance report: U.S. HIV and AIDS cases reported through June 1999.* Retrieved on May 6, 2003, from *www.cdc.gov/hiv/stats/hasr1101 .pdf.*

Chesney, M. A., and Folkman, S. (1994). Psychological impact of HIV disease and implications for intervention. *Psychiatric Clinics of North America, 17*(1), 163–182.

Douailhy, A., and Singh, N. (2001). Patient care factors affecting quality of life in patients with HIV infection. *The AIDS Reader, 11*(9), 450–454.

Duan, N., Fox, S. A., Derose, K. P., and Carson, S. (2000). Maintaining mammography adherence through telephone counseling in a church-based trial. *American Journal of Public Health, 90*(9), 1468–1471.

Fleishman, J. A., and Fogel, B. (1994). Coping and depressive symptoms among people with AIDS. *Health Psychology, 13,* 156–169.

Flunder, Y. A. (2001). My people are destroyed for lack of knowledge: Ministering and HIV. *Focus, 16*(10), 5–6.

Herek, G. M. (1999). AIDS and stigma. *American Behavioral Scientist, 42,* 1106–1116.

Ickovics, J. R., Hamburger, M. C., Vlahov, D., Schoenbaum, E. E., Schuman, P., Boland, R., and Moore, J. (2001). Mortality, CD4 cell count decline, and depressive symptoms among HIV-seropositive women: Longitudinal analysis from the HIV Epidemiology Research Study. *Journal of the American Medical Association, 285,* 1466–1474.

Ironson, G., Soloman, G. K., Balbin, E. G., O'Cleirigh, C., George, A., Kumar, M., Larson, D., and Woods, T. E. (2002). The Ironson-Woods Spirituality/Religiousness Index is associated with long survival, health behaviors, less distress, and low cortisol in people with HIV/AIDS. *Annals of Behavioral Medicine*, 24(1), 34–48.

Jenkins, R. A. (1995). Religion and HIV: Implications for research and intervention. *Journal of Social Issues*, 51, 131–144.

Kumanyika, S. K., and Charleston, J. B. (1992). Lose weight and win: A church-based weight loss program for blood pressure control among Black women. *Patient Education and Counseling*, 19, 19–32.

McFarlane, M., Bull, S. M., and Rietmeijer, C. A. (2000). The Internet as a newly emerging risk environment for sexually transmitted diseases. *Journal of the American Medical Association*, 284, 443–446.

Pargament, K. I. (1997). *The Psychology of Religion and Coping: Theory, Research, Practice*. New York: Guilford Press.

Pargament, K. I., Ensing, D. S., Falgout, K., Olsen, H., et al. (1990). God help me: I. Religious coping efforts as predictors of the outcomes of significant negative life events. *American Journal of Community Psychology*, 18(6), 793–824.

Preston, J. D. (2001). *You Can Beat Depression*. San Luis Obispo, CA: Impact Publishers.

Preston, J. D., O'Neal, J. H., and Talaga, M. (2001). *Handbook of Clinical Psychopharmacology for Therapists*. Oakland, CA: New Harbinger.

Puerto Rico Health Department. (1998). *Reported AIDS cases in Puerto Rico*. San Juan: Puerto Rico Health Department.

Radloff, L. S. (1977). The CES-D scale: A self-report depression scale for research in the general population. *Applied Psychological Measurement*, 1, 385–401.

Simoni, J. M., and Ortiz, M. Z. (2003). Mediational models of spirituality and depressive symptomatology among HIV-positive Puerto Rican women. *Cultural Diversity and Ethnic Minority Psychology*, 9(1), 3–15.

Somlai, A. M., Kelly, J. A., Kalichman, S. C., Mulry, G., Sikkema, K. J., McAuliffe, T., Multhauf, K., and Davantes, B. (1996). An empirical investigation of the relationship between spirituality, coping, and emotional distress in people living with HIV infection and AIDS. *Journal of Pastoral Care*, 50(2), 181–191.

Taylor, R., and Chatters, L. (1986). Church-based informal support among elderly Blacks. *Gerontologist*, 26, 637–642.

Wells, K., Golding, J. M., and Burnam, M. A. (1988). Psychiatric disorder and limitations in physical functioning in a sample of Los

Angeles general population. *American Journal of Psychiatry*, 145, 712–717.

Woods, T. E., Antoni, M. H., Ironson, G. H., and Kling, D. W. (1999). Religiosity is associated with affective and immune status in symptomatic HIV-infected gay men. *Journal of Psychosomatic Research*, 46(2), 165–176.

Young, J. L., Griffith, E. E. H., and Williams, D. R. (2003). The integral role of pastoral counseling by African American clergy in community mental health. *Psychiatric Services*, 54(5), 688–692.

Hysterectomy

"She turned away in tears"

F umi greeted Rev. Jackson with a smile and a "hello" as she always
did when she came to the church office. She had been teaching
Sunday school for the past four years and frequently ran into
the minister when she visited the church's library of children's books.
Today, however, the pastor was surprised at Fumi's unusual response
to his usual polite inquiry, "How are you today, Fumi?" It unexpect-
edly resulted in tears springing to her eyes, and she quickly turned away
from him. After gently questioning her, Rev. Jackson realized that whatever was troubling Fumi, she did not want to talk about it with him.
Acting on a hunch, he asked if she would like to talk to the associate
pastor, Rev. Janet Vaughn — a woman a few years older than Fumi's
41 years. Fumi hesitated, but then decided to make an appointment to
see Rev. Vaughn.

At the scheduled visit two days later, after a brief chat about church
business, Fumi again teared up when asked how she was doing. She
told Rev. Vaughn that she was having health problems and had recently
been told by her doctor that she needed a hysterectomy. The prospect of
major surgery was looming, but the toll that several years of persistent
and life-disrupting symptoms had taken on her was equally disturbing.
She described pain, restrictions in her normal life activities, excessive
bleeding, and resultant embarrassing situations. Fumi had quit her exercise class, missed days of work, curtailed social activities, and was
feeling the effects of disrupted sleep for four or five days a month. In
addition, she worried about the effects of her current problems and
of the surgery on her relationship with her husband, John; they had
only been married three years and had no children. Their sex life was
now virtually nonexistent, and they had talked very little about that or
about the ramifications of the surgery. She admitted to being afraid —
and felt alone and uncertain.

Pastoral Care Assessment

Rev. Jackson was perceptive in recognizing the verbal and nonverbal indications of Fumi's discomfort and her reluctance to talk with him about her problem. He accurately surmised that she might open up to a female and made a referral to a clergywoman.

Rev. Vaughn assessed Fumi's situation and recognized the broad scope of the issues involved:

Medical — The decision of whether or not to have surgery; the need for further information regarding alternatives, options, risks, and benefits; the need for answers to her questions about the surgical procedure, recovery time, and probable results; the possibility of, or more information about, hormone replacement therapy.

Social — Fumi's increasing withdrawal from activities due, at times, to almost debilitating conditions.

Psychological — Her feelings of fear, confusion, uncertainty, sadness, grief (for loss of reproductive organs, a chance to have a child, a sense of herself as a woman); she had not developed the skills necessary to directly and assertively talk with her doctor about her questions and concerns.

Relationship — The affects on her sexual functioning and possible feelings of inadequacy; her lack of communication with John about significant aspects of their lives and the resultant loss of both sexual and emotional intimacy.

Spiritual — Questioning of the strength of her faith for the first time because she was experiencing feelings of fear (of surgery, of death).

Rev. Vaughn evaluated Fumi for depressive symptoms. She had no personal or family history of depression, and her current emotional response was assessed as being directly and proportionally related to her situation.

The associate pastor communicated her recognition of the seriousness of the situation. In doing so, she validated Fumi's response as understandable and reasonable. She helped Fumi realize that since there was no evidence of her condition being life-threatening, her decision need not be made immediately. Fumi had been coping with this for several years, and with guidance and support, she could take time to address the multiple identified issues — and arrive at a plan based on reasoned and educated decisions. Rev. Vaughn assured Fumi that help and hope existed.

Fumi is a third-generation Japanese American. Though very "Westernized," she is also strongly influenced by her mother and maternal grandmother (second- and first-generation immigrants, respectively). She was taught to be quiet, nonassertive, and obedient. She internalized the Japanese virtue of accepting problems quietly and courageously, without tears or outward emotional expression (Kishimoto, 1967). This made discussion of her situation difficult for Fumi, and she experienced her tearfulness as embarrassing.

Fumi had graduated from college and married soon afterward. Her way of coping with what she eventually understood as her husband's verbally abusive behavior was to keep quiet and try to avoid conflict. With the help of a therapist, eventually she was able to extricate herself from the marriage, despite family pressure to stay. She married John, a kind and loving man, three years ago. Both came from large families, but they have no children. Early in their relationship they talked about their plans to have a family, but possibly due to Fumi's health problems, she never became pregnant. Fumi has been employed for 15 years as a caseworker in a social service agency; she is dependable and a hard worker, although she rarely expresses herself in meetings or with her boss. She has no history of mental illness, nor has anyone in her family ever been diagnosed with it.

Relevant History

Fumi is experiencing what has become a chronic medical condition in which her symptoms of excessive bleeding, pelvic pain, sleep disturbance, fatigue, painful intercourse, and urinary stress incontinence had a significant negative effect on her overall health and well-being. Determining conclusively the medical necessity for the recommended surgery is a first step. Hysterectomies are most often performed due to fibroid tumor, endometriosis (uterine lining tissue that has formed in abnormal areas), uterine prolapse (abnormal protrusion of the uterus through the pelvic floor) or chronic pelvic pain (National Women's Health Resource Center, 2002). Hysterectomy is the second most frequently performed surgery among reproductive-aged women (Centers for Disease Control, 2002; Haas and Puretz, 2002; Richter et al., 2000; Lambden et al., 1997), and more than 25 percent of all women will have this surgery by age 60 (Centers for Disease Control, 2002). Rates are highest in women 40 to 44 years old; fibroids are the most frequent reason in the 35–54 age group, and uterine prolapse or cancer the most common causes in those over age 55 (Centers for Disease Control, 2002).

Diagnostic Criteria

Fumi's problems are the result of uterine fibroids, and cancer is not suspected. This condition occurs in approximately 25 percent of women over age 34, and in 40 percent of women over the age of 40.

Hysterectomy is not the only treatment for symptoms of fibroids. Myomectomy is the surgical removal of fibroid tumors while leaving the uterus intact. Uterine artery embolization involves the injection of tiny particles into the uterus which then lodge in the fibroid-feeding blood vessels and result in the tumors decreasing in size over time (National Women's Health Resource Center, 2002; Haas and Puretz, 2002). Another option is anti-estrogen hormone therapy to decrease the size of fibroids and the severity of endometriosis. Exploring the viability of alternatives to hysterectomy is important in order to avoid unnecessary major surgery, particularly when future pregnancy is still desired. Obtaining a second opinion from another gynecologist is recommended (Haas and Puretz, 2002); this helps with decision making and is another step which helps prevent surgery that is not necessary. Though hysterectomy is considered a low-risk procedure, possible complications and risks exist in any surgery; these can be explained by the physician. Preexisting conditions are generally the main reason for complications — and so one's other medical problems need to be considered when making decisions regarding surgery (Haas and Puretz, 2002).

The Ethnicity, Needs, and Decisions of Women (ENDOW) project is a five-year study of ethnic and racial variations in attitudes about hysterectomy and related issues. ENDOW research found that females want to discuss the issues with their partners and want support prior to deciding and during the surgery/recovery, but clearly women make the decisions themselves (Richter et al., 2000). Multiple factors enter into the decision-making process, including symptom relief, medical need, insurance coverage or ability to pay, recovery time, partners' attitudes regarding the surgery's effects (such as on sexual relations and child-bearing), religious beliefs (such as an understanding that the couple is one and the woman cannot make the decision unilaterally), and quality of life (Richter et al., 2000). When couples reported that they communicate well, even about the hysterectomy, research indicated that in fact little communication actually occurred (Bernhard and Harris, 1977). Interventions suggested to improve communication are couples counseling; education to clarify both women's and men's perceptions, feelings, and attitudes about hysterectomy and treatment options; communication skills training; values clarification; and provision of medical information (Richter et al., 2000). Education and psychosocial support interventions have been implemented at some hospitals to address the often unmet needs of women pre- and postsurgically (Dulaney, Crawford, and Turner, 1989).

The results of hysterectomy are mixed, but in most cases are positive (Lewis et al., 2000; Galavotti and Richter, 2000; Kritz-Silverstein et al., 2002). Women generally experience alleviation of pelvic pain, incontinence, and sleep disturbance; sexual functioning is unchanged (Rannestad et al., 2001b); and energy level improves. Older studies suggested increased mental health problems (such as high rates of depression) in females after hysterectomy; newer, more methodically sound research contradicts this position (Khastgir and Studd, 1998; Khastgir, Studd, and Catalan, 2000). Several studies, as summarized by Williams and Clark, have shown that hysterectomy does not lead to psychiatric problems; it is not the surgery, but the preexistence of psychological problems that is the best predictor of postsurgery mental health difficulties. Other factors that affect psychological health are age and reason for the surgery. Depression is more likely in women of childbearing age whose possibility of pregnancy is removed and in females whose surgery is precipitated by cancer (Shephard and Shephard, 1990). Overall, the general health of women with gynecological disorders is significantly improved after hysterectomy (Rannestad et al., 2001a; Haas and Puretz, 2002; Mingo et al., 2002; Lambden et al., 1997; National Women's Health Resource Center, 2002).

With the assistance and support of a clergywoman with whom she felt comfortable, Fumi was able to make a plan about how to proceed. Rev. Vaughn helped her locate several good books to learn about treatment options, medical facts, decision making, risks/benefits, and possible outcomes of surgery. Fumi began to see the importance of better communication with both her doctor and her husband about these issues. She enrolled in a six-week class on assertiveness training for women offered at the local community college and developed the skills to effectively communicate with her physician and spouse. Having more information about hysterectomy from her self-education process allowed Fumi to feel more confident discussing the possible surgery. The reading also somewhat desensitized her, making it easier to talk about such personal topics with her male doctor. She met a woman in the assertiveness training who had had a hysterectomy several years ago — and they talked about the experience. Fumi was able to role-play conversations with her physician in the class and eventually was armed with the knowledge, communication skills, and confidence to approach her doctor with a list of questions that she and her husband had prepared. This served to involve John more in the decision-making process, opened lines of communication between them, and in turn strengthened their relationship. Fumi was leaning toward surgery, but decided to get another opinion. The second gynecologist concurred that

Response to Vignette

hysterectomy was indicated, and Fumi returned to her physician to schedule the procedure.

Treatment within the Faith Community

The referral by Rev. Jackson to his associate pastor was a wise move by a perceptive clergyman. Fumi was able to talk more easily and openly to another female. She received guidance and encouragement from Rev. Vaughn to reach out to other community resources. She developed a strong tie with the clergywoman, who also provided spiritual support on an ongoing basis. They prayed together about the decision and later prior to the surgery. Fumi experienced a strengthening of her religious faith as a result of her personal contact with the minister. At the suggestion of Rev. Vaughn, she became involved with one of the congregation's women's circles. Through their fund-raising and service projects, she met a number of other females and developed a social network at the church. The circle provided outreach to church members of the congregation who are elderly, grieving, ill, or experiencing difficult life situations. They provided spiritual and social support to Fumi before and after surgery and helped her in other ways (such as preparing food, driving her to follow-up appointments) during the initial stage of her recovery. In turn, Fumi became involved in doing the same for others in the church after she had recovered. She developed stronger in her personal ties and a deeper Christian commitment throughout this process. Religious faith and social support networks are both sources of comfort and strength for those coping with stressful situations. Findings of the ENDOW project "support the importance of spiritual care" (Williams and Clark, 2000) and found that some females expressed a reliance on prayer and meditation for support (Galavotti and Richter, 2000).

Fumi's medical problems began with her feeling isolated, frightened, and alone — and resulted in her feeling more connected to her church, to her faith, to other women in her church, and to her husband.

Indications for Referral

A referral for a second medical opinion is suggested (Haas and Puretz, 2002) and has been shown to decrease the number of elective hysterectomies (Haas and Puretz, 2002; Shephard and Shephard, 1990; Lewis et al., 2000). The amount of information a female has and her involvement in the decision-making process increase patient satisfaction (Lewis et al., 2000). Hospitals and other community agencies often provide cancer support groups that are appropriate referrals for women whose surgery revealed malignancy; these groups are often also open to family members.

Hospital-based comprehensive nursing intervention programs for those undergoing hysterectomy, where available, can be valuable in assisting females with coping. This type of program offers presurgery classes, provides educational information and support during hospitalization, and offers postdischarge support groups (Dulaney et al., 1989). Encouraging women to research the availability of such a program by talking with their physicians and by calling area hospitals can result in the utilization of valuable services.

Sexual adjustment is often a concern post-hysterectomy. Counseling in this area is best reserved for medical and mental health experts. However, some preliminary discussion is appropriate to determine if a referral is indicated. Postsurgery sexual problems can include pain, "mechanical" difficulties, decrease in libido, a female's sense of loss (of reproductive organs and reproductive abilities), and a partner's negative attitude regarding the effects of a hysterectomy on a woman and on their sex life (Rudy and Bush, 1992). Postsurgery sexual functioning is one of the least discussed associated issues; validating the importance of a female's concern and steering her in the right direction(s) for help in addressing these matters is an appropriate intervention. Medical experts (such as gynecologists, RNs, or hysterectomy support program staff) can answer questions and address issues regarding physical changes, such as thinning/dryness/atrophy of the vaginal mucosa causing intercourse to be painful and other tissue changes that might cause urinary stress incontinence or other vaginal or urinary problems. A decrease in libido may occur, and concerns about this can also be addressed by medical experts and/or mental health professionals. The latter can also help a woman and her partner communicate about and cope with any sexuality-related fears, concerns, and uncertainties. The uterus is a symbol of motherhood, femininity, and youth, and its loss can trigger emotional responses in a female and in her partner. Both should have the opportunity before and after surgery to get medical answers and psychological support (Rudy and Bush, 1992).

None of the women in the cultures studied in the ENDOW project reported being referred for evaluation or support to mental health services prior to surgery (Galavotti and Richter, 2000). Research indicates that females who had or were scheduled to have hysterectomies want treatment choices, a part in decision making, factual and useful information on illness/treatment/after-effects, referrals, and professional and lay emotional support (Wade et al., 2000; Lindberg and Nolan, 2001; Corney et al., 1992). By being aware of the signs and symptoms of mental health and relationship problems and by knowing about locally available psychological and other services, clergy are equipped to provide much-needed referrals.

Treatment by Mental Health Specialist   Despite an often reported decline in psychological functioning after a hysterectomy, the current scientific literature does not support this (Khastgir and Studd, 1998). Preoperative depression is generally improved after surgery, perhaps due to the relief of symptoms (Centers for Disease Control, 2002; Khastgir and Studd, 1998). Gynecological disorders alone do not predict increased psychiatric problems in women. A study that used the Quality of Life Index to measure several areas found that females with gynecological disorders experienced a lower quality of life in the health/functioning domain, but not in the psychological/spiritual domain (Rannestad et al., 2000).

However, depression can occur or continue after hysterectomy. The surgery precludes pregnancy — and in women for whom this might be of special concern (those who are young, childless, or with a new partner), the psychological effect may be negative (Centers for Disease Control, 2002; National Women's Health Resource Center, 2002; Shephard and Shephard, 1990; Dulaney et al., 1989; Williams and Clark, 2000). If the surgery is performed due to a life-threatening medical condition such as uterine cancer, depression is more likely and professional counseling may be indicated (Shephard and Shephard, 1990). A female who has experienced past psychological problems unrelated to presurgery medical symptoms is at greater risk of future psychiatric illness (Khastgir and Studd, 1998). Symptoms of depression include depressed mood, diminished interest or pleasure in activities, unexplained marked weight loss or gain, sleep disturbance, persistent postrecovery fatigue, significant feelings of worthlessness and/or guilt, difficulty concentrating, recurrent thoughts of death, and impairment in social/occupation functioning (American Psychiatric Association, 2000). If they develop or persist, that is a strong indication for referral to a mental health professional. Timely and effective treatment is vital since medical recovery can be negatively affected or prolonged by depression. Treatment for depression, including "talk" therapies and medication, are effective in most cases.

Anxiety and issues related to preparing psychologically for surgery can be addressed by clinicians who specialize in the treatment of anxiety disorders, relaxation techniques, and cognitive-behavioral preparation for surgery.

Any related marital issues (sexual, financial, communication) that are evident might best be addressed by a referral to a marriage counselor or a psychologist who specializes in couples' issues. Values clarification, communication skills training, and cognitive-behavioral approaches (Gottman, 1994; McKay et al., 1994) can be used to address marital issues that might arise from or be exacerbated by the stressors (medical, relationship, financial) associated with the situation.

The ENDOW project collected data on African American, European American, Hispanic, and Navajo women's experiences with and attitudes toward hysterectomy. The study found that decision-making patterns and experiences with health care providers differed among ethnic groups; however, females classified as "traditional" across ethnic groups (those whose lifestyle was most like that of a previous generation) had more in common with each other than with the least traditional women in her own ethnic group. They reported few or no menopausal symptoms after hysterectomy, and many had never even heard of hormone replacement therapy. Conversely, the symptoms of menopause were more prevalent in the "modern" women (most isolated from their culture) in all ethnic groups (Mingo et al., 2002). African American women undergo hysterectomy at younger ages than European American women — possibly due to differences in decision-making processes, rather than differences in age at onset of symptoms. Spiritual support was most often cited by African American and low-income women as a means of coping with the experience of a hysterectomy. They were less likely to talk with coworkers than were European American females, but were more likely to consult with a male relative. European American women more often talked with female relatives and friends (Williams and Clark, 2000). Acculturation and assimilation barriers (modesty, language limitations, views toward authority figures) are thought to hinder traditional Hispanic females from readily entering into the medical system (Lewis et al., 2000).

Some African American women in the study believed that their male partners had negative attitudes about hysterectomy. They expressed beliefs that the surgery could result in the breakup of the relationship due to their resultant inability to have children and to anticipated negative effects on female sexual functioning (Williams and Clark, 2000).

One study of the fears, misconceptions, and psychological trauma associated with the prospect of hysterectomy found that Mexican American women were most affected, followed by African American, French Canadian, and European females; Anglo-Americans and Asians were found to be least affected (Lalinec-Michaud and Englesmann, 1989).

Cross-Cultural Issues

Resources American College of Obstetricians and Gynecologists; 409 Twelfth Street, SW, P.O. Box 96920, Washington, DC 20090; (202)683-5577; (800)762-2264; *www.acog.org*; an organization of obstetricians and gynecologists dedicated to the advancement of women's health through education, advocacy, practice, and research.

Centers for Disease Control and Prevention; 1600 Clifton Road, Atlanta, GA; (800)311-3435; *www.cdc.gov*; an agency of the U.S. Department of Health and Human Services; provides hysterectomy facts and statistics; Web site provides links to related topics.

Endometriosis Research Center; 630 Ibis Drive, Delray Beach, FL 33444; (800)239-7280, (561)274-7442; *www.endocenter.org*; a nonprofit organization for education, support, raising awareness, and research. Information regarding treatment alternatives is provided. *How to Choose a Doctor* fact sheet and a newsletter are available. An online bookstore is provided.

Ethnicity, Needs, and Decisions of Women (ENDOW) Coordinating Center; Division of Preventive Medicine, University of Alabama at Birmingham, 1717 Eleventh Avenue South, Room 730, Birmingham, AL 35205; (205)934-6383; *www.dopm.uab.edu/endow*; a four-center, collaborative project sponsored by the Women's Health Initiative of the National Institutes of Health and the Centers for Disease Control and Prevention to focus on women's attitudes, experiences, and decisions about hysterectomy/surgical menopause and questions about menopause and hormone replacement therapy across racial/cultural groups. Investigators developed a video (*Hysterectomy: The Decision Is Yours*), an information brochure in English and Spanish, and two other brochures (*The Wise Woman's Guide to Making Decisions and The Decision Is Yours: Talking to Your Doctor*); material is available from ENDOW at cost.

Fibroid Treatment Collective; 100 UCLA Medical Plaza, Suite 310, Los Angeles, CA 90024; (866)362-6463, (310)208-2442; *www.fibroids.com*; a medical group consisting of health care professionals dedicated to improving the quality of life of women with uterine fibroids. Information is focused on fibroid embolization, an outpatient treatment that preserves the uterus and fertility.

Hysterectomy Educational Resources and Services Foundation; 422 Bryn Mawr Avenue, Bala Cynwyd, PA 19004; (610)667-7757, (888)750-4377; *www.hersfoundation.com*; an independent, nonprofit, international health organization for women who have had or who are considering having a hysterectomy. Physician referrals are available, and the organization publishes a newsletter.

National Institute of Mental Health; (301)443-4513; *www.nimh.gov*; information on anxiety disorders and depression, with fact sheets and booklets in English and Spanish.

National Institutes of Health; 9000 Rockville Pike, Bethesda, MD 20892; *www.nih.gov*; (301)496-4000, toll-free numbers available at *www.nih.gov/health/infoline.htm*; provides health information, consumer brochures, and information on NIH-supported research studies. Links to Medline searches of all related topics.

National Uterine Fibroids Foundation; P.O. Box 9688, Colorado Springs, CO 80932-0688; (877)553-6833, (719)633-3454; a non-profit corporation for charitable, educational, and scientific activities related to the care and treatment of women with fibroids. It promotes alternatives to hysterectomy.

National Women's Health Information Center; 8550 Arlington Boulevard, Suite 300, Fairfax, VA 22031; (800)994-9662; *www.4woman.gov*; a project of the U.S. Department of Health and Human Services. Offers a toll-free call center and a Web site health topics search with links to related topics.

National Women's Health Resource Center; 120 Albany Street, Suite 820, New Brunswick, NJ 08901; (877)986-9472; *www.healthywomen.org*; a nonprofit organization to help women make informed decisions regarding their health. Includes "Questions to Ask" your doctor and information on diagnoses, treatment options, and preparing for surgery. Related resources and recommended books are listed.

Helpful Books

The Fibroid Book (Francis L. Hutchins, Bala Cynwyd, PA: The Fibroid Center, 1997).

Fibroids: The Complete Guide to Taking Charge of Your Physical, Emotional, and Sexual Well-Being (Johanna Skilling and Eileen Hoffman, New York: Marlowe and Co., 2000).

Health, Happiness and Hormones: One Woman's Journey towards Health after a Hysterectomy (Arlene Swaney, Lancaster, PA: Starburst, 1996).

Hysterectomy: Before and After: A Comprehensive Guide to Preventing, Preparing for and Maximizing Health after Hysterectomy (Winnifred B. Cutler, New York: HarperCollins, 1990).

Hysterectomy: Woman to Woman (Sue Ellen Barber, Wilsonville, OR: Book Partners, 1996).

Just As Much a Woman: Your Personal Guide to Hysterectomy and Beyond (Nancy Rosenfeld and Dianna W. Bolen, Rocklin, CA: Prima, 1999).

Uterine Fibroids: What Every Woman Needs to Know (Nelson H. Stringer, Glenville, IL: Physicians and Scientists Publishing, 1996).

The Woman's Guide to Hysterectomy: Expectations and Options (revised ed.). (Adelaide Haas and Susan L. Puretz, Berkeley, CA, Celestial Arts, 2002).

References American Psychiatric Association. (2000). *Diagnostic and Statistical Manual of Mental Disorders* (4th ed. text revision). Washington, DC: American Psychiatric Association.

Bernhard, L. A., and Harris, C. R. (1977). Partner communication about hysterectomy. *Health Care for Women International*, 12(4), 73–85.

Centers for Disease Control and Prevention. (2002). *Women's Reproductive Health: Fact Sheet: Hysterectomy in the United States, 1980–1993*. Retrieved February 11, 2002, from *www.cdc.vog*, Atlanta: CDC.

Corney, R., Everett, H., Howells, A., and Crowther, M. (1992). The care of patients undergoing surgery for gynecological cancer: The need for information, emotional support and counseling. *Journal of Advanced Nursing*, 17(6), 667–671.

Dulaney, P. E., Crawford, V. C., and Turner, G. (1989). A comprehensive education and support program for women experiencing hysterectomies. *Journal of Obstetric, Gynecologic, and Neonatal Nursing*, 19(4), 319–325.

Galavotti, C., and Richter, D. L. (2000). Talking about hysterectomy: The experiences of women from four cultural groups. *Journal of Women's Health and Gender-Based Medicine*, 9(Supplement 2), S63–S67.

Gottman, J. (1994). *Why Marriages Succeed or Fail*. New York: Fireside-Simon and Schuster.

Haas, A., and Puretz, S. L. (2002). *The Women's Guide to Hysterectomy: Expectation and Options* (revised ed.). Berkeley, CA: Celestial Arts.

Khastgir, G., and Studd, J. (1998). Personal perspectives: Hysterectomy, ovarian failure, and depression. *Journal of the North American Menopause Society*, 5(2), 113–122.

Khastgir, G., Studd, J. W., and Catalan, J. (2000). The psychological outcome of hysterectomy. *Gynecological Endocrinology*, 14(2), 132–141.

Kishimoto, H. (1967). Some Japanese cultural traits and religions. In C. A. Moore (ed.), *The Japanese Mind: Essentials of Japanese*

Philosophy and Culture (pp. 110–121). Honolulu: University of Hawaii Press.

Kritz-Silverstein, D., Wingard, D. L., and Barrett-Connor, E. (2002). Hysterectomy status and life satisfaction in older women. *Journal of Women's Health and Gender-Based Medicine*, 11(2), 181–190.

Lalinec-Michaud, M., and Englesmann, F. (1989). Cultural factors and reaction to hysterectomy. *Social Psychiatry and Psychiatric Epidemiology*, 24, 165–171.

Lambden, M. P., Bellamy, G., Ogburn-Russell, L., Preece, D. K., Moore, S., Pepin, T., Croop, J., and Culbert, G. (1997). Women's sense of well-being before and after hysterectomy. *Journal of Obstetric, Gynecologic, and Neonatal Nursing*, 26(5), 540–548.

Lewis, C. E., Groff, J. Y., Herman, C. J., McKeown, R. E., and Wilcox, L. S. (2000). Overview of women's decision making regarding elective hysterectomy, oophorectomy, and hormone replacement therapy. *Journal of Women's Health and Gender-Based Medicine*, 9(Supplement 2), S5–S14.

Lindberg, C. E., and Nolan, L. B. (2001). Women's decision-making regarding hysterectomy. *Journal of Obstetric, Gynecologic, and Neonatal Nursing*, 30(6), 607–616.

McKay, M., Fanning, P., and Paley, K. (1994). *Couples Skills*. Oakland, CA: New Harbinger.

Mingo, C., Herman, C. J., and Jasperse, M. (2002). Women's stories: Ethnic variations in women's attitudes and experiences of menopause, hysterectomy, and hormone replacement therapy. *Journal of Women's Health and Gender-Based Medicine*, 9(Supplement 2), S27–S38.

National Women's Health Resource Center. (2002). *Hysterectomy*. Retrieved February 11, 2002, from *www.healthywoman.org*.

Rannestad, T., Eikeland, O. J., Helland, H., and Qvarnstrom, U. (2000). Quality of life, pain, and psychological well-being in women suffering from gynecological disorder. *Journal of Women's Health and Gender-Based Medicine*, 9(8), 897–903.

Rannestad, T., Eikeland, O. J., Helland, H., and Qvarnstrom, U. (2001a). Are the physiologically and psychosocially based symptoms in women suffering from gynecological disorders alleviated by means of hysterectomy? *Journal of Women's Health and Gender-Based Medicine*, 10(6), 579–587.

Rannestad, T., Eikeland, O. J., Helland, H., and Qvarnstrom, U. (2001b). The general health in women suffering from gynaecological disorders is improved by means of hysterectomy. *Scandinavian Journal of Caring Sciences*, 15(3), 264–270.

Richter, D. L., McKeown, R. E., Corwin, S. J., Rheaume, C., and Fraser, J. (2000). The role of male partners in women's decision making regarding hysterectomy. *Journal of Women's Health and Gender-Based Medicine*, 9(Supplement 2), S51–S61.

Rudy, D. R., and Bush, I. M. (1992). Hysterectomy and sexual dysfunction: You can help. *Patient Care*, September 30, 67–82.

Shephard, B. D., and Shephard, C. A. (1990). *The Complete Guide to Women's Health* (2nd ed.). New York: Plume.

Wade, J., Pletsch, P. K., Morgan, S. W., and Menting, S. A. (2000). Hysterectomy: What do women need and want to know? *Journal of Obstetric, Gynecologic, and Neonatal Nursing*, 9(1), 33–42.

Williams, R. D., and Clark, A. J. (2000). A qualitative study of women's hysterectomy experience. *Journal of Women's Health and Gender-Based Medicine*, 9(Supplement 2), 33–42.

Infertility

"Excitement and optimism gradually turned into concern"

Simon appeared at Rev. James Hiller's office at a time he knew his pastor would be free. He felt comfortable talking frankly and openly with the minister. After all, they had shared cooking duties at many parish suppers and played on the church softball team together. They were close in age and interests and had developed an easy rapport over the years. Because of this, Simon was able to talk about a very personal and troubling issue with his pastor. Simon sat down and said, "I want to talk with you, James — as my minister and spiritual counselor." Initially Rev. Hiller was taken aback by the uncharacteristically serious tone in Simon's voice, but he responded, "Fire away, Simon."

The story he told was of joy and anticipation turned to emotional pain and fear. Simon and Anna had been trying to conceive for the past two years. Initial excitement at the prospect of being parents resulted in frequent romantic and sexual encounters that had drawn the couple closer together and had strengthened their marriage. However, Anna did not become pregnant. Excitement and optimism gradually turned into concern ("Is something wrong with me?"), fears ("We're going to be too old soon to be new parents"), anger ("Why can't we do this? Everyone else seems to have no problem"), and then resignation ("It's never going to happen").

Simon believed that Anna blamed him, and he was seriously considering the possibility that it was his fault. He recently experienced several incidents of impotence for the first time, which resulted in his developing performance anxiety and a decrease in sexual desire. Sexual encounters became unromantic, awkward, and discouraging, and because of this, much less frequent. Emotional closeness had deteriorated into psychological distance, and the lighthearted and playful tone that had characterized their relationship was gone. Where the marriage had initially flourished with their conception attempts, it was now showing signs of the stress of failure. Anna began to avoid social activities, especially those involving children. "Life is no longer fun. Anna and I walk on eggshells around each other — and at times tempers flair. I've always felt in control of my life. And now it's out of control!"

Rev. Hiller was relieved to finally learn what was causing the periodic sadness and irritability he had noticed in recent months. He had also recognized a distancing between Simon and Anna when he saw them together and had been concerned. Though the problem was serious, he perceived it as being in the relatively early stages and therefore able to be addressed in helpful and relationship-saving ways. The pastor understood that the negative impact of their infertility was affecting them and that without some type of intervention their relationship and the quality of their lives would be likely to continue to deteriorate. Since the problem clearly involved both Anna and Simon, he suggested that they come together to talk about their concerns.

Pastoral Care Assessment

Anna and Simon met in college, married in their mid-20s, and have been establishing their careers for the past decade. He is a schoolteacher and coach of the boys' basketball team; she is a financial officer at a bank. They are financially secure, own a nice home, and have had a happy and fulfilling marriage. Anna was raised in the United Methodist Church, and Simon's family was Presbyterian. During college and the first few years of their marriage, neither regularly attended any church. They have weathered many situations in their lives together, including the long illnesses and eventual deaths of both Anna's mother and Simon's father. Those confrontations with mortality contributed to a renewed interest in their spiritual lives. They joined Anna's childhood church five years ago and began attending regularly. Both enjoy working with children, and they eventually gravitated to the youth program. They have led the United Methodist Youth Fellowship for the past four years. Financial security, a solid relationship, their ticking biological clocks, and their positive experiences with the young people all contributed to their decision a year ago to begin a family.

Diagnostic Criteria

Infertility in a woman is defined as the inability to become pregnant after at least one year of sexual relations without the use of contraception (Weschler, 2002) — or more specifically, as the inability to produce a pregnancy which culminates in a live birth after one year for a woman less than 35 years old or after six months over the age of 35 (Domar and Kelly, 2002). It is a relatively common condition affecting between 10 and 20 percent of women of reproductive age (Domar and Kelly,

2002; Edwards, 1989; Liebmann-Smith, Egan, and Stangel, 1999; RE-SOLVE, 2003). In 1995, 15 percent of women of reproductive age used some type of infertility service (Liebmann-Smith et al., 1999).

Infertility is a result of the "male factor" (conditions in a man that contribute to or cause infertility) about 35 percent of the time, the result of the "female factor" about 35 percent, and a combination of both approximately 20 percent of the time. The cause of infertility is unexplained in about 10 percent of cases (Liebmann-Smith et al., 1999; RESOLVE, 2003). Infertility can be either a temporary or a permanent condition, depending on the etiology and the availability of treatment. Causes of infertility and conditions affecting fertility include anatomical abnormalities, hormonal problems, other medical conditions (such as sexually transmitted diseases and other infections, diabetes, cystic fibrosis, sickle-cell disease, renal disease), impotence, smoking, alcohol consumption, illicit drug use, environmental toxins, and prescription medications and treatments (such as chemotherapy, radiation therapy, anabolic steroids, and medications for hypertension, seizure disorder, and ulcers) (Liebmann-Smith et al., 1999). Age is also a factor: fertility declines in both men and women as they become older.

The number of women seeking infertility treatment increased by 30 percent between 1988 and 1995, due in part to baby-boom-generation women and couples delaying attempts to have children until they were in their 30s and 40s (Liebmann-Smith et al., 1999). With accurate diagnoses and adequate treatment (drug therapy, surgery, and assisted reproductive technologies such as in vitro fertilization), 50 to 75 percent of couples seeking help are able to conceive (Liebmann-Smith et al., 1999; Sher, Davis, and Stoess, 1998). Low-technology lifestyle changes related to such lifestyle matters as smoking, diet, exercise, general health, clothing, toxins, and drugs might also increase a couple's chance of conceiving (Robin, 1993; Wesson, 1999). Observation and charting of fertility signs to increase the likelihood of conception is another low-tech possibility (Weschler, 2002), and some individuals choose to explore alternative therapies such as acupuncture, cranial osteopathy, herbal medicine, and homeopathy (Wesson, 1999). Mind/body strategies (such as relaxation-inducing practices, cognitive therapy, stress management/coping training, and communication skills) and infertility support group interventions have been shown to decrease distress levels in infertile women (Domar et al., 2000a) and positively affect fertility (Domar et al., 2000b).

If low-tech, inexpensive, and less invasive methods do not work, fertility drugs, surgery (male and female), and in vitro fertilization (IVF) are options. If these methods do not work, some couples might choose to pursue a third-party reproductive method such as using donated sperm, eggs, embryos (from another couple's IVF procedure), or a uterus (a surrogate mother is artificially inseminated with the sperm of the male of the infertile couple, and she carries the baby to term for them). Third-party reproductive options can raise serious issues in the personal, medical, relationship, social, ethical, legal, financial, and religious arenas; careful consideration and expert medical, legal, psychological, and religious guidance is indicated if this path is chosen (Liebmann-Smith et al., 1999).

Emotional Aspects

In the quagmire of diagnostic tests, medical issues, lifestyle alterations, and financial concerns, the emotional toll of infertility can get lost. Recognizing and addressing this is important. Infertility can be a "life crisis" (Edwards, 1989) that can create chronic stress (Newton et al., 1999), resulting in feelings of anger, guilt, anxiety, fear, inadequacy, depression, and grief (Wesson, 1999). Frequency of sexual activity and satisfaction has also been shown to be negatively affected by infertility (Oddens et al., 1999). Women report more distress related to infertility than do men; studies have shown infertile females to be as depressed as women with life-threatening illnesses. This depression peaks after two to three years of unsuccessful conception attempts. Unfortunately, while infertility apparently causes depression, depressive symptoms also apparently hinder conception (Domar and Kelly, 2002).

Response to Vignette

Rev. Hiller talked to Anna and Simon together. He assured them that their problem was not uncommon and that they were not the first couple in the congregation to discuss infertility with him. He talked with them about some of the low-tech strategies to increase fertility and realized that they had not yet explored them. He referred them to both local and national infertility resources so they could begin the process of self-education about treatment options. Both Anna and Simon seemed to relax during their hour-long conversation with their pastor. His acceptance, basic knowledge, and frank discussion about infertility helped normalize their situation and gave them the support and encouragement they needed to move from being scared, angry, and defeated to feeling hopeful and empowered.

He validated for them that the emotional impact of infertility was significant and offered to be available for ongoing support. He also suggested that they might consider attending a support group or seeing a therapist knowledgeable about infertility. His assessment was that they were in the initial stages of a potentially long-term process and that their issues and responses would change over time. He assured them that he would be there for them — to listen, counsel, support, encourage, make referrals if needed, help with any religious concerns, and to pray with and for them.

Infertility can cause an "intense spiritual crisis." Women sometimes report that infertility results in a questioning of their faith when their prayers are not answered or in a belief that they are being punished by God (Domar and Kelly, 2002). Others might find a new or renewed interest in religious faith as a result of infertility and turn to it to help them cope (Liebmann-Smith et al., 1999). The results of one study led to the recommendation that "the nurturing of a spiritual or philosophical life to enhance coping and personal growth" should be one of the therapeutic interventions for women struggling with infertility (Gonzalez, 2000). **Treatment within the Faith Community**

Though people often look to their religion as a source of support in life crises, doing so to cope with infertility-related issues can be problematic. Faith communities are often quite child- and family-centered; some even promote large families and espouse the view that a woman's primary role is that of mother. Children are often omnipresent at church services, activities, and holidays. This can result in infertile members feeling angry, hurt, and alienated from their faith community (Domar and Kelly, 2002). Difficulties are sometimes created by religious doctrines that prohibit assisted reproductive technologies or certain other infertility treatment procedures. Some tenets might be misunderstood, and a religious leader can help elucidate their meaning. Some are clearly prohibitive, and a couple might choose to ignore a doctrine; this can result in guilt or a turning away from one's faith. Helping persons grapple with questions of conscience if they decide to go outside of the dictates of their faith is an appropriate pastoral role (Robin, 1993). Alternately they might choose to follow prohibitive tenets and then become resentful toward their religion.

These situations require someone with a sensitivity to the issues and to the potential severity of the related emotional trauma, and one who can provide guidance in helping the infertile member(s) use their religious beliefs in a way that facilitates effective coping — regardless of a couple's choices and of the outcome of any fertility treatment. A pastoral counselor can help them use the situation as an opportunity to reexamine their faith, to learn and grow spiritually, and to accept and embrace new paths when necessary (such as adoption or a child-free life). Faith communities sensitive to the issues related to infertility make room in their congregations for childless church members. Spiritual guidance can help individuals recognize opportunities in their lives provided by the challenges of infertility.

Indications for Referral
Referrals most often would be related to education about the specialized and complex area of infertility and treatment options. Clergy cannot be expected to have comprehensive knowledge about infertility unless they have personally experienced a similar situation. Having basic knowledge of the medical, emotional, financial, and relationship issues involved and an understanding of how traumatic and far-reaching the effects can be on people's lives should be a reasonable expectation of pastors. Clergy can familiarize themselves with the educational materials, specialists, and support organizations that exist to provide encouragement and suggestions as to where and how to begin the process of pursuing education and support.

When a marital relationship is suffering as a result of infertility or stressors related to treatment, a referral for marriage counseling can be made if the situation is more complicated than the minister is competent to address. The longer infertility has been a problem and a couple has been pursing medical or alternative treatment, the greater the toll is likely to be and the more likely couple therapy is indicated. A referral for counseling should also be considered if a couple has experienced miscarriages or stillbirths during the process of trying to conceive. Individual referrals to mental health specialists might be made if there is an assessment of depression in either partner.

Treatment by Mental Health Specialist
Mental health professionals who specialize in reproductive issues and infertility can be located through fertility clinics or specialists. Psychologists who have expertise in these areas might be located by contacting the state professional psychological association. Mental health clinicians will assess the severity of any symptoms of depression and treat or refer accordingly. They will also provide emotional support and can use cognitive-behavioral therapy approaches to assist couples in coping with their lives.

A recent study of infertile women found five key themes that were the most troubling: (1) failure to fulfill a prescribed social norm to become pregnant; (2) assault on one's personal identity triggering feelings of powerlessness, or alienation from others, and stigmatization for the inability to create "ties of descent"; (3) mourning; (4) transformation (i.e., facing reality); and (5) restitution, found in relinquishing the hope of bearing a child (Gonzalez, 2000). Loss or fear of loss is a major issue for individuals facing infertility. Missing out on the birth experience, creation of descendants, parenting, marital relationship, work productivity, self-esteem, hope, and religious beliefs are all possible losses (RESOLVE, 2003).

A cognitive therapist can help a woman identify negative or irrational beliefs about herself, her life, the marriage, or her partner, and help her challenge and modify them, which would then result in a change in her emotional responses (such as decreased anger or depression). In addition to cognitive restructuring, a mental health specialist can encourage a woman to make behavioral changes and to develop communication and coping skills and strategies. Joining an infertility support group, learning how to assertively communicate feelings and needs to friends and family, selectively avoiding people and places that trigger painful emotions, practicing meditation, and self-nurturing are some of the many things a skilled mental health professional can teach, encourage, and facilitate (Domar and Kelly, 2002).

Couples therapy is a specialized field of psychological treatment. Though many pastors and mental health clinicians offer marriage counseling, few are well-trained to provide it (Doherty, 2002). Having an established referral relationship with one or more competent couple therapists can be invaluable for situations in which more specialized intervention is necessary.

Psychological counseling is recommended prior to infertility treatment (Lukse and Vacc, 1999) and is mandated by the Human Fertilization and Embryology Authority, which regulates assisted reproduction in the United Kingdom for anyone seeking IVF or donor insemination (Boivin et al., 1999). Professional associations in the field of infertility, as well as patients themselves, express the need for psychosocial counseling and emotional support for those undergoing infertility treatments (RESOLVE, 2003; Souter et al., 1998; Sundby et al., 1994).

Women and couples undergoing assisted reproductive treatments are not the only ones who might benefit from counseling. One study found that approximately 32 percent of females even in the initial stages of pursuing infertility services were at risk for developing associated psychological problems (Souter et al., 2002). Other researchers found that infertile women's scores on a measure of psychological symptoms were equivalent to patients with cancer, heart disease, and HIV (Domar et al., 1993). Any female or couple experiencing the distress of infertility, regardless of treatment choices, is a candidate for counseling. The type and specificity of the therapeutic service should be determined by the needs of the clients, and anyone who provides the services should be cognizant of the emotional impact of infertility and should be able to offer (or refer for) ongoing evaluation and grief counseling (Kennedy et al., 1998).

Cross-Cultural Issues   Infertility affects women and couples across all socioeconomic, racial, and ethnic groups (RESOLVE, 2003). Although 1995 government statistics of married women in the United States aged 16 to 44 show non-Hispanic black women as having a higher percentage of infertility (10.5 percent) than Hispanic (7 percent) or non-Hispanic white (6.4 percent) women, the statistics of *all* women in the same age group in the same year do not show this difference; all three groups had "impaired fecundity" at about 10 percent (Abma et al., 1997).

"Cultural" issues related to infertility affect nontraditional prospective parents such as unmarried women or lesbians, persons with disabilities or illnesses that complicate the picture, and those whose religion forbids or restricts fertility treatment. To qualify as infertile and therefore eligible for treatment can be difficult because females who are not having unprotected, heterosexual relations do not meet the definition of being infertile. Some doctors will not provide infertility treatment to unmarried women. Lesbians can face even more challenges, with family members possibly not accepting their sexuality and then blatantly discouraging parenthood (Domar and Kelly, 2002).

Prospective parents who have a disability (such as paraplegia), who are being treated for another medical problem (such as radiation or chemotherapy for cancer), or who carry genes for a genetic disease often have major conception-related complications; these issues can be medical, emotional, legal, ethical, and/or practical, but do not necessarily preclude pregnancy, childbearing, or parenting (Robin, 1993).

Religious beliefs can complicate one's approach to infertility treatment because they introduce moral considerations to the multifarious issues already faced by an infertile woman or couple. The tenets of some faiths prohibit certain procedures such as any medical technology that produces conception outside of a woman's body or the use of donated sperm or eggs. Couples might look to their pastor for guidance and interpretation of religious doctrine to help them decide their course of action.

Resources   Adoptive Families of America; 3333 Highway 100 North, Minneapolis, MN 55422; (800)372-3300.

American Society for Reproductive Medicine; 1209 Montgomery Highway, Birmingham, AL 35216-2809; (205)978-5000; *www.asrm .org*; is an organization which offers patient information and fact sheets, a list of infertility counselors, state-by-state insurance law information, assisted reproductive technology success rates, and advice about locating a physician specializing in infertility.

Centers for Disease Control and Prevention; 1600 Clifton Road, Atlanta, GA 30333; (800)311-3435; (404)639-3534; *www.cdc.gov*; an agency of the U.S. Department of Health and Human Services; provides infertility facts and statistics; Web site provides links to related topics.

Childless by Choice, P.O. Box 695, Leavenworth, WA 99926; (509)763-2112; *www.now2000.com/cbc*.

Mind/Body Center for Women's Health at Boston IVF; 40 Second Avenue, Suite 300, Waltham, MA 02451; (781)434-6500; *www .bostonivf.com*.

National Adoption Information Clearinghouse; 11426 Rockville Pike, Rockville, MD 20852; (301)231-6512.

National Center for Health Statistics; U.S. Department of Health and Human Services, Centers for Disease Control and Prevention, Division of Data Services, 6525 Belcrest Road, Hyattsville, MD 20782-2003; *www.cdc.gov/nchs/fastats/fertile.htm*; (301)458-4636; provides government statistics on infertility and assisted reproductive technology success rates.

National Institutes of Health (NIH); 9000 Rockville Pike, Bethesda, MD 20892; *www.nih.go*; (301)496-4000; toll-free numbers available at *www.nih.gov/health/infoline.htm*; as well as links to its institutes, centers, and divisions, including the National Institute of Mental Health. Provides health information, consumer brochures, and information on NIH-supported research studies. Links to Medline searches of all related topics.

North American Council on Adoptable Children; 1821 University Avenue #498 North, St. Paul, MN 55104; (612)644-0336.

RESOLVE, The National Infertility Association; 1310 Broadway, Somerville, MA 02144-1731; (888)623-0744; *www.resolve.org*; a nonprofit organization that offers information on infertility, fertility medications and treatment options, and advice about finding a physician specializing in infertility treatment. RESOLVE also sponsors local chapters, support groups, and lectures.

Society for Assisted Reproductive Technology; 1209 Montgomery Highway, Birmingham, AL 35216; (205)978-5000; affiliated with the American Society for Reproductive Medicine, which provides information about in vitro fertilization including a list of IVF programs with success rate statistics.

Helpful Books *Conquering Infertility* (Alice Domar and Alice Lesch Kelly, New York: Viking Penguin, 2002).

Enhancing Fertility Naturally: Holistic Therapies for a Successful Pregnancy (Nancy Wesson, Rochester, VT: Healing Arts Press, 1999).

How to Be a Successful Fertility Patient (Peggy Robin, New York: William Morrow, 1993).

In Vitro Fertilization: The A.R.T. of Making Babies (updated ed.). (Geoffrey Sher, Virginia Marriage Davis, and Jean Stroess, New York: Facts on File, 1998).

Motherhood After 35: Choices, Decision, Options (Maggie Jones, Tucson, AZ: Fisher Books, 1998).

A Stairstep Approach to Fertility (Margot Edwards, ed., Freedom, CA: Crossing Press, 1989).

Taking Charge of Your Fertility: The Definitive Guide to Natural Birth Control, Pregnancy Achievement, and Reproductive Health (revised ed.) (Toni Weschler, New York: HarperCollins, 2002).

The Unofficial Guide to Overcoming Infertility (Joan Liebmann-Smith, Jacqueline Nardi Egan, and John Stangel, New York: Macmillan, 1999).

References Abma, J., Chandra, A., Mosher, W., Peterson, L., and Piccinino, L. (1997). Fertility, family planning, and women's health: New data from the 1995 national survey of family growth *www.cdc.gov/nchs/data/series/sr_23/sr23_019.pdf.*

Boivin, J., Scanlan, L. C., and Walker, S. M. (1999). Why are infertile patients not using psychosocial counseling? *Human Reproduction*, 14, 1384–1391.

Doherty, W. (2002). Bad couples therapy. *Psychotherapy Networker*, November–December, 26–33.

Domar, A. D., Clapp, D., Slawsby, E. A., Dusek, J., Kessel, B., and Freizinger, M. (2000a). The impact of group psychological interventions on pregnancy rates in infertile women. *Fertility and Sterility*, 73, 805–811.

Domar, A. D., Clapp, D., Slawsby, E. A., Kessel, B., Orav, J., and Freizinger, M. (2000b). The impact of group psychological interventions on distress in infertile women. *Health Psychology*, 19, 568–575.

Domar, A., and Kelly, A. L. (2002). *Conquering Infertility.* New York: Viking Penguin.

Domar, A. D., Zuttermeister, P. C., and Friedman, R. (1993). The psychological impact of infertility: A comparison with patients with other medical conditions. *Journal of Psychosomatic Obstetrics and Gynaecology*, 14(Suppl.), 45–52.

Edwards, M. (Ed.). (1989). *A Stairstep Approach to Fertility.* Freedom, CA: Crossing Press.

Gonzalez, L. O. (2000). Infertility as a transformational process: A framework for psychotherapeutic support of infertile women. *Issues in Mental Health Nursing*, 21, 619–633.

Kennedy, H. P., Griffin, M., and Frishman, G. (1998). Enabling conception and pregnancy: Midwifery care of women experiencing infertility. *Journal of Nurse-Midwifery*, 43, 190–207.

Liebmann-Smith, J., Egan, J. N., and Stangel, J. (1999). *The Unofficial Guide to Overcoming Infertility.* New York: Macmillan.

Lukse, M. P., and Vacc, N. A. (1999). Grief, depression, and coping in women undergoing fertility treatment. *Infertility Counseling*, 93, 245–251.

Newton, C. R., Sherrard, W., and Glavac, I. (1999). The fertility problem inventory: Measuring perceived infertility-related stress. *Fertility and Sterility*, 72, 54–62.

Oddens, B. J., den Tonkelaar, I., and Nieuwenhuyse, H. (1999). Psychosocial experiences in women facing fertility problems — a comparative study. *Human Reproduction*, 14, 225–261.

RESOLVE, *The National Infertility Association Web site.* (2003). Retrieved April 3, 2003, from *www.resolve.org*.

Robin, P. (1993). *How to Be a Successful Fertility Patient.* New York: William Morrow.

Sher, G., Davis, V. M., and Stoess, J. (1998). *In Vitro Fertilization: The A.R.T. of Making Babies* (updated ed.). New York: Facts on File.

Souter, V. L., Hopton, J. L., Penney, G. C., and Templeton, A. A. (2002). Survey of psychological health in women with infertility. *Journal of Psychosomatic Obstetrics and Gynaecology*, 23, 41–49.

Souter, V. L., Penney, G., Hopton, J. L., and Templeton, A. A. (1998). Patient satisfaction with the management of infertility. *Human Reproduction*, 13, 1831–1836.

Sundby, J., Olsen, A., and Schei, B. (1994). Quality of care for infertility patients: An evaluation of a plan for a hospital investigation. *Scandinavian Journal of Social Medicine*, 22(2), 139–144.

Weschler, T. (2002). *Taking Charge of Your Fertility* (rev. ed.). New York: HarperCollins.

Wesson, N. (1999). *Enhancing Fertility Naturally.* Rochester, VT: Healing Arts Press.

Infidelity

"It was a symptom of their other marital problems"

Pastor Grace Sanchez saw it time and time again: infidelity that brought pain not only to individual lives, but also to her whole church community. It always hit her especially hard, because when she was a child her father had had an affair and it ultimately led to her parents' divorce. She had two friends who had had affairs, although both wives were married to disturbed husbands. One was abusive and violent, and the other was an extremely aloof and cold alcoholic. In both instances, the women were dying from emotional starvation and had, in desperation, turned to men who were more decent and loving to them. For the pastor, adultery was a profoundly complicated and confusing matter. It was not simply a case of right or wrong, but something that could occur in many different contexts. She did her best to help people struggling with this issue, but she was always conflicted inside.

Sheila came to see Rev. Sanchez in tears. She had just discovered that her husband was having an affair, and he had told her that for at least five years he had felt no attraction or love for her. She stated that this came as a complete surprise to her: "My whole world has crashed down around me."

Pastoral Care Assessment

As with all other areas when sexuality is involved, the dynamics of each case are unique and often complex (Olson et al., 2002). There is widespread condemnation of adultery, but regardless of whether you are counseling those who have been unfaithful or their spouses, it is important to listen in a balanced and noncritical way. Rev. Sanchez was alert to hearing Sheila's story and looked for signs of depression or other serious emotional distress. In this case, Sheila was clearly upset, but presented no signs of a psychological disorder. However, late in their conversation, Sheila cautiously admitted that she had had a very brief affair about 10 years ago. Had Pastor Sanchez quickly taken a judgmental stance, it would have likely closed the door to Sheila's sharing of her own infidelity. Rev. Sanchez had said, "I am here to listen, not to pass judgment. Please take your time and tell me anything that you want, so I can try to understand and help you."

Relevant History

Sheila's initial portrayal of a good marriage with the affair being a complete surprise turned out to be not completely true. Her husband, Jerry, had been preoccupied with his work almost from the beginning of their 14-year marriage. He was frequently late coming home, and within months of their wedding, Sheila began to feel all intimacy evaporating. "For such a long time, it's been like he was having an affair with his job."

Upon closer inspection, often infidelity is just one outward sign of dysfunctional relationship patterns. Especially if reconciliation is a possibility, these issues need to be fully explored and understood.

Understanding the Nature of Infidelity Experiences

Diagnostic Criteria

To best help people either repair a relationship or come to terms with a devastating experience like adultery, it is important to understand and explore the many possible factors that can underlie infidelity. Crisis intervention and the addressing of urgent concerns (for example, serious depressive reactions) are the first order of business. Beyond this, it is often helpful for a couple to carefully explore the history of their relationship. It may be best to consider the following common factors leading to adultery. In doing so, one will have to ask oneself and those one counsels, "Do motives matter?" Quick condemnation can often eliminate the possibility of healing. The following are issues that often emerge:

- Development of emotional distance, or lack of intimacy or trust in a relationship

- Significant sexual mismatch, that is, one person has a high sex drive and the other has a low one or even sexual aversion (not rare among survivors of childhood molestation or other sexual trauma)

- Loss of intimacy and/or reduced sexual interactions due to depression, serious or chronic illness, or drug/alcohol abuse

- Abuse (domestic violence, psychological or sexual abuse in the marriage)

- Loneliness, low self-esteem, or need for emotional reassurance

- Desire to punish the other partner

People will vary considerably regarding their interest in reconciliation. In the wake of infidelity, a number of issues that must be addressed often emerge:

- Scope of betrayal and lack of trust (will I ever be able to trust him/her again?). For some, the breach of trust hurts so much and runs so deep that it can result in long-lasting fears of abandonment and reluctance to regain intimacy with the partner (or in some cases, reluctance to ever trust anyone again).

- Sexual incompatibility can be addressed by sex therapy aimed at improving a couple's sexual relationship.

- Guilt and pleas for forgiveness: are these genuine or feigned? The issue of forgiveness deserves some attention. Psychiatrist M. Scott Peck states that in order to pardon someone, you must first find him or her guilty. Without this, words of forgiveness are shallow and meaningless. At times, authentic forgiveness is possible and can be a beginning point for rebuilding a relationship (Weaver and Furlong, 2000). But this is usually best accomplished if it is approached at a slow pace, taking ample time to explore the various factors that contributed to the rift in the relationship. Forgiveness rarely means forgetting. Rather, it can be fashioned out of one's ability to understand, to accept, and to commit to openly dealing with relationship problems. Under the best of circumstances, ongoing mistrust is the rule and not the exception, and it generally requires months or years to fully repair a relationship after an affair. Trust must be won, not just promised.

Response to Vignette

Grace Sanchez had two meetings with Sheila. During this time, the pastor learned more about what was a very troubled relationship. As is often the case, the extramarital affair was just the tip of the iceberg. In Sheila's case the emotional void that existed between her and her husband was huge, and he refused to go with her for marital counseling. However, Rev. Sanchez's nonjudgmental and compassionate stance allowed Sheila to feel comfortable in opening up to her (unlike her relationship with her husband, she was gradually able and willing to feel vulnerable and trusting with the pastor).

Due to the increasingly apparent emotional issues in Sheila's life, Rev. Sanchez referred her to a psychologist. After six months of therapy and during a follow-up visit with her pastor, Sheila stated that she was feeling much better. "The affair was devastating, but I've come to see that the real problem was that I was married to an emotionally unavailable man. I had been fooling myself into believing that my marriage was fine. Now it is clear that it never was." Sheila and Jerry separated and later divorced. For them reconciliation was not the pathway, but within a year, Sheila started to feel a growing sense of her own strength and the first sense of vitality she had felt in years.

A theme that runs throughout this book is that sexual problems or indiscretions are often quickly condemned in faith communities. Understandably, most religions have strong prohibitions regarding infidelity. Yet adultery is often but one manifestation of problematic or disturbed relationships. Understanding the complex nature of personal and interpersonal psychological factors underlying infidelity is the key to offering an atmosphere that facilitates healing. In a broader sense, it is equally important to teach and preach about forgiveness and to help parishioners develop attitudes of compassion for fellow church members going through this difficult experience.

Treatment within the Faith Community

Two issues are important to assess in the aftermath of experiences of infidelity, in order to determine if referral to a mental health professional is warranted. The first is to note if there are significant psychological symptoms present, such as depression. The second matter is often harder to assess: in addition to the response to an extramarital affair, are there serious relationship problems that underlie the current crisis? In either case, therapy may be helpful or necessary.

Indications for Referral

If the couple is willing to work together in counseling, the focus can either be on reconciliation or on helping each partner to cope with the emotions associated with the affair and the disruption of their relationship. As mentioned earlier, there are serious interpersonal problems at the heart of many marriages where infidelity occurs. A number of approaches have been developed and refined to help couples function more successfully, including family therapy, interpersonal therapy, and behavioral family therapy (Weaver et al., 2002). Each approach involves not only a forum for open discussion of problems in the relationship, but also techniques designed to improve communication skills, promote more productive problem solving, and facilitate intimate interactions. A conclusion often made is that adultery is just about sex. Often it is but one of several relationship problems that may require intensive psychological treatment.

Treatment by Mental Health Specialist

Cross-Cultural Issues

Adultery is a crime in 26 American states. These laws were based upon the idea that women were property belonging to men, and thus adultery is a violation of property rights. In 1997, a North Carolina woman successfully sued her husband's lover for $1 million for breaking up their marriage (King, 1999).

Resources

Face Reality, *www.facereality.com/about/index.html*, focuses on the difficulties of bringing the trauma of cheating and affairs to the surface of everyday conversation.

Heartchoice, *www.heartchoice.com*, offers advice, information, and resources about how to deal with sexual intimacy, infidelity, divorce, and other marital issues.

Refuge for the Soul, *www.geocities.com/HotSprings/Villa/9645*, was created for people who are trying to recover and heal emotionally after a relationship breakup or separation, such as the ending of a marriage, an extramarital affair, or grieving the loss of a loved one.

2-in-2-1, *www.2-in-2-1.co.uk/index.html*, discusses marriage topics, such as enhancing couple relationships, support through marital problems, and working through the challenges of breakdown and divorce.

Helpful Books

Adultery: The Forgivable Sin (Bonnie Eaker Weil, Ruth Winter, and Thomas Fogarty, New York: Hastings House, 1994).

How Could You Do This to Me? (Jane Greer, Jackson, TN: Main Street Books, 1998).

Love Affairs: Marriage and Infidelity (Richard Taylor, New York: Prometheus Books, 1997).

Make Up, Don't Break Up (Bonnie Eaker and Harville Hendrix, Holbrook, MA: Adams Media Corporation, 2000).

Repairing Your Marriage after His Affair: A Woman's Guide to Hope and Healing (Emily Brown and Marcella Bakur Weiner, New York: Random House, 1998).

Straight Talk about Betrayal: A Self-Help Guide for Couples (Donna R. Bellafiore, Naperville, IL: DRB Alternatives, 1999).

Surviving an Affair (Willard F. Harley Jr. and Jennifer Harley Chalmers, Grand Rapids: Revell, 1998).

Surviving Betrayal: Hope and Help for Women Whose Partners Have Been Unfaithful — 365 Daily Meditations (Alice May, San Francisco: Harper, 1999).

Surviving Infidelity: Making Decisions, Recovering from the Pain (Rona Subotnik and Gloria Harris, Holbrook, MA: Adams Media Corporation, 1993).

King, B. M. (1999). *Human Sexuality Today.* Upper Saddle River, NJ: **References**
Prentice Hall.

Olson, M. M., Russell, C. S., Higgins-Kessler M., and Miller R. B. (2002). Emotional processes following disclosure of an extramarital affair. *Journal of Marital and Family Therapy*, 28(4), 423–434.

Weaver, A. J., and Furlong, M. (eds.). (2000). *Reflections on Forgiveness and Spiritual Growth*. Nashville: Abingdon Press.

Weaver, A. J., Revilla, L. A., and Koenig, H. G. (2002). *Counseling Families Across the Stages of Life: A Handbook for Pastors and Other Helping Professionals*. Nashville: Abingdon Press.

Masturbation

*"She had gotten a clear message
that it was bad and sinful"*

Most clergy have been exposed to an array of feelings, values, beliefs, and opinions about masturbation in their families of origin and often in their faith communities. Almost all have had to come to terms with their own responses to sexual urges that accompanied entry into puberty. This is an area of human experience often fraught with guilt, shame, and sometimes, religious admonitions. In the period of one month Rev. Margaret Olsen had two parishioners raise concerns about masturbation: one, the single mother of a 14-year-old boy, and the other, a lonely widow.

While avoiding direct eye contact, Angela admitted, "I don't know how to talk about this. I'm embarrassed, but I'm worried about my son, Josh. Recently, I've seen him a couple of times touching himself, you know, his private parts." She said that she was completely at a loss to know how to respond to her son. She was also confused about the issue of masturbation. She had gotten a clear message from her mother that it was bad and sinful. She has recently been feeling uneasy and now has come for spiritual guidance.

Ginger's 39-year-old husband, Gary, died one year ago in a traffic accident. She also went to Rev. Olsen, initially talking with her about her ongoing grief. But at one point, she confessed that she was having a lot of guilty feelings over having had sexual longings and masturbating. "I don't know what's wrong with me — it just doesn't seem right."

Pastoral Care Assessment With the onset of puberty and the rise of sex hormones, sexual curiosity is intensified and masturbation increases. The frequently conflicting pressures of establishing adolescent sexual identity and controlling sexual impulses create a strong physiological sexual tension in teenagers, and masturbation is a normal way to reduce these tensions.

In general, males learn to masturbate earlier than females, and males do so more frequently. The better educated a person is, the more likely it is that he or she masturbates (Laumann et al., 1994). In addition, couples in a sexual relationship do not abandon masturbation entirely. When coitus is unsatisfactory or is unavailable because of illness or the absence of the partner, self-stimulation often serves an adaptive purpose, combining sensual pleasure and tension release (King, 2001).

Masturbation is a subject that most people find difficult to discuss with others. Yet it does, on occasion, come to the attention of pastors. Like many human behaviors, masturbation can be seen in a number of different contexts, and this must be gently explored and understood if a clergyperson is to know what to say and how to proceed.

A good starting point is to ask, "What is there about this that concerns you the most?" It is important to come to an understanding of the reasons this subject is being brought to a pastor. Often there are worries similar to those expressed by Ginger and Angela (such as guilt, shame, or concerns over sinful behavior). However, other issues include:

+ Misinformation about masturbation's physical or psychological effects. The stories about it making a person go blind or insane may sound outrageous these days, but many people harbor fears that it is harmful in either physical or emotional ways. It is important to encourage people to be as open as they can about their fears.

+ Some see masturbation as a sign of sexual perversion or deviance. Statistics vary, but it is generally agreed that approximately 50–60 percent of women and 90 percent of men masturbate and rarely are people involved in sexual deviance.

+ If it is discovered that a spouse is masturbating, it may lead to fears that this reflects a lack of love for or attraction to one's partner. This is a possibility in some instances, but often it is not the case.

Relevant History

Ancient Chinese culture condemned male masturbation as a waste of *yang* (male essence), and writers of Hebrew scriptures considered it "spillage of seed," punishable by death. The early church deemed the only legitimate function of sex to be for procreation, and sexual behaviors that did not have this as a goal were considered immoral. In Victorian times, many physicians also believed that loss of semen was as harmful to a male's health as loss of blood. The American physician, Dr. Sylvester Graham, wrote in 1834 that if a boy masturbated, he would turn into "a confirmed and degraded idiot" (King, 2001).

Diagnostic Criteria   More than a half a century ago, Kinsey and his colleagues published research that showed that masturbation was a common sexual activity. Ninety-two percent of the men in their sample reported having masturbated (Kinsey et al., 1948). In a more recent survey of sexual behavior in the United States, 52 percent of men and 42 percent of the women reported that they had masturbated in the preceding year (Laumann et al., 1994). Today, it is well recognized within science that the supposed ill-health effects of masturbation are baseless (Kaplan and Sadock, 1998).

For example, there is no evidence that masturbation is physically harmful; in fact, in some instances it may have positive health consequences. It is also a normal manifestation of human sexuality (APA, 2000). Although masturbation, per se, does not cause psychological problems, there are some emotional disturbances that are associated with masturbation.

- Some people who are suffering from significant psychological problems (such as depression) turn to activities or behaviors that temporarily reduce distress or function as a distraction (such as alcohol use, gambling, overeating, or frequent masturbation). Here masturbation is not the core problem, but rather is a solution of sorts — that is, an attempt to reduce suffering. What really needs to be addressed is the underlying problem.

- Masturbation may generate unhealthy levels of guilt or shame or lead to unrealistic conclusions about the self (such as, "I must be a pervert"). In this way, masturbation may lead to unnecessary emotional suffering.

- Masturbation may be associated with certain obsessions (such as a preoccupation with Internet pornography) or, *on occasion*, deviant sexual fantasies (such as fantasies about sex with animals or dead bodies, or sadistic sexual fantasies in which a person imagines hurting or humiliating another human being). Such preoccupations are a sign of significant psychopathology.

- In many marriages sexual problems abound. A common example of this is when one partner in an intimate relationship has a low sex drive or sexual aversion. Another problem is ignorance about sexuality or a lack of clear communication about what does or does not feel good sexually. Some couples are too inhibited to openly discuss this, resulting in years of unsatisfying sexual interactions. In these instances the sexual problems can occur in the context of an otherwise healthy relationship, but unmet sexual needs may be addressed by masturbation.

Noted psychologist Dr. Albert Ellis has written about a number of positive benefits of masturbation (Ellis, 1965; DeMartino, 1979), including the following:

- For young persons it can be a safe way to explore their sexuality, rather than engaging in premature sexual relations with others. And it may also help to protect a youngster from such adverse consequences as teenage pregnancy or sexually transmitted diseases.

- For those with marked sexual inhibitions, sexual aversion, or the lack of an intimate interpersonal relationship, masturbation can provide an outlet for sexual urges.

- As noted above, in some marriages when one spouse has a low sex drive or marked sexual inhibition, masturbation may allow the other partner to get some sexual needs met without imposing on the other partner.

- For some persons with physical disabilities or other limitations that preclude more usual interpersonal sexual relationships, this may be an outlet.

- Masturbation may be an acceptable outlet for sexual needs when one's partner is unable to participate in sexual intercourse (such as during the late stages of pregnancy, while physically ill, or during recovery from surgery).

- When persons are forced to be apart from a partner, masturbation may partially reduce some pangs of loneliness (such as when a soldier is deployed away from home).

- Masturbation can reduce tension and anxiety and promote more restful sleep. Some women also experience a reduction in premenstrual tension through masturbation.

- Masturbation may help a person to avoid involvement in a destructive relationship. One example of this is a woman who has separated from a husband who has been abusive. Sexual longings may contribute to a temptation to reengage with the spouse, which she clearly knows would be a poor decision. Masturbation can help to reduce such sexual urges, helping a woman resist the urge to return to an abusive husband.

In addition to this list, what was discovered to be a primary motive for Ginger was that her sexual/masturbatory fantasies were of being with her late husband. For her it was a way to maintain a connection with her soul mate.

Given such motives as addressed above, it is clear that any critical or judgmental conclusions would likely have failed to take into account the understandable and legitimate needs being met through masturbation. This is why it is crucial to explore the context in which this subject is raised. As with all issues involving sexuality, a stance of compassion and the desire to fully understand can go a long way in opening the door to meaningful discussions regarding aspects of the personal and emotional lives of those who turn to clergy for help.

Response to Vignette

Even the most experienced pastoral caregivers, as well as physicians, nurses, and psychotherapists may feel uncomfortable discussing the topic of masturbation. For this reason, it is often helpful to begin by admitting to your own uneasiness. Here is what Rev. Olsen said to both Angela and Ginger, "Practically everybody has a difficult time talking about masturbation, including me. But I want you to know that it is fine with me to discuss this. I will listen without any judgment; I simply want you to help me understand your concerns."

Her openness to discussing these matters helped Ginger understand that what for her had been a significant worry was both a normal human experience and a manifestation of her ongoing attachment to her late husband. The pastor's compassionate and supportive approach helped to transform Ginger's understanding and to increase self-acceptance.

Angela had been so worried about even bringing up the subject that she experienced tremendous relief when she saw that Rev. Olsen was comfortable talking and showed no hint of judgment. She reassured Angela and also referred her to a book that explained adolescent sexuality. Angela subsequently spoke with her son, and although both felt somewhat tense during the conversation, it was clear to Angela that Josh was relieved and was able to feel more acceptance for his completely normal adolescent behavior.

Treatment within the Faith Community

Faith communities play a crucial role in the lives of many individuals and families facing all sorts of human problems, including sexual concerns (Weaver et al., 2002). Given that clergy are often the first professionals sought for help, those in ministry need to understand the key issues to be addressed regarding sexual matters such as masturbation. Through suggesting books and articles to read, clergy can offer guidance and direction on issues including normal adolescent sexual development. The faith community can foster preventive care through adequate and appropriate sex education within the community of faith.

Taboos against masturbation have produced folklore that it causes mental illness. No scientific evidence supports this belief. Masturbation is a maladaptive symptom only when it becomes a compulsion beyond a person's willful control (APA, 2000). Then it is an indication of emotional disturbance, not because it is sexual but because it is compulsive. Masturbation is almost certainly a universal and predictable aspect of psychosexual development and, in the great majority of cases, positively adaptive. If a clergyperson feels uncomfortable counseling a person about sexual matters like masturbation, having a pastoral counselor or mental health professional to whom one can refer an individual or family is a good plan.

Indications for Referral

Mental health professionals who specialize in counseling on sexual issues endeavor to eliminate myths and negative attitudes about masturbation. The basic task is "normalizing" it. Many sexologists, however, are interested in going beyond reducing "unease" and trying to help people enjoy and feel pleasure during masturbation. Human sexual expression is diverse, and there are numerous forms. Persons engage in a lot of sexual activities that have no other purpose than pleasure. Too many people experience guilt and shame over their sexuality because they believe that they deviate from what is normal.

Treatment by Mental Health Specialist

A study conducted at the University of Memphis found that European American women had a greater acceptance of masturbation than African American females (Shulman and Horne, 2003). The National Health and Social Life Survey (Laumann et al., 1994) also found that more European American women (44 percent) report ever having masturbated than African American females (32 percent). Among women, positive attitudes about sexuality and orgasmic capacity have been positively correlated to masturbation (Kelly et al., 1990).

Cross-Cultural Issues

American Association of Retired Persons; 601 E Street, NW, Washington, DC 20049; (202)434-AARP; *www.aarp.org*; is the nation's leading organization for people over the age of 50. It has information on health and sexual related topics for older adults.

American Association of Sex Educators, Counselors, and Therapists; P.O. Box 5488, Richmond, VA 23220-0488; (212)819-9770; *www.aasect.org*; promotes understanding of human sexuality and healthy sexual behavior.

Resources

Families Are Talking: Safer Sex, *www.familiesaretalking.org/teen/ teen0011.html*, information for teenagers about abstinence, alternatives to sex, and safe sex.

Family Project, *www.familiesaretalking.org*, is a Web site and newsletter put out by the Sexuality Information and Education Council of the U.S. This project is meant to empower parents and caregivers to communicate with their children about sexuality-related issues, to provide tools to help families communicate about these matters, and to encourage parents, caregivers, and young people to become advocates on the local, state, and national levels for comprehensive sexuality education programs in the schools.

National Women's Health Information Center; 8550 Arlington Boulevard, Suite 300, Fairfax, VA 22031; (800)994-9662; *www .4woman.gov*; a project of the U.S. Department of Health and Human Services. Offers a toll-free call center and a Web site health topics search with links to related topics.

Sexuality Information and Education Council of the U.S. (SIECUS), *www.siecus.org/index.html*, is an organization that develops and disseminates information, promotes comprehensive education concerning sexuality, and advocates responsible sexual choices.

Sexuality Websites for Teens, online at *www.familiesaretalking.org/teen/ teen0014.html*, provides a list of Web sites for teens dealing with sexual issues and questions.

SIECUS: Religion and Sexuality, *www.siecus.org/toc.html#RELI*, provides a list of Web sites that deal with issues concerning religion and sexuality and a list of links to fact sheets, community resources, and policy issues related to sexuality and sexual education.

SIECUS: Sexuality Education Curricula, *www.siecus.org/pubs/biblio/ bibs0010.html*, describes sexual education curricula for elementary through high school students.

SIECUS: Sexuality Education in the Home, *www.siecus.org/pubs/biblio/ bibs0011.html*, provides a list of books to help parents understand and talk to their children and teens about sexual issues, including abuse, pregnancy, and STDs.

Helpful Books   *Changing Bodies, Changing Lives* (Ruth Bell, New York: Three Rivers Press, 1998).

From Boys to Men: All about Adolescence and You (Michael Gurian, East Rutherford, NJ: Price Stern Sloan, 1999).

Guy Book: An Owner's Manual (Mavis Jukes, New York: Crown Books for Young Readers, 2001).

Human Sexuality (William H. Masters, Virginia E. Johnson, and Robert C. Kolodny, Reading, MA: Addison-Wesley, 1997).

Human Sexuality Today (Bruce M. King, Upper Saddle River, NJ: Prentice Hall, 2001).

It's Perfectly Normal: Changing Bodies, Growing Up, Sex, and Sexual Health (Robie H. Harris, Cambridge, MA: Candlewick Press, 1996).

New Male Sexuality (Bernie Zilbergeld, New York: Random House, 1999).

Sex Matters for Women: A Complete Guide to Taking Care of Your Sexual Self (Sally Foley, Sally A. Kope, and Dennis P. Sugrue, New York: Guilford Publications, 2001).

What's Going on Down There? Answers to Questions Boys Find Hard to Ask (Karen Gravelle, Nick Castro, and Chava Castro, New York: Walker Books, 1998).

"What's Happening to My Body?" Book for Girls: A Growing-up Guide for Parents and Daughters (Lynda Madaras and Area Madaras, New York: Newmarket Press, 2000).

References

American Psychiatric Association. (2000). *Diagnostic and Statistical Manual of Mental Disorders* (4th ed. text revision). Washington, DC: American Psychiatric Association.

DeMartino, M. F. (1979). *Human Autoerotic Practices.* New York: Human Sciences Press.

Ellis, A. (1965). *Sex Without Guilt.* Hollywood: Wilshire Books.

Kaplan, H. I., and Sadock, B. J. (1998). *Synopsis of Psychiatry: Behavioral Sciences/Clinical Psychiatry* (8th ed.). Baltimore: Williams and Wilkins.

Kelly, M. P., Strassberg, D. S., and Kircher, J. R. (1990). Attitudinal and experiential correlates of anorgasmia. *Archives of Sexual Behavior,* 19(2), 165–167.

King, B. (2001). *Human Sexuality Today.* Upper Saddle River, NJ: Prentice Hall.

Kinsey, A., Pomeroy, W., and Martin, C. (1948). *Sexual Behavior in the Human Male.* Philadelphia: W. B. Saunders.

Laumann, E. O., Gagnon, J. H., Michael, R. T., and Michaels, S. (1994). *The Social Organization of Sexuality: Sexual Practices in the United States.* Chicago: University of Chicago Press.

Oliver, M. B., and Hyde, J. S. (1993). Gender differences in sexuality: A meta analysis. *Psychological Bulletin* 114(1), 29–51.

Shulman, J. L., and Horne, S. G. (2003). The use of self-pleasure: Masturbation and body image among African American and European American women. *Psychology of Women Quarterly*, 27, 262–269.

Weaver, A. J., Revilla, L. A., and Koenig, H. G. (2002). *Counseling Families Across the Stages of Life: A Handbook for Pastors and Other Helping Professionals*. Nashville: Abingdon Press.

Menopause

"Will I still be attractive to my husband?"

Mary went to her pastor, Wendy Myers. Both Mary and her husband had been active in the church for several years and knew the clergywoman well. Since Mary was an attractive 51-year-old woman who was confident and articulate, Rev. Myers was somewhat surprised to hear Mary express self-doubt. She began to describe her fears about the changes to her body as a result of menopause. The pastor listened as Mary wondered out loud, "Will I still be attractive to my husband as everything begins to sag and the fine lines become wrinkles?" Mary said that she was having minor sleep disturbance and some headaches, but was generally in a good mood. Rev. Myers knew the importance of communicating with Mary in an accepting, patient manner and the value of being a good listener.

Pastoral Care Assessment

During menopause many women begin to feel insecure about their body and sexuality. They may ask themselves, am I still attractive? Will my husband still have erotic feelings for me? Such thoughts that can hamper sexual activity and enjoyment are usually without merit, since it is one's attitude toward sexuality that is important and not appearance (King, 2001). It is also important to remember that men have their own concerns in middle age — whether it is the fear of becoming bald or doubts about sexual performance. Women who have a supportive network of family, friends, and others (such as clergy) with whom they can talk about menopause are more positive about this midlife transition than are those without such a support network (Theisen et al., 1995).

Relevant History

Hormonal shifts during menopause can cause sleep disturbances, irritability, and frequent headaches. While there is no clear evidence showing a direct link between menopause and emotional symptoms that occur during this time, some women do experience mood swings. In addition, passing through this transition may make women somewhat more vulnerable to stress. So if a woman is stressed in her family or at work, it may be more difficult for her to cope with menopause.

Diagnostic Criteria   Menopause usually occurs between the ages of 45 and 55 and is the name given to the last menstrual period of a woman's life. There are three stages of the cycle: premenopause, defined as menstruating regularly for the past 12 months; perimenopause, defined as menstruating during the past 12 months but experiencing cycle irregularity; and postmenopause, defined as no menstruation within the past 12 months (King, 2001).

Perimenopause is the stage when women may experience physical changes such as hot flashes and problems sleeping (Rosenthal, 1999). Symptoms usually last between two to five years and are due to a decrease in the amount of estrogen in the body. Hot flashes are the most common symptom, usually occurring at night. About 20 percent of menopausal women notice increased vaginal dryness, even when feeling aroused. This is the body's normal response to a decreased level of the hormone estrogen. Other symptoms include insomnia, mood swings/irritability, anxiety/panic attacks, poor memory/lack of concentration, joint/muscle pains, loss of self-esteem, atrophy of the vagina, urinary infections and pain on urinating, loss of libido, and dry hair and skin. Postmenopause is the time that follows the last menses (Rosenthal, 1999).

Menopause may lead women to consider the use of hormone replacement therapy (HRT). Recent research has left many females confused over whether HRT is likely to do them more harm than good. When a woman nears menopause her ovaries produce fewer and fewer female hormones (King, 2001). HRT is the name given to a group of drugs, in a variety of preparations, that are a substitute for these female hormones. The most common form of HRT is a combination of estrogen and progestogen. Women use HRT around the time of menopause and beyond to relieve menopausal symptoms and for its protective effects.

HRT is often effective at relieving hot flashes (Greendale et al., 1998). It can also alleviate other early problems. The increase in estrogen levels keeps the lining of the vagina soft and healthy, making intercourse more comfortable. HRT is also recognized for its long-term benefits, including aiding in the prevention of osteoporosis (Eichner et al., 2003). This is because of the important role estrogen plays in maintaining the levels of calcium in bones.

HRT is not suitable for every woman because of an increased risk of breast cancer. A large study in the United Kingdom found that long-term use of HRT is associated with a small increased risk of breast cancer (Beral, 2003). Researchers found that 10 years' use of a combined estrogen/progestogen preparation of HRT resulted in an estimated five additional breast cancer cases per 1,000 users. A large study in the United States showed that females taking combined HRT had a 26 percent higher risk of breast cancer (Rossouw et al., 2002). It is imperative that women who seek clergy counsel about the effects of menopause and the possible use of HRT be directed to the expertise of a medical doctor.

Response to Vignette

Sexuality exists in one form or another throughout life — it is a natural and healthy part of being human. People are now living longer and are healthier than ever before. This has resulted not only in a sizeable growth in the elderly population, but also in an increasing emphasis on the normal aspects of aging, including issues relating to menopause and changing sexuality. When sex is pleasurable and fulfilling, it can enhance the later years. The pattern of one's sex life before menopause and the quality of a marriage are strongly associated with sexual activity and satisfaction.

The physical changes associated with aging can negatively affect the sexual response cycle. However, problems involving intimacy usually are a greater concern to menopausal women than are physical changes. Those who perceive aging as negative have greater difficulties with emotional problems. For many of these females, the stereotype of older age as being sexually detached and indifferent becomes the key problem (Rosenthal, 1999). Affirmative attitudes can have a positive effect on sexuality. Women who look forward to menopause for its freedom from pregnancy and child-rearing generally report an increase in sexual feelings and heightened sexuality.

The chief reason for declining sexuality in older females is the unavailability of a partner — there are 84 men for every 100 women in the population between 65 and 69 years of age. This number decreases to only 44 males for every 100 females in those 85 years of age or older (U.S. Bureau of the Census, 1996). With the availability of a partner, sexual interest and activity can be sustained throughout life. With aging there is a trend toward viewing the quality of sexual experience over quantity as a measure of satisfaction. The need for closeness, caring, and companionship is lifelong (Byyny and Speroff, 1990).

Treatment within the Faith Community

One advantage that faith communities have when addressing health issues among older adults (especially among females) is that they are the most likely group by age and gender to be affiliated with congregations and to attend religious services (Saad and Gallup, 2003). Women and older Americans provide the backbone for organized religion with both groups significantly more likely than men and young adults to say religion is very important to them or to attend religious services on a regular basis. More than two-thirds of females (69 percent), in comparison to just over half of males (53 percent), say religion is very important in their lives. The religiousness gap is even larger with respect to age. Three-quarters of Americans aged 65 and older (76 percent) say religion is very important to them. Similarly, the percentage who say they have attended church in the last seven days rises from 32 percent among the youngest adult age group to 54 percent among the oldest one. Furthermore, attendance at religious services has been found to be even higher among ethnic minorities than in the nation as a whole (Saad and Gallup, 2003).

Contemporary American society tends to define midlife and aging in negative terms, contributing to the demoralization many women feel at menopause. Factors that influence the experience of sexuality, menopause, and self-worth in elderly females include negative societal attitudes, cultural roles, and beliefs. Faith communities can play a positive role by providing accurate information for people regarding these issues. Congregations have long-established communication networks that allow them to stay in touch with their members who need education and support on this and other health issues that affect older women. Accurate information can be disseminated to members through these networks. In every congregation there are persons who are willing to be of service to others.

Indications for Referral

Mary is a healthy, well-adjusted woman who needed a caring pastor, like Rev. Myers, who has good listening skills and can share accurate information about menopause. Mary experienced the sort of self-doubts that many females have at that time in life. She had no signs of depression or other mental health problems, and the pastoral care was sufficient to address the issues that concerned her. There was no need for a referral in this case.

Treatment by Mental Health Specialist

Some women do experience significant depression during menopause that requires the intervention of a mental health professional. It is found more often in nonmarried than married women, although married females who are unhappy with their marriages are at greater risk of depression than those in a happy marriage (Robinson-Kurpius et al., 2001).

Of all mental health problems, depression is the most common and the most treatable. Symptoms of a major depression can include depressed mood, inability to enjoy things, difficulty sleeping, changes in patterns of sleeping and eating, problems in concentration and decision making, feelings of guilt, hopelessness, and decreased self-esteem (Preston, 2001). Depression has been linked to abnormal levels of neurotransmitters in the brain, and treatment using medications seeks to correct the imbalance. There are several groups of drugs available to treat this illness, and they can affect individuals differently (Preston et al., 2001). It is necessary for patients to work with their physicians to find the most beneficial choice. Medication for depression is usually prescribed in conjunction with therapy (Preston et al., 2001).

It is important to note that most mental health professionals do not address menopause during their sessions with midlife women. According to Wilk and Kirk (1995) only 16 percent regularly discuss menopause with their clients who are experiencing menopause. Mental health professionals clearly need to better recognize the importance of menopause and of addressing pertinent issues, such as sexuality, in working with females in midlife.

Cross-Cultural Issues

Researchers studied the effect of menopause in 185 U.S. women over a 7-to-9-year period (Bromberger et al., 1997). The median age at menopause was 51.5 years for the overall group. However, the median age at menopause was earlier for females who were African American (49.3 years), were smokers (50.6 years), or were currently on a weight reduction diet (50.5 years). Stress was associated with an earlier age at menopause in African Americans (48.4 years). Results suggest that premenopausal women in their 40s who are smokers, are dieting, or are African American are likely to experience menopause earlier than their contemporaries. This study suggests that African American females may have a different "biological clock" than European American women, especially when under stress, or they may experience more stress of longer duration (Bromberger et al., 1997).

Resources

A Friend Indeed, *www.afriendindeed.ca*, is a newsletter that provides information and support to women about the menopausal and midlife transitions. It is published six times yearly and distributed free.

American College of Obstetrics and Gynecology, *www.acog.org*, is an independent nonprofit organization that provides information and resources for females, including research on menopause and midlife health changes.

Menopause-Online, *www.menopause-online.com*, is a site that provides current, easy-to-understand information about menopause.

Midlife sexuality, *www.nurseweek.com/ce/ce206a.html*, is a page that provides useful information about sexuality for menopausal and midlife women.

North American Menopause Society, *www.menopause.org*, is a nonprofit scientific organization devoted to promoting women's health during midlife and beyond, through an understanding of menopause. This site contains information on perimenopause, early menopause, menopause symptoms, long-term health effects of estrogen loss, and a variety of therapies to enhance health during and after menopause.

OBGYN.Net, *www.obgyn.net/women/women.asp*, is a site that provides information, news, research, answers to frequently asked questions, and articles about menopause and postmenopausal life, in addition to many other important women's medical issues. It also provides a free monthly e-mail newsletter.

Planned Parenthood, Women's Health; *www.plannedparenthood.org/~WOMENSHEALTH/menopause.htm*; provides information about the symptoms and effects of menopause, as well as resources on coping with the difficulties of menopause, including changing sexuality, stressors, and general health.

Powersurge, *www.power-surge.com/intro.htm*, is a nonprofit online menopause support group providing online chat forums, message boards, information, news, research, articles, medical advice, coping tips, and links to other resources for females experiencing changes from menopause.

PRIME PLUS/Red Hot Mamas, *www.primeplususa.com/index2.html*, provides menopause education to broaden the base of women's knowledge about menopause and its management. It has comprehensive health-related information and tools to support menopausal females.

Sexuality Tutor, *www.sexualitytutor.homestead.com/SeniorIssues.html*, provides information about a variety of topics on sexuality. It has links to articles, research, and information about coping with changing menopausal sexuality.

Sexualityandu.ca, *www.sexualityandu.ca/eng*, is a Canadian Web site devoted to sexuality education and information. It provides guidance and resources about important women's topics, including menopause and postmenopausal sexuality.

Women's Health Hotline, *www.libov.com/info/sources/index.html*, provides news and resources about menopause and other women's health issues.

Women's Health Initiative, *www.nhlbi.nih.gov/whi/resources.htm*, is a major research program associated with the National Institutes of Health that addresses the most common causes of disability, death, and poor quality of life in postmenopausal women.

Helpful Books

Flying Solo: Single Women in Midlife (Carol Anderson, Sona Dimidjian, and Susan Stewart, New York: Norton, 1995).

The Fountain of Age (Betty Friedan, New York: Simon and Schuster, 1993).

The Hormone of Desire: The Truth about Sexuality, Menopause, and Testosterone (Susan Rako, New York: Three Rivers Press, 1996).

The New Ourselves, Growing Older: Women Aging with Knowledge and Power (Paula Doress-Worters and Diana Siegal, New York: Touchstone/Simon and Schuster, 1996).

The New Sex Over 40 (Saul Rosenthal, New York: J. P. Tarcher, 1999).

The Pause: Positive Approaches to Menopause (Lonnie Barbach, New York: Plume/Penguin, 1995).

Questions and Answers about Sex in Later Life (Margot Tallmer, Philadelphia: Charles Press, 1995).

Sex Over 50 (Joel Block and Susan Crain Bakos, New York: Prentice Hall, 1999).

Sexuality in Mid-life (Stephen Levine, New York: Plenum, 1998).

Still Doing It: Women and Men over 60 Write about their Sexuality (Joani Blank, San Francisco: Down There Press, 2000).

References

Beral, V. (2003). Breast cancer and hormone replacement therapy in the million women study. *The Lancet*, 362, 419–427.

Bromberger, J. T., Matthews, K. A., Kuller, L. H., Wing, R. R., Meilahn, E. N., and Plantinga, P. (1997). Prospective study of the determinants of age at menopause. *American Journal of Epidemiology*, 145, 124–133.

Byyny, R. L., and Speroff, L. (1990). *A Clinical Guide for the Care of Older Women*. Baltimore: Williams and Wilkins.

Eichner, S. F., Lloyd, K. B., and Timpe, E. M. (2003). Comparing therapies for postmenopausal osteoporosis prevention and treatment. *The Annals of Pharmacotherapy*, 37(5), 711–724.

Greendale, G. A., Reboussin, B. A., Hogan, P., Barnabei, V. M., Shumaker, S., Johnson, S., and Barrett-Connor, E. (1998). Symptom relief and side effects of postmenopausal hormones: Results from the Postmenopausal Estrogen/Progestin Interventions Trial. *Obstetrics and Gynaecology*, 92(6), 982–988.

King, B. (2001). *Human Sexuality Today*. Upper Saddle River, NJ: Prentice Hall.

McKinlay, S. M. (1996). The normal menopause transition: An overview. *Maturitas*, 23(2), 137–45.

Preston, J. D. (2001). *You Can Beat Depression*. San Luis Obispo, CA: Impact Publishers.

Preston, J. D., O'Neal, J. H., and Talaga, M. (2001). *Handbook of Clinical Psychopharmacology for Therapists*. Oakland, CA: New Harbinger.

Robinson-Kurpius, S. E., Nicpon, M. F., and Maresh, S. E. (2001). Mood, marriage and menopause. *Journal of Counseling Psychology*, 48(1), 77–84.

Rosenthal, S. H. (1999). *The New Sex Over 40*. Rockland, MA: Wheeler Publishing.

Rossouw, J. E., Anderson, G. L., Prentice, R. L., La Croix, A. Z., et al. (2002). Risks and benefits of estrogen plus progestin in healthy postmenopausal women. *Journal of the American Medical Association*, 288(3), 321–323.

Saad, L., and The Gallup Organization. (2003). *Religion is very important to majority of Americans*. Retrieved April 8, 2004, from *www.gallup.com/content/login.aspx?ci=9853*.

Theisen, S. C., Mansfield, P. K., Seery, B. L., and Voda, A. (1995). Predictors of midlife women's attitudes toward menopause. *Health Values*, 19, 22–31.

U.S. Bureau of the Census. (1996). *Current population reports, special studies. 65+ in the United States*. Washington, DC: Government Printing Office.

Wilk, C. A., and Kirk, M. A. (1995). Menopause: A developmental stage, not a deficiency disease. *Psychotherapy*, 32, 233–241.

Pedophilia

"They could not believe an adult
would do that to a child"

A former youth worker was sentenced to 10 years in prison after pleading guilty to 28 counts of taking indecent liberties with minors. The Protestant youth director, 32, had engaged in sexual activity with three 12-year-old girls, over a period of 2 years. He met his victims through the youth praise team that he led at the church, and his behavior included caressing the girls, fondling their genitals, and performing oral sex. On about 10 occasions, he engaged in games of "truth or dare" on the Internet using a Web camera, which involved him watching the girls engage in oral sex and other sexual acts initiated by his "dares." Authorities seized more than 200 videotapes and 15,000 computer files from the youth leader's home, some of which depicted very young and preadolescent children posed or engaged in sexual conduct. It was discovered that the youth director previously had been convicted in another state of sexually abusing a child. He had been released from prison after serving five years. The senior pastor resigned when it was found that he had not screened the youth worker as the church required.

Pastoral Care Assessment

The families of the girls and other church members were shattered by the revelation of child sexual abuse by a leader in their congregation. Nothing can prepare a family or faith community for the devastation of finding out that a child has been abused. Although adults understand the words, they are often emotionally unable to handle what they are hearing; it is so horrible that they want it to be a mistake. But adult rationality recognizes that the situations being described are beyond a child's knowledge and experience. Children do not know the terminology for sexual contact, but victims are nevertheless able to describe in detail what was done to them and the acts that they were made to perform.

The three girls disclosed the abuse gradually. Each new piece of information brought more sorrow and horror as the families and members of the church realized that these children had been violated at such a tender age. The adults were overwhelmed by the thoughts of what the girls had endured. For a long time their parents could think of nothing else. In private moments, they cried their hearts out. There was a period entirely lacking in joy or any pleasure in life for the parents and grandparents. On some days family members walked around like zombies, only going through the motions of living. They began to question whether they could ever return to normal thought patterns or ever feel happy again.

Coupled with the grief the parents and church members were experiencing over the children's loss of innocence was a growing rage at the perpetrator and the pastor who did not check the youth worker's references, which might have protected the children. The families' feelings toward the perpetrator became a desire for violent retribution, ranging from wanting to beat him up to wanting to kill him. However, they maintained restraint through their Christian beliefs and did not act on their urges. They also realized that further violence only would have caused more destruction to their families. That was something that they had to remind themselves of often because these thoughts did not easily subside. Having extremely violent feelings can cause great distress and drive persons to question their sanity.

Relevant History According to an extensive *New York Times* survey of documented church sex abuse cases through December 2002, the crisis that has affected the Roman Catholic Church involves every American diocese and includes more than 1,200 priests (Goodstein and Zirilli, 2003). These men are known to have victimized more than 4,000 minors over the last six decades, although experts say there are surely many more who have remained silent. Their position is supported by a study of the criminal behavior of 453 pedophilic offenders, recruited through outpatient treatment programs, which found that each offender admitted to an average of 148 victims and 236 acts of molestation (Abel and Osborne, 1992).

Child sexual abuse by a religious leader is a violation of trust that has an enormous impact on all members of the faith community. One study explored the effects of priests publicly being accused of child sexual abuse on adult Roman Catholics' feelings of trust in the priesthood, the church, and God (Rossetti, 1997). Over 1,800 active Catholics in the United States and Canada fell into one of three groups: those who had no awareness of priests being charged with child sexual abuse in their parish or diocese (501), those who had a priest in their diocese accused (1,097), and those whose own parish priest had been charged (177). From the first to the second to the third group, there was a steady decline in trust in the priesthood and the church, but not in trust in God. The study expanded the concept of victim to include parishes and the wider church when priests are charged with child sexual abuse, and it highlighted the need to extend pastoral and psychological care to these groups.

A diagnosis of the disorder of pedophilia requires sexual activity with a prepubescent child (generally age 13 years or younger). An individual with pedophilia must be 16 years of age or older and at least 5 years older than the victim. Persons with this disorder usually report an attraction to children of a particular age range (APA, 2000). Some individuals prefer males, others females, and some are aroused by both sexes, although pedophilia involving female victims is reported more often than pedophilia with male victims. Some perpetrators are sexually attracted only to children (exclusive type), while others are sometimes attracted to adults (nonexclusive type). **Diagnostic Criteria**

Pedophiles who act on their urges may limit their activity to undressing a child and looking, exposing themselves, masturbating in a child's presence, or touching a child. Others, however, perform oral sex on a child or penetrate a child's vagina, mouth, or anus with their fingers, foreign objects, or penis, using varying degrees of force to do so (APA, 2000). These actions are commonly explained with excuses or rationalizations that they have "educational value" for the child, that the child derives "sexual pleasure" from them, or that the child was "sexually provocative" — themes that are also common in child pornography. Because pedophiles often do not understand that what they are doing is wrong, many do not experience significant distress. It is important to note that distress about having the fantasies, urges, or behaviors is not necessary for a diagnosis of pedophilia. Those who have a pedophilic arousal pattern and act on those fantasies or urges with a child fit the diagnosis (APA, 2000).

Some pedophiles limit their activities to their own children, stepchildren, or relatives, while others victimize children outside of their families. Some threaten the child to prevent disclosure. Others, particularly those who are frequent victimizers, develop complicated techniques for obtaining access to children, which may include winning the trust of a child's mother or marrying a woman with an attractive child (APA, 2000). A perpetrator may be attentive to a child's needs in order to gain the child's affection, interest, and loyalty and to prevent the child from reporting the sexual activity. The frequency of pedophilic behavior can fluctuate with the degree of stress in a perpetrator's life. Pedophilia is usually a chronic disorder, especially in those attracted to males. The recidivism rate for pedophiles with a preference for males is roughly twice that of those attracted to females. In addition to their pedophilia, a significant number of the perpetrators are also involved in exhibitionism, voyeurism, or rape (Kaplan and Sadock, 1998).

Response to Vignette

Bishop Marvin Martin met with the leaders of the congregation and then held a special worship service for the children and families who had been victimized. After consulting with the leaders of the church, the bishop assigned a denominational Response Team of experts that included social workers, psychologists, and guidance counselors. They offered individual and group counseling services to the adults and youth of the church in response to the crisis. An interim pastor, Rev. Anna Murray, with specialized training in conflict resolution and advanced pastoral counseling was assigned to the congregation.

The interim minister and the Response Team taught church members about possible feelings, reactions, and needs of the victims and their families. They educated the congregation about psychological trauma and traumatic grief that may be experienced by the families and the church members who knew the victims. Rev. Murray offered special programs and workshops on several topics including "Grief and Loss," "Anger," "Healing," and "Where is God in Crises?" The interim pastor facilitated healing with her nonanxious presence, psychological skills, and wise counsel. She helped the church regroup and prepare for a new minister to arrive. The crisis combined with a new awareness of child abuse motivated several members to become involved in giving assistance to children from abusive family situations at a foster care home near the church. The congregation also provided practical and emotional support to the families of the children during the trial by providing transportation to the courthouse and companionship during the ordeal.

Treatment within the Faith Community

Sexual abuse is a reality in our society, and the faith community must face this issue by taking steps to protect children. Guidelines for the prevention of sexual misconduct in churches can help safeguard youngsters while promoting a positive environment for ministry. The following guidelines can help protect children and youth and those supervising them.

- Screening of adult workers must be mandatory. Interviews with prospective leaders, checking of references, and criminal background checks are essential. No adult with any prior incident of child sexual abuse can be involved in any capacity with a youth ministry or other program that provides access to children.

- All workers with children or youth should be required to take a rigorous workshop on the prevention of child sexual abuse and have a complete understanding of the material covered in the workshop.

- Persons who are sexually promiscuous or in a state of active addiction to alcohol or drugs cannot be permitted to work in ministry with minors. Youth leaders should be mentally healthy with a good dose of self-esteem and solidly grounded in faith.

- An open-door policy is important at all children's and youth activities. Clergy, staff, parents, and church members have a right to observe any program.

- Adult workers with children and youth must meet on a regular basis with the clergy supervisors to openly discuss problems, accountability, policy clarification, personal feelings, and issues that affect their ministry. It is also highly recommended that counseling and/or spiritual direction be provided.

- A young person should never be left in the primary care of a single adult. Teams of adults (preferably male and female) should supervise children's and youth activities. This protects both youngsters and adults from false accusations and questionable situations. Furthermore, it diffuses the possibility of an adult having too much influence over an individual child. A ratio of five youth to one adult is recommended as a minimum.

- At least two adults should be present at any overnight activity. If the participants include both boys and girls, the chaperones must be both male and female. It is never appropriate for an adult leader who is not a family member to share a bed with a young person. Males and females should sleep in separate rooms at all events and have access to separate bathroom facilities or separate times for use. Adult workers experienced with children or youth should be included with adults who are newcomers to the ministry.

- Avoid dropping off and/or picking up young persons without being accompanied by another adult. Encourage families to arrange their own transportation, if possible.

- At times when one-to-one conversations are needed, notify another adult of the place of consultation and with whom you are counseling.

Try to meet in a public place where you can talk privately but are still in view of others. Guard yourself against seclusion. Make every attempt to have adult females counsel girls and adult males counsel boys. Another option is team counseling, a male and female adult working with an individual together.

- Many times in counseling youth, issues of abuse, alcoholism, and neglect are raised. One must be aware of these issues and be ready to refer youth who have such problems to qualified professionals. A leader also needs to be sure that he or she is following the legal requirements for reporting instances of abuse or criminal activity.

- Older minors should never be given responsibility for the care of younger children. Older teens can assist in supervision but must not be solely responsible. An adult's presence is required.

- No adult leaders should give a personal gift or money privately to a young person without first notifying the parent(s) and the ministry or clergy supervisor, since gifts can be easily misinterpreted.

- No adult youth worker may be romantically or sexually involved with a minor under any circumstances. Sexual misconduct can be devastating to the parties involved and can lead to civil action as well as criminal prosecution and imprisonment.

Indications for Referral The intense anxiety or severe depression after finding out that your child or grandchild has been sexually exploited by a leader of your faith community can warrant mental health treatment (Weaver et al., 2003). Such traumatic events can provoke severe psychological reactions in persons with preexisting vulnerability, but such symptoms can occur in otherwise emotionally healthy individuals as well. This point should be made with those experiencing traumatic reactions. Such persons must be strongly encouraged to accept a referral to a mental health professional.

Pedophilia is extremely difficult to treat. A team of specialists should be involved. This disorder requires intensive and comprehensive treatment, involving pharmacological and psychological interventions over months or years, often with lifetime follow-up. A large study conducted by the Canadian government found that on average the sexual offense recidivism rate was fairly low at 13.4 percent. However, among those offenders who failed to complete treatment, a much higher risk of offending again was discovered than among those who had completed treatment (Hanson and Bussière, 1998). The rate of repeat offenses was also significantly higher among those who had deviant sexual preferences and prior sexual offenses.

Pedophilia is a serious, chronic, and very often lifelong mental disorder. Many people with this illness have other sex-related disorders as well as depression, anxiety, and addictions (Raymond et al., 1999). In offenders, cognitive distortions and denial of the implications of aberrant sexual behavior have been widely seen. Pedophiles routinely minimize the deviant nature of their behavior and its destructive impact on the children involved, and such distortions can reach delusional intensity.

Treatment by Mental Health Specialist

Cognitive behavioral treatments have been used to reduce pedophilic sexual desire and increase age-appropriate sexual behavior (Leiblum and Rosen, 2000). Conditioning techniques, such as changing patterns of behavior to reduce exposure to risk and aversive conditioning, are also employed. Training in interpersonal skills, assertiveness, and empathy are used to improve relationships with adults. Finally, confrontation of denial, particularly in a group format, cognitive restructuring of distortions in thinking, and training in empathy for victims are all used to reduce the risk of pedophilic behavior (Leiblum and Rosen, 2000). In cases where internal motivation is lacking, external restraints, such as surveillance networks or the threat of incarceration, are used to bolster inhibition. Relapse prevention programs that identify risk, develop alternative responses to risk, and use supportive resources are important.

Ninety-five percent of pedophile offenders are heterosexual, and 50 percent consume alcohol to excess at the time of the incident (Kaplan and Sadock, 1998).

Cross-Cultural Issues

FaithTrust Institute; 2400 North Forty-fifth Street #10, Seattle, WA 98103; (206)634-1903; *www.faithinstitute.org*. The center offers training, consultation, videos, and publications to clergy, laity, seminary faculty, and students.

Resources

Interfaith Sexual Trauma Institute; St. John's Abbey and University, Collegeville, MN 56321; (320)363-3931; *www.csbsju.edu/isti*.

National Coalition Against Sexual Assault; 125 North Enola Drive, Enola, PA 17025; (717)728-9764; is a membership organization committed to the prevention of sexual violence through intervention, education, and public policy.

National Committee to Prevent Child Abuse; 323 South Michigan Avenue #950, Chicago, IL 60604; (800)55-NCPCA; will provide information on child abuse and prevention.

National Council on Child Abuse and Family Violence; 1025 Connecticut Avenue, NW, Suite 1012, Washington, DC 20036; (202)429-6695; *www.nccafv.org.*

National Organization against Male Sexual Victimization; P.O. Box 207823, West Palm Beach, FL 33416; (800)738-4181; online at *www.malesurvivor.org.*

National Organization for Victim Assistance; 1730 Park Road, NW, Washington, DC 20010; (800) TRY-NOVA; *www.try-nova.org.* This group, founded in 1975, provides support, referrals, and advocacy for victims of violent crime and disasters.

Rape, Abuse & Incest National Network; 635-B Pennsylvania Avenue, SE, Washington, DC 20003; (800)656-4673; *www.rainn.org.*

Survivors Network of Those Abused by Priests; P.O. Box 6416, Chicago, IL 60680; (312)409-2720; *www.survivorsnetwork.org.* This is an international group founded in 1990 to support men and women who were sexually abused by Roman Catholic leaders. It provides extensive phone networking, information, and support groups.

Victims Of Incest Can Emerge Survivors (VOICES) in Action, Inc.; P.O. Box 13, Newtonsville, OH 45158; (800)7-VOICE-8; *www.voices-action.org.*

Helpful Books *Advocacy Training Manual: Advocating for Survivors of Sexual Abuse by a Church Leader/Caregiver* (Heather Block, Winnipeg, Canada: Mennonite Central Committee Canada, 1996).

Behind Closed Doors: Child Sexual Abuse and the Church is a 57-minute videotape accompanied by a training manual. It was developed as a joint project of the mission arm of the Anglican Church in the Sydney Diocese and TAMAR (Towards a More Appropriate Response), an advisory educational and advocacy group working within the Anglican Church. For more information contact: Public Affairs Unit, AngliCare NSW, P.O. Box 427, Parramatta, NSW, 2124, Australia; (61)(02) 9895–8000.

Breach of Trust: Sexual Exploitation by Health Care Professionals and Clergy (John C. Gonsiorek, Thousand Oaks, CA: Sage Publications, 1995).

Facing the Unthinkable: Protecting Children from Abuse is a package of materials. It includes two manuals — *Facing the Unthinkable:*

Protecting Children from Abuse and *Guidance to Churches: Protecting Children and Appointing Children's Workers* — and a 58-minute videotape entitled *Facing the Unthinkable*. This package was produced by the Churches Child Protection Advisory Service. For more information contact: PCCA, P.O. Box 133, Swanley, Kent BR8 7UQ, England.

How to Keep Your Church Out of Court (Stephen P. Chawaga, St. Louis: Concordia Publishing House, 2002).

Interim Pastor's Manual (Alan G. Gripe, Louisville: Westminster John Knox, 2000).

Lead Us Not into Temptation: Catholic Priests and the Sexual Abuse of Children (Jason Berry, Chicago: University of Illinois Press, 2000).

Not If, But When: A Crisis Management Manual (United Methodist Communications, Nashville: Abingdon Press, 1997).

Restoring the Soul of a Church: Congregations Wounded by Clergy Sexual Misconduct (Nancy M. Hopkins and Mark Laaser [eds.], Collegeville, MN: Liturgical Press, 1995).

Safe Connections: What Parishioners Can Do to Understand and Prevent Clergy Sexual Abuse (Jan Erickson-Pearson, Minneapolis: Augsburg Fortress, 1996).

Safety Tips on a Sensitive Subject: Child Sexual Abuse is a 16-page booklet especially useful in highlighting preventive measures that can be taken in the process of employment and enlistment of volunteers within a local parish. It is available free from Church Mutual Insurance Company, 3000 Schuster Lane, Merrill, WI 54452; (715)536-5577.

Sexual Abuse Prevention: A Course of Study for Teenagers (Rebecca Voelkel-Haugen and Marie M. Fortune, Cleveland: United Church Press, 1996).

Survivor Prayers: Talking with God About Childhood Sexual Abuse (Catherine J. Foote, Louisville: Westminster John Knox, 1994).

Taking Care: Monitoring Power Dynamics and Relational Boundaries in Pastoral Care and Counseling (Carrie Doehring, Nashville: Abingdon Press, 1995).

Telling the Truth: Preaching about Sexual and Domestic Violence (John S. McClure and Nancy J. Ramsay [eds.], Cleveland: Pilgrim Press, 1999).

Violence in the Family: A Workshop Curriculum for Clergy and Other Helpers (Marie M. Fortune, Cleveland: United Church Press, 1991).

References   Abel, G. C., and Osborne, C. (1992). The paraphilias: The extent and nature of sexually deviant and criminal behavior. *Clinical Forensic Psychiatry*, 15, 675–687.

American Psychiatric Association. (2000). *Diagnostic and Statistical Manual of Mental Disorders* (4th ed. text revision). Washington, DC: American Psychiatric Association.

Cohen, L. J., and Galynker, I. I. (2002). Clinical features of pedophilia and implications for treatment. *Journal of Psychiatric Stress*, 8(5), 276–289.

Goodstein, L., and Zirilli, A. (2003, January 12). Decades of damage: Trail of pain in church crisis leads to nearly every diocese. *New York Times*. Retrieved January 22, 2003, from *www.nytimes.com*.

Hanson, R. K., and Bussière, M. T. (1998). Predicting relapse: A meta-analysis of sexual offender recidivism studies. *Journal of Consulting and Clinical Psychology*, 66(2), 348–362.

Kaplan, H. I., and Sadock, B. J. (1998). *Synopsis of Psychiatry: Behavioral Sciences/Clinical Psychiatry* (8th ed.). Baltimore: Williams and Wilkins.

Leiblum, S. R., and Rosen, R. C. (eds.) (2000). *Principles and Practice of Sex Therapy* (3rd ed.). New York: Guilford Press.

Raymond, N. C., Coleman, E., Ohlerking, F., Christenson, G. A., and Miner, M. (1999). Psychiatric comorbidity in pedophilic sex offenders. *American Journal of Psychiatry*, 156(5), 786–788.

Rossetti, S. J. (1997). The effects of priest-perpetration of child sexual abuse on the trust of Catholics in priesthood, Church, and God. *Journal of Psychology and Christianity*, 16(3), 197–209.

Weaver, A. J., Flannelly, L. T., and Preston, J. D. (2003). *Counseling Survivors of Traumatic Events: A Handbook for Pastors and Other Helping Professionals*. Nashville: Abingdon Press.

OTHER PARAPHILIA

The term "paraphilia" comes from two Greek words meaning "to the side of" and "love." It is a condition in which a person's sexual arousal and gratification depend on fantasizing about and engaging in sexual behavior that is unusual, intense, and recurrent (Kaplan and Sadock, 1998). A paraphilia can be focused on a particular object (such as children, animals, underwear) or around a particular act (such as inflicting pain, exposing oneself). Most of the paraphilias are far more common in men than in women. The focus of a paraphilia is usually very specific and does not change.

For some individuals paraphilic fantasies or stimuli are necessary for erotic arousal. In other cases, the paraphilic preferences occur only episodically (for example, during periods of stress).

The paraphilias described here include: fetishism (use of non-living objects), exhibitionism (exposure of genitals), transvestism (a male dressing in women's garments), voyeurism (observing unsuspecting individuals), sexual sadism (inflicting humiliation or suffering on another), sexual masochism (receiving humiliation or suffering), frotteurism (touching and rubbing against a nonconsenting person), and telephone scatologia (making obscene telephone calls). It is rare that a pastor would have the clinical experience to treat these conditions, and clergy should not try to do so unless they have specialized training. However, pastors should be able to recognize the disorder and refer persons to appropriate mental health professionals as needed.

Most paraphiliacs describe themselves as heterosexual, but they generally have poor social skills, low self-esteem, histories of childhood abuse or neglect, or were raised in families where sex was thought of as evil and normal erotic development was inhibited. Conventional sexual relationships are too complex and threatening for most of these individuals, who need to have a great deal of control in order to become sexually aroused. As a result, paraphiliacs have difficulties with intimacy, especially when they attempt to have sexual relationships (Kaplan and Sadock, 1998).

Treatment may include cognitive-behavioral therapy, psychotherapy, behavior modification, antidepressant drugs, and medications that alter hormone production, particularly of testosterone (Kaplan and Sadock, 1998). However, the cause and treatment of paraphilias is poorly understood, and treatment is rarely effective. Most mental health professionals prefer not to pathologize sexual behavior that involves only willing adults, even if the behavior might be deemed deviant in mainstream society. In cases where the behavior is potentially criminal, as in pedophilia, treatment is usually offered within the penal system.

Exhibitionism is a compulsive act of exposing one's sex organs to unsuspecting strangers for the purpose of sexual arousal and gratification. Also known as "indecent exposure" and "flashing," this paraphilia is found almost exclusively in males, most commonly in their 20s. For some, the primary intent of exhibitionism is to evoke shock or fear in their victims, not necessarily to achieve an erection or to ejaculate. They derive their pleasure from the visible reaction of their victims. Generally, an exhibitionist is unlikely to rape or assault his victims, but there are exceptions to this rule, especially when an exhibitionist is unsatisfied with his victim's response. Police catch more exhibitionists than any other category of paraphiliacs. Few arrests are made in the older age groups, which may suggest that the condition becomes less severe after 40 years of age (APA, 2000).

Fetishism is a fixation on an object or body part (the "fetish") that is not primarily sexual in nature and a compulsive need for its use in order to obtain sexual gratification. The fetish object is usually used during masturbation and may also be incorporated into sexual activity with a partner in order to produce sexual excitation. Fetishists usually collect the object of their favor and may go to great lengths, including theft, to acquire just the "right" addition to their collection. Some of the more common objects that have served as fetishes include women's undergarments, stockings, shoes, or specific materials, like silk, leather, or fur. Some people have a fetish for particular body parts such as feet, hair, or legs. Usually fetishism begins by adolescence and once established tends to be lifelong (APA, 2000).

Frotteurism (French, meaning rubbing) involves rubbing one's genitals against other people in public while fully clothed. The behavior usually occurs in crowded places from which the individual can more easily escape arrest (for example, on busy sidewalks or on public transportation). He rubs his genitals against the victim's thighs and buttocks or fondles her genitalia or breasts with his hands. While doing this he usually fantasizes an exclusive, caring relationship with the victim. However, he recognizes that to avoid possible prosecution, he must escape detection after touching his victim. Usually the paraphilia begins by adolescence. Most acts of frottage occur when the person is between the ages of 15 and 25, after which there is a gradual decline in frequency.

Sexual masochism involves the act (real, not simulated) of being humiliated, beaten, bound, or otherwise made to suffer. This condition is named after Leopold von Sacher-Masoch (1835–1895), a practicing masochist who wrote novels about people getting sexual pleasure by having pain inflicted on them.

Some individuals act on the masochistic sexual urges by themselves (such as binding themselves, sticking themselves with pins, shocking themselves electrically, or self-mutilation, or with a partner. Masochistic acts that may be sought with a partner include restraint (physical bondage), blindfolding (sensory bondage), paddling, spanking, whipping, beating, electrical shocks, cutting, "pinning and piercing" (infibulation), and humiliation (such as being forced to crawl and bark like a dog or being subjected to verbal abuse). Forced cross-dressing may be sought for its humiliating associations. The individual may have a desire to be treated as a helpless infant and clothed in diapers (infantilism). One particularly dangerous form of sexual masochism, called "hypoxyphilia," involves sexual arousal by oxygen deprivation obtained by means of chest compression, noose, ligature, plastic bag, mask, or chemical (often a volatile nitrite that produces a temporary decrease in brain oxygenation by peripheral vasodilation). Oxygen-depriving activities may be engaged in alone or with a partner. Because of equipment malfunction or other mistakes, accidental deaths sometimes occur. Some males with the condition of sexual masochism also experience fetishism, transvestic fetishism, or sexual sadism. The age at which masochistic activities with partners first begins is variable, but commonly occurs by early adulthood. Sexual masochism is usually chronic, and a person tends to repeat the same masochistic act. Some individuals may engage in masochistic activity for many years without increasing the potential injuriousness of their acts. Others, however, increase the severity of the masochistic acts over time or during periods of stress, which may eventually result in injury or even death (APA, 2000).

Sexual sadism involves acts (real, not simulated) in which the individual derives sexual excitement from inflicting psychological or physical suffering (including humiliation) on a victim. The term "sadism" derives from the Marquis de Sade (1740–1814), a French aristocrat and novelist who wrote stories, supposedly based on his own experiences, of beating and torturing women while being sexually stimulated himself.

Some individuals with this paraphilia act on the sadistic sexual urges with a consenting partner (who may have sexual masochism), who willingly suffers pain or humiliation. Others with this disorder act on their sadistic sexual urges with nonconsenting victims. In all of these cases, it is the suffering of the victim that is sexually arousing. Sadistic fantasies or acts may involve activities that indicate the dominance of the person over the victim (such as forcing the victim to crawl or keeping the victim in a cage). They may also involve restraint, blindfolding, paddling, spanking, whipping, pinching, burning, rape, cutting, stabbing, strangulation, torture, mutilation, or killing. The age at onset of sadistic activities is variable, but is commonly by early adulthood. Sexual sadism is usually chronic. When it is practiced with nonconsenting partners, the activity is likely to be repeated until the person with sexual sadism is apprehended. When sexual sadism is severe, and especially when it is associated with antisocial personality disorder, individuals with this paraphilia may seriously injure or kill their victims (APA, 2000).

Telephone scatologia is the making of obscene telephone calls for sexual pleasure, which is classed as a paraphilia from a medical viewpoint, although from the viewpoint of the law, it is considered a form of sexual harassment. Obscene phone calls exploit the potential of the telephone system for real or apparent anonymous communication. The relative safety and one-sided anonymity of the telephone provides an idealized setting for masturbatory fantasies with no worries about face-to-face contact.

There are three basic types of obscene phone calls. In the first, the caller boasts about himself and describes in detail his masturbatory act. In the second type, the caller directly threatens the victim ("I've been watching you" or "I'm going to find you"). In the third type, the caller tries to get the victim to reveal intimate details about her life. Sometimes the obscene phone caller repeatedly calls the same victim, but more often, unless the victim shows a willingness to stay on the phone and play his game, he will move on to others.

The advent of telephone caller ID has greatly reduced the number of obscene calls. Generally, recipients of such phone calls are advised to simply put the telephone down on obscene callers and to report the caller's identity to the police. If caller ID is not available, victims should still report the call to the police. In the event of repeated or extreme cases, the authorities will get the telephone company to reveal the true calling number, which is logged by the telephone company computers, regardless of caller ID settings.

Transvestism is a paraphilia in which heterosexual males repeatedly and persistently get sexual pleasure from dressing in women's clothing. Transvestism is not simply dressing up in the other sex's garments for fun or for temporary effect. The transvestite needs to cross-dress to achieve full sexual and emotional release. In many cases, sexual arousal is produced by the accompanying thought or image of the person as a female (referred to as "autogynephilia"). Women's garments are arousing primarily as symbols of the individual's femininity, not as fetishes with specific objective properties (for example, objects made of rubber). The condition typically begins with cross-dressing in childhood or early adolescence. In many cases, the cross-dressing is not done in public until adulthood. This is different from the female impersonator or the drag queen (male homosexuals who occasionally dress in women's clothing), both of whom are usually playing social roles rather than expressing sexual needs (APA, 2000).

Voyeurism involves deriving sexual satisfaction from the act of repeatedly observing unsuspecting individuals who are naked, in the process of disrobing, or engaging in sexual activity. Voyeurs (from the French verb meaning "to see") or "Peeping Toms" are usually unmarried males in their 20s and 30s. They generally prefer to watch women who are strangers, and they are often most sexually excited when the risk of being discovered is high. Frequently these individuals have the fantasy of having a sexual experience with the observed person, but in reality, this rarely occurs. Many voyeurs confine their sexual activity to masturbation while watching or while fantasizing about previous peeping episodes. In its severe form, peeping constitutes the exclusive form of sexual activity. The onset of voyeuristic behavior is usually before 15 years of age. The disorder tends to be chronic.

American Psychiatric Association. (2000). *Diagnostic and Statistical Manual of Mental Disorders* (4th ed., text revision). Washington, DC: American Psychiatric Association.

Kaplan, H. I., and Sadock, B. J. (1998). *The Comprehensive Textbook of Psychiatry* (8th ed.). Baltimore: Williams and Wilkins.

Rape

"She felt terrified, overwhelmed, and ashamed"

Paula was accompanied by her friend Shelley as she walked into Rabbi Max Schoenfeld's office. She immediately began to tremble and sob. She said that she had been raped ten days ago and only now was able to come in to see her rabbi after Shelley had insisted. She felt terrified, overwhelmed, and most of all, ashamed. She was afraid to tell anyone, but since the assault, she has been "falling apart," unable to attend college or her job, or even to leave her apartment unaccompanied.

Rabbi Schoenfeld has seen this all too many times — an innocent person violated, threatened with the loss of her life, brutalized, and yet, what plagued her the most was shame.

Pastoral Care Assessment

If a sexual assault has just occurred the victim must be referred immediately to a medical facility for a physical examination and be encouraged to contact a law enforcement agency or rape crisis center, if she has not already done so. However it is not unusual, as in Paula's case, that sexual assault survivors only come to the attention of clergy after a passage of time. Many victims, largely due to feelings of shame and guilt, never tell anyone and do not report the event to the police. Thank goodness that Paula has a good friend like Shelley.

In initially speaking with rape survivors, a clergyperson must be carefully attuned to the issues of shame and guilt. It is often the case that rapes involve two assaults: the physical act of violence and the later assault by others who "blame the victim." This is a peculiar, but all too common, experience when totally innocent people are assumed to have somehow played a role in the crime (Frazier and Haney, 1996). Equally common is the tendency for self-blame. When doing an assessment, it is important to listen carefully for any comments that might reveal either personal shame or experiences of having significant others lay blame on the victim. Hearing the story and maintaining a nonjudgmental and compassionate stance is crucial for creating the kind of safe and supportive interaction that rape survivors need. It is also important to know that many such people may consciously or unconsciously anticipate shaming and rebuke from their spiritual caregiver. This expectation is often projected on a clergyperson, even if he or she has never come across in a judging/shaming way. It is a common human manifestation of one's own shame to anticipate judgment from others.

Sexual assaults are almost always highly traumatic (Rothbaum et al., 1992). A common mistake made by counselors is to initially delve too deeply into the events, only to have this result in the survivor experiencing an overwhelming emotional response, which in itself is retraumatizing. Thus it is helpful to say something like this: "I know this was overwhelming for you. I want to know about what happened, but be gentle with yourself and only tell me what you feel comfortable in sharing. There will be time to talk in more detail if you wish, but for now only tell me what you want to."

Some survivors will want to share a lot, and that may be appropriate, but it is important to help persons pace themselves so they do not become overwhelmed. It is also helpful to ask at some point, "How do you feel about telling me what happened?" This provides an opportunity to assess whether a person is experiencing shame, guilt, or embarrassment. If so, this is where compassionate reassurance can be a great help.

In getting initial information, it is important to determine who constitutes their support system. Remember that, unfortunately, even loving and otherwise supportive friends and relatives may be judgmental toward a sexual assault victim, and a survivor may be reluctant to tell loved ones (for example, a husband). This must be listened to carefully, understood, and respected.

Relevant History

Rape can trigger lasting, disturbing existential issues. For many victims, the world never again seems safe, or others are no longer to be trusted (Herman, 1992). For some, the consequences are etched into their character in the form of continuous vigilance, mistrust, and fear, or in a lifestyle in which closeness or intimacy is impossible. One survivor said, "What disturbed me most about the rape was looking into his eyes and seeing that he was getting off on seeing me be terrified. I just never imagined human beings could be that way! That's what haunts my dreams."

Diagnostic Criteria

Sexual assault is the most rapidly growing violent crime in the United States, with 261,000 victims of rape, attempted rape, or sexual assault reported in the year 2000 (NCVS, 2000). The National Women's Study

(Resnick et al., 1993) estimated that 12.1 million (12.7 percent) of adult American women have experienced a completed rape at some point in their lives.

What is often not understood by others, but witnessed firsthand by victims, is that rape is much more than a forced sexual encounter. Although sexuality is an element of rape, at the heart of most rapes is violence. The gratification the rapist experiences comes largely from his ability to overpower, terrorize, and humiliate the victim. Obviously, the sexual component of rape cannot be ignored, but what must be understood is that it is essentially an act of violence. The experience of being raped is also accompanied by a profound sense of helplessness and powerlessness, and often the fear of loss of one's life. It is overwhelmingly traumatic and results in severe post-traumatic stress disorder (PTSD) in many individuals (Rothbaum et al., 1992).

Many victims never report sexual assaults for a number of reasons. The three most common causes are personal shame, anxiety that others will judge or blame them, or fear of the effect of reporting on one's safety. This last factor is most likely to occur if the assault is committed by a family member, such as child molestation by a relative or rape by a spouse. It must be emphasized that even in the context of marriage, rape occurs; sexual assault in this context is a version of domestic violence. Often such acts are prompted by the need to punish, dominate, scare, or control the spouse.

Some unwanted sexual encounters are termed "acquaintance rape" or "date rape." This occurs in the context of a friendship or dating relationship where one person coerces the other to have sex against her will.

Common complications of sexual assault also include contracting sexually transmitted diseases (STDs) or pregnancy. If PTSD follows a sexual assault, it may have the following symptoms (Weaver et al., 2003):

- Nightmares and disturbed sleep.

- Intense anxiety and persistent hyperarousal.

- Recurring intensive memories of the event. Especially intense memories are referred to as "flashbacks," during which an individual feels as if the rape is happening in the present and responds with fear or terror.

- Times of feeling detached, numb, or slightly disoriented (a symptom referred to as *dissociation*).

- Depression and/or alcohol/substance abuse.

Rabbi Schoenfeld listened carefully to Paula's story. Her emotional response was intense, and her descriptions of the rape were graphic (many clergy as well as mental health professionals experience their own version of PTSD when listening to survivors of assaults, since such material can be intense). The rabbi was shaken by Paula's story, but was able to remain a steadfast and compassionate listener. He reassured Paula that her self-blame and shame were unwarranted, yet he wisely let her know that many rape victims experience these feelings. She was tremendously relieved to see in his eyes kindness without judgment.

Rabbi Schoenfeld learned that Paula was having frightening nightmares and flashbacks. He strongly encouraged her to see a therapist, which she did the following day.

Response to Vignette

The two greatest barriers to recovery from a sexual assault are personal shame and silence. Survivors need to be able to talk about the traumatic event, but only if they are responded to with understanding and without criticism. This dynamic of blaming the victim runs deep in some cultures. Even today in some communities, totally innocent female rape victims are brutally punished or killed ostensibly for their "sin."

Strong statements in discussions and sermons can do a lot to help an entire faith community know where its spiritual leaders stand on such issues and may open the door for many people to seek pastoral care. A problem present in some faith communities is the tacit approval of sexual abuse within marriage. Such experiences can be profoundly harmful and should be openly addressed in churches and synagogues. Also, remember that some males (mostly youngsters) are victims of sexual assault. In many settings this is not recognized or is minimized.

Treatment within the Faith Community

If an assault has recently occurred, it is important to encourage a survivor to contact a local law enforcement agency and to seek medical attention. A medical evaluation is necessary to gather forensic evidence and to evaluate for physical trauma, STDs, and pregnancy. Acute stress reactions, PTSD, and depression are often seen in the wake of sexual assault. If treated early, these psychological responses can often be resolved more easily. Thus, referral for mental health treatment should be offered to all survivors.

Indications for Referral

More than half of sexual assault victims develop PTSD (Rothbaum et al., 1992). This can be a devastating disorder and one that can lead to chronic, lifelong suffering. Treatments for PTSD include psychotherapeutic (in particular, an empirically validated exposure-based

Treatment by Mental Health Specialist

cognitive behavioral therapy) and medical (psychiatric drugs) ones (Foa and Rothbaum, 1998). Medications that are commonly used to treat PTSD include antidepressants (such as Prozac, Paxil, Lexapro, Serzone, Celexa, Zoloft), a-2 agonists (such as Catapres), and mild tranquilizers (such as Ativan, Klonopin, Xanax). All of these classes of medications have research support of efficacy in reducing anxiety, flashbacks, sleep disturbances, and nightmares (Preston et al., 2001).

Cross-Cultural Issues   Rape victims belong to both sexes, all races and ethnic groups, various economic backgrounds, and all ages. However, African Americans are about 10 percent more likely to be attacked than European Americans. In 2000, there were 1.1 victimizations per 1,000 European Americans and 1.2 victimizations per 1,000 African Americans (NCVS, 2000).

Resources   FaithTrust Institute; 2400 North Forty-fifth Street, Suite 10, Seattle, WA 98103; (877)860-2255; *www.faithinstitute.org*; offers training, consultation, videos, and publications for clergy, laity, seminary faculty, and students. Resources are available in Chinese, Korean, Laotian, Spanish, and Vietnamese.

Incest Survivors Anonymous; P.O. Box 17245, Long Beach, CA 90807; (562)428-5599; *www.lafn.org/medical/isa*; is an international association based on the 12-step approach. Women, men, and teens meet to share experiences, strength, and hope so they recover peace of mind. Send a self-addressed stamped envelope for information, if you are a survivor.

Interfaith Sexual Trauma Institute; St. John's Abbey and University, Collegeville, MN 56321; *www.csbsju.edu/isti*; (877)672-3257.

Male Survivor; PMB 103, 5505 Connecticut Avenue, NW, Washington, DC 20015-2601; (800)738-4181; *www.malesurvivor.org*; is an organization of diverse individuals committed through research, education, advocacy, and activism to the prevention, treatment, and elimination of all forms of sexual victimization of boys and men.

Men Can Stop Rape; P.O. Box 57144, Washington, DC 20037; (202)265-6530; *www.mencanstoprape.org*.

National Organization for Victim Assistance; 1757 Park Road, NW, Washington, DC 20010; (800) TRY-NOVA; *www.try-nova.org*; founded in 1975, provides support, referrals, and advocacy for victims of violent crime.

National Sexual Violence Resource Center; 125 North Enola Drive, Enola, PA 17025; *www.nsvrc.org*; (877)739-3895; is a national information and resource hub relating to all aspects of sexual violence.

Rape, Abuse and Incest National Network; 635-B Pennsylvania Avenue, SE, Washington, DC 20003; (800)656-4673; *www.rainn.org*.

Survivors Connections; 52 Lyndon Road, Cranston, RI 02905; *www.members.cox.net/survivorconnections*; is a grassroots activist organization for survivors of sexual assault.

VOICES in Action, 8041 Hosbrook Road, Suite 236, Cincinnati, OH 45236; (800)7-VOICE-8; *www.voices-action.org*.

Helpful Books

The Gift of Fear: Survival Signals That Protect Us from Violence (Gavin De Becker, New York: Dell Publishing, 1998).

If You Are Raped: What Every Woman Needs to Know (Kathryn M. Johnson, Holmes Beach, FL: Learning Publications, 1985).

Rape Victim: Clinical and Community Interventions (Mary P. Koss and Mary R. Harvey, New York: Sage Publications, 1991).

Recovering from Rape, 2nd edition (Linda E. Ledray, New York: Henry Holt and Company, 1994).

Recovery: How to Survive Sexual Assault for Women, Men, Teenagers, and Their Friends and Families (Helen Benedict and Susan Brison, New York: Columbia University Press, 1994).

Sexual Violence: The Sin Revisited (Marie M. Fortune. Cleveland: The Pilgrim Press, 2005).

Stopping Rape: Successful Survival Strategies (Pauline B. Bart and Patricia H. O'Brian, New York: Pergamon Press, 1993).

Trauma and Recovery: The Aftermath of Violence from Domestic Abuse to Political Terror (Judith L. Herman, New York: Basic Books, 1997).

References

Foa, E. B., and Rothbaum, B. O. (1998). *Treating the Trauma of Rape.* New York: Guilford Press.

Frazier, P. A., and Haney, B. (1996). Sexual assault cases in the legal system: Police, prosecutor, and victim perspectives. *Law and Human Behavior*, 20, 607–628.

Herman, J. L. (1992). *Trauma and Recovery.* New York: Basic Books.

National Crime Victimization Survey. (2000). Bureau of Justice Statistics. Washington, DC: U.S. Department of Justice.

Preston, J. P., O'Neal, J. H., and Talaga, M. (2001). *Handbook of Clinical Psychopharmacology for Therapists.* Oakland, CA: New Harbinger.

Resnick, H. R., Kilpatrick, D. G., Dansky, B. S., Saunders, B. E., and Best, C. B. (1993). Prevalence of civilian trauma and post-traumatic stress disorder in a representative national sample of women. *Journal of Consulting and Clinical Psychology*, 61, 984–991.

Rothbaum, B. O., Foa, E. B., Riggs, D. S., Murdock, T., and Walsh, W. (1992). A prospective examination of post-traumatic stress disorder in rape victims. *Journal of Traumatic Stress*, 5, 455–475.

Weaver, A. J., Flannelly, L. T., and Preston, J. D. (2003). *Counseling Survivors of Traumatic Events: A Handbook for Pastors and Other Helping Professionals*. Nashville: Abingdon Press.

Sexual and Emotional Distress: Hypoactive Sexual Desire Disorder

"She lost all feelings of sexual desire"

F ather Stevens had noticed a change in Virginia's demeanor over the past few months. The liveliness had left her eyes, and she looked tired and care-worn. She also left immediately after mass instead socializing afterwards as usual. Something was happening in her life, but he did not know what. When Virginia came for a pastoral visit, initially her concerns were not for herself but for her husband, Jim. "I really don't know how to tell you this. My husband is upset about our sex life. I don't know what is happening, but over the past 3 or 4 months, I've lost all feelings of sexual desire. I love him dearly, but he thinks I don't care anymore. He even asked me if I was seeing another man. I would never do that — I love him. I just don't know what is wrong with me!"

Virginia was quite tense, fatigued, and sad. The priest asked her to tell him more about what generally had been happening in her life. During their visit Virginia recounted how she had begun to feel increasingly depressed and distraught since the previous summer. Over a period of two months, her elderly mother had died and her oldest son had left for college. Both of these events were significant and painful losses. Father Stevens was aware that emotional distress — especially depression — often takes its toll on sexual desire and functioning.

Virginia, in fact, was quite depressed. She told the priest that she had been having crying spells nearly every day and that she experienced restless sleep, had lost ten pounds during the past two months, and had no energy for her regular activities. He told her that it was likely that she was clinically depressed and that a loss of sexual desire was a common symptom. She did not know this and felt relief as she began to understand the reasons for the change in her sexual feelings.

Pastoral Care Assessment   Sexual problems (decreased sexual desire/drive, difficulty with arousal, and erectile dysfunction) are common symptoms that occur for people experiencing significant life stress and/or psychological disorders (such as depression, anxiety disorders, bipolar illness). Likewise, primary sexual problems (such as erectile dysfunction) can be the source of considerable emotional distress. It is important to be aware of this since sexual dysfunctions often occur in the context of otherwise healthy and loving relationships. However, many people do not know this and are prone to inaccurate conclusions, as was the case with Virginia's husband.

Thus it is very important to inquire about a parishioner's general life circumstances and to be alert to the signs of emotional distress or psychological disorder and to make appropriate referrals when indicated.

Relevant History   Virginia experienced a serious bout of depression when she was 21, but not again until this past summer. Two-thirds of people who experience clinical depression will have two or more episodes (Preston, 2001). After her recent life stressors, she first felt sadness, but within weeks other symptoms began to emerge, such as sleep disturbances, poor appetite, fatigue, and loss of sex drive. Many cases of depression are accompanied by such physical symptoms (Preston, 2001).

Father Stevens inquired in some detail about her marital relationship. Depression was a likely cause of the sexual problem, but he wanted to determine if marriage difficulties were a contributing factor. A host of relationship-based problems can lead both to sexual dysfunction and to depression.

Common relationship issues to be alert to include: lack of intimacy, poor communication skills, psychological abuse (such as humiliating, belittling, shaming, ridicule, coercion, hostility, and dominance), domestic violence, substance abuse, and poor communication regarding sex and sexual interactions. In Virginia's case, none of these problems were evident, and in all likelihood her sexual problems were due primarily to the clinical depression.

Diagnostic Criteria   Virginia's symptoms meet the criteria for Hypoactive Sexual Desire Disorder, which is marked by a deficiency or lack of sexual fantasies and desire for sexual activity (APA, 2000). A person may experience low desire for either all forms of sexual expression or particular sexual activities (for example, intercourse but not masturbation). An individual with this disorder usually does not initiate sexual activity or may only engage in it reluctantly when it is initiated by the partner. Frequently, the disorder is associated with psychological distress, stressful life events, or interpersonal difficulties. Low sexual desire is also often associated with depressive disorders, as in this case (APA, 2000).

Almost any significant stressful life event can lead to sexual dysfunction. This is especially true for disorders of sexual arousal and erectile dysfunction. Normal hormonal changes that occur in response to stress are often the cause. Sexual problems are commonly seen in almost all forms of psychological disorders (Kaplan and Sadock, 1998). A comprehensive discussion of the diagnostic criteria for psychiatric disorders is beyond the scope of this book, but listed below are the common signs and symptoms to watch for in people seeking counseling for sexual problems:

- *Depression*
  - Sadness
  - Irritability
  - Loss of interest in usual life activities
  - Low self-esteem
  - Excessive or inappropriate guilt
  - Suicidal thoughts or impulses
  - Pessimism, negativity, hopelessness
  - Physical symptoms of depression
  - Sleep disturbances
  - Appetite and weight changes (increased *or* decreased)
  - Fatigue
  - Agitation and/or anxiety
  - Loss of sex drive

- *Anxiety Disorders or Situational Stress*
  - Nervousness, tension, apprehension
  - Constant worry
  - Panic attacks (sudden, very intense surges of anxiety, lasting 1–20 minutes)
  - Obsessive preoccupation with cleanliness or intense fear of germs, dirt, and contamination

- Extreme uneasiness in social situations
- Physical symptoms of anxiety
- Muscle tension, tension headaches
- Trembling
- Difficulty going to sleep
- Racing heart
- Shortness of breath
- Restlessness

- *Substance Abuse Disorders:* (often cause sexual dysfunction)

  - Alcoholism
  - Abuse of illicit drugs: marijuana, amphetamines, cocaine, etc.

- *Post-Traumatic Stress Disorder*

  - Intense anxiety
  - Nightmares
  - Recurring intrusive memories of traumatic events
  - Hyperarousal; startled easily
  - Feeling numb, "spacey," mildly confused, withdrawn
  - Note: if the post-traumatic stress disorder is related to traumatic sexual events such as rape or childhood sexual molestation, significant fear of and aversion to sexual encounters is common (see cases 2 and 13).

- *Severe Mental Illness*

  - Schizophrenia: hallucinations (hearing voices or seeing things that are actually not there), delusions (extremely unrealistic or bizarre beliefs), disorganized speech and thinking, peculiar behavior
  - Dementias (such as Alzheimer's disease or advanced Parkinson's disease): memory impairment, confusion, disorientation, and apathy. Sexual desire and behavior is often profoundly impaired in dementing illnesses. One of the most common manifestations of this is that a person who is ill gradually begins to initiate sexual contact, but does so in a rude or inappropriate manner (for example, being insensitive to the other partner's feelings or a lack of tenderness). Often the spouse will comment that the ill person's sexual behavior is significantly different than has been experienced

before. Note: depression is a common occurrence in Parkinson's disease (and the depression certainly is treatable).

- Bipolar (manic-depressive) illness: severe depression (with symptoms as noted above), marked mood swings, and mania (high energy, agitation, rapid speech, decreased need for sleep, impulsivity, and poor judgment). Note: during manic episodes, sexual drive may *increase* dramatically, and marked sexual promiscuity may be seen in otherwise sexually responsible and monogamous individuals.

Psychiatric Medications That May Cause Sexual Problems

Although psychiatric medication can often play an important role in recovery from psychological disorders, some of these drugs can also have sexual side effects (Preston et al., 2001). Listed below are some common medications (most are registered trademarks) and possible sexual side effects.

Antidepressants: erectile dysfunction and loss of sexual desire are rare, but inorgasmia (difficulty in achieving an orgasm) may be seen in up to 30 percent of people treated.

Prozac	Celexa	Anafranil
Paxil	Lexapro	MAO inhibitors
Zoloft	Effexor	Parnate
Remeron	Norpramin	Nardil
Luvox	Tofranil	Tricyclics
Pamelor	Sinequan	Elavil

Note: Very low rates of inorgasmia occur with Serzone and Wellbutrin.

Antipsychotics: may cause decreased sex drive

Haldol	Mellaril
Thorazine	Risperdal

Mood stabilizers: used to treat bipolar illness (may cause menstrual irregularities or decreased sex drive)

Lithium	Neurontin
Tegretol	Lamictal
Trileptal	Topamax
Depakote	

Response to Vignette

Father Stevens suggested that Virginia ask her husband to come with her to see him in a few days. The priest shared his opinions with Jim. He was relieved and supportive of Virginia seeking a mental health professional for treatment of her depression. She began therapy and was given an antidepressant. Depression generally requires several weeks of treatment before symptoms improve. This was true for Virginia. Within four weeks, her sleep began to improve and her normal energy returned. By the end of three months, she had fully recovered. The medication helped, in conjunction with grief work that she did to come to terms with her experiences of loss. The sexual dysfunction disappeared, and Father Stevens saw a marked change in Virginia when she came to church. She had come back to life. Jim looked better as well.

Treatment within the Faith Community

Most people assume that if they are in a loving relationship, it will include sexual feelings and behavior. However, when individuals are stressed or suffering psychological disorders, sexual functioning often suffers. Parishioners need to understand this to help them avoid inaccurate conclusions regarding sexual dysfunction. Such information is important to include in premarital counseling, in couples counseling, and in marriage enrichment programs. Also, since sexual problems are enormously common during times of emotional stress or psychiatric illness, it is often helpful for a clergyperson to broach the topic when providing pastoral care. Many individuals and couples experience stress-related sexual difficulties but are too embarrassed to mention it to clergy. One can say something like, "Many people who go through stressful times encounter sexual problems, and I want you to know that it is very common. If this is an issue for you, we can discuss it."

Indications for Referral

Providing information about common sexual problems associated with stress or psychological disorders may provide considerable reassurance to many people who are counseled. However, all individuals with significant psychiatric symptoms should be referred for mental health treatment. Most people being treated with psychiatric medications receive their prescriptions from primary care doctors. In many instances the treatment provided in a primary care setting is inadequate (especially the lack of good patient follow-up). Thus, if parishioners are taking psychiatric drugs and indicate that they are having sexual problems, it is appropriate to encourage them to check with the prescribing physician to make sure the symptoms are not due to medication side effects. Sometimes it is difficult to determine if a sexual dysfunction is due to the drug or to the disorder itself (Preston et al., 2001). This distinction is best left to a physician, but people should know about the possibility of adverse medication effects so they can check this out with their doctor.

If it is determined that sexual problems are due primarily to a psychological disorder, then almost without exception, treatment is initially focused on the resolution of the psychological problem (and often the sexual dysfunction is resolved in the process). However, even if the sexual difficulties are mainly due to stress or a psychiatric problem, secondary sexual and relationship problems can often develop. Virginia and Jim's experience is a common example of this. Both were unaware that depression frequently reduces sex drive, and Jim began to draw inaccurate conclusions regarding the cause of the sexual problems. At times, these difficulties can be resolved relatively easily by providing information and reassurance. However, often such concerns have a great impact on individuals or couples, especially if they have been long-lasting. This is where in-depth marital counseling may be necessary.

Treatment by Mental Health Specialist

Some couples may require joint counseling to address interpersonal issues and communication styles. Therapy may be important to address anxieties, inhibitions, or negative body image. The prognosis depends on the form of sexual dysfunction (Leiblum and Rosen, 2000). In general, the probable outcome is good for physical (organically caused) dysfunctions resulting from treatable or reversible conditions. In sexual problems resulting from either relationship problems or psychological factors, the prognosis may be good for temporary or mild dysfunction associated with situational stressors or lack of accurate information. Unfortunately, those cases associated with chronically poor relationships or deep-seated emotional problems have less optimistic outcomes (Leiblum and Rosen, 2000).

Epidemiological studies in the United States, the United Kingdom, and Sweden indicate that about 40 percent of women aged 18–59 have significant concerns about their sexual lives. In these countries the majority of complaints concern low sexual desire (Seagraves, 2003). Major depression is twice as likely among women as men and appears to be a significant risk factor for low sexual desire (APA, 2000).

Cross-Cultural Issues

American Academy of Family Physicians; P.O. Box 11210, Shawnee Mission, KS 66207; (800)274-2237; *www.aafp.org/afp/20000701/127.html*; is a national medical organization, representing more than 94,300 physicians, residents, and medical students. Its members provide quality, cost-effective health care for patients of all ages.

Resources

American Association of Retired Persons; 601 E Street, NW, Washington, DC 20049; (202)434-AARP; *www.aarp.org*; is the nation's leading organization for persons over the age of 50. It has information on health and sexual-related topics for older adults.

American Association of Sex Educators, Counselors, and Therapists; P.O. Box 5488, Richmond, VA 23220-0488; (212)819-9770; *www.aasect.org*; promotes understanding of human sexuality and healthy sexual behavior.

American College of Obstetricians and Gynecologists; 409 Twelfth Street, SW, P.O. Box 96920, Washington, DC 20090; (202)683-5577, (800)762-2264; *www.acog.org*; an organization of obstetricians and gynecologists dedicated to the advancement of women's health through education, advocacy, practice, and research.

Centers for Disease Control and Prevention; 1600 Clifton Road, Atlanta, GA 30333; (800)311-3435, (404)639-3534; *www.cdc.gov*; an agency of the U.S. Department of Health and Human Services, provides information about sexual dysfunction and links to related topics.

Center for Sexual and Relationship Health; Robert Wood Johnson Medical School, 675 Hoes Land, Piscataway, NJ 08854-5635; (733)235-4273; *www2.umdnj.edu/csrhweb*; provides evaluation and treatment services for a variety of sexual dysfunction and relationship issues.

Female Sexual Psychology Laboratory; University of Texas, Sarah M. and Charles E. Seay Building, 3rd floor, Austin, TX; (512)232-4805; *homepage.psy.utexas.edu/homepage/group/MestonLAB/about_us/meston.htm*; provides information and resources about women's sexual issues, including sexual dysfunction.

Heartchoice, *www.heartchoice.com*, offers advice, information, and resources on how to deal with sexual and other marital issues.

Kinsey Institute for Research in Sex, Gender, and Reproduction; University of Indiana, Morrison Hall 313, Bloomington, IN 47405-2501; *www.indiana.edu/~kinsey;* is devoted to research on sexual issues.

Med Help International; 6300 North Wickham Road, Suite 130, PMB #188, Melbourne, FL 32940; (321)259-7505; *www.medhelp.org/HealthTopics/Sexual_Dysfunction.html*; helps patients find medical information and the tools to make informed treatment decisions.

National Institutes of Health; 9000 Rockville Pike, Bethesda, MD 20892; *www.nih.gov*; (301)496-4000, toll-free numbers available at *www.nih.gov/health/infoline.htm*. Provides health information, consumer brochures, and information on NIH-supported research studies. Links to Medline searches of related topics.

National Women's Health Information Center; 8550 Arlington Boulevard, Suite 300, Fairfax, VA 22031; (800)994-9662; *www .4woman.gov*; a project of the U.S. Department of Health and Human Services. Offers a call center, information on health topics, and links to related topics.

National Women's Health Resource Center; 120 Albany Street, Suite 820, New Brunswick, NJ 08901; (877)986-9472; online at *www .healthywomen.org*; a nonprofit organization to help women make informed decisions regarding their health. Includes "Questions to Ask" your doctor and information on diagnoses, treatment options, and preparing for surgery. Related resources and recommended books are listed.

Society for the Scientific Study of Sexuality; c/o David Fleming, P.O. Box 416, Allentown, PA 18105; (610)530-2483; *www.ssc.wisc .edu/ssss*; is dedicated to the advancement of research on sexual issues.

Society for Sex Therapy and Research; 409 Twelfth Street, SW, P.O. Box 96920, Washington, DC 20090; (202)863-1648; *www.sstarnet.org*; has a range of professionals with clinical or research interests in human sexual concerns. It provides the latest research and information about sexual issues. Its goal is to treat problems of sexual identity, sexual function, and reproductive life, and to provide a forum for caregivers and researchers.

2-in-2-1, *www.2-in-2-1.co.uk/index.html*, discusses sexual and relationship topics, such as enhancing couple relationships, support through marital problems, and working through challenges.

Handbook of Clinical Psychopharmacology for Therapists (John D. **Helpful Books** Preston, John H. O'Neal, and Mary C. Talaga. Oakland, CA: New Harbinger, 2001).

Human Sexuality (William H. Masters, Virginia E. Johnson, and Robert C. Kolodny, Reading, MA: Addison-Wesley, 1997).

Human Sexuality Today (Bruce M. King, Upper Saddle River, NJ: Prentice Hall, 2001).

New Male Sexuality (Bernie Zilbergeld, New York: Random House, 1999).

Resurrecting Sex: Resolving Sexual Problems and Rejuvenating Your Relationship (David Morris Schnarch, New York: HarperCollins, 2002).

Sex Matters for Women: A Complete Guide to Taking Care of Your Sexual Self (Sally Foley, Sally A. Kope, and Dennis P. Sugrue, New York: Guilford Publications, 2001).

The Sex-Starved Marriage: A Couple's Guide to Boosting Their Marriage Libido (Michele Weiner-Davis, New York: Simon and Schuster, 2001).

You Can Beat Depression (John D. Preston, San Luis Obispo, CA: Impact Publishers, 2001).

References

American Psychiatric Association. (2000). *Diagnostic and Statistical Manual of Mental Disorders* (4th ed., text revision). Washington, DC: American Psychiatric Association.

Kaplan, H. I., and Sadock, B. J. (1998). *Synopsis of Psychiatry: Behavioral Sciences/Clinical Psychiatry* (8th ed.). Baltimore: Williams and Wilkins.

Leiblum, S. R., and Rosen, R. C. (eds.) (2000). *Principles and Practice of Sex Therapy* (3rd ed.). New York: Guilford Press.

Preston, J. D. (2001). *You Can Beat Depression.* San Luis Obispo, CA: Impact Publishers.

Preston, J. D., O'Neal, J. H., and Talaga, M. (2001). *Handbook of Clinical Psychopharmacology for Therapists.* Oakland, CA: New Harbinger.

Segraves, R. T. (2003). Emerging therapies for female sexual dysfunction. *Expert Opinions on Emerging Drugs*, 8(2), 515–522.

Sexuality and Illness — Heart Attack

"She had felt an uncomfortable pressure in her chest"

When Sophie woke and became aware of her surroundings she realized she was not in her own bed, but was in the hospital. Her husband, Mario, was sitting in a chair beside her. She had been transferred to this room four days ago from the Coronary Care Unit (CCU). Sophie thought back on the events of the past week. Six days had passed since the day she arrived home from work feeling nauseous. She remembered on that night while she was fixing dinner she had felt an uncomfortable, though not painful, pressure in her chest. Mario walked into the kitchen and could tell by her expression that she was not feeling well. But Sophie said she was all right and that she must be coming down with the virus that was going around at her office. Mario went outside to do some chores, and Sophie continued preparing dinner. Twenty minutes later she began feeling light-headed. She called outside and told Mario that she was going to lie down and rest for a while, and he came inside to finish making dinner. When Sophie came to the dinner table she was adamant that nothing was seriously wrong — but the light-headedness and pressure in her chest persisted. Mario became concerned and finally insisted they go to the emergency room "just to be safe." Sophie rolled her eyes, saying, "It's nothing, really," but agreed to go.

Since the hospital was within a mile of their home, in 15 minutes Sophie was being monitored in the ER. To her amazement an EKG indicated that she was having a heart attack. Emergency procedures were immediately initiated to stabilize her. Extreme fear gripped her while she watched wide-eyed as the ER staff rapidly went into action.

Fortunately, serious heart damage was averted by the timely medical attention Sophie received. She spent the next 24 hours being closely monitored in the loud, bustling, and frightening CCU. Now, six days later, Sophie was looking at Mario, and while she said nothing, her quiet countenance belied her wildly spinning thoughts.

Pastoral Care Assessment

Though Sophie considered herself to be a "spiritual" person, she did see herself as "religious" since she didn't subscribe to the beliefs of any particular organized religion. She did not attend church, although she prayed regularly and thought of her garden as her own sanctuary. Her social service career and her fair, kind, and generous actions toward others were her spiritual practice.

However, the recent developments had touched her to her core, and she felt the need to talk with someone about the nonmedical aspects of it all. The doctors and nurses provided her with important medical information, but now she felt an almost desperate need to process what had happened to her on a very personal and even spiritual level. Sophie soon requested a visit from the hospital chaplain.

Over the next several days, Chaplain Amy DeFranco visited Sophie in the afternoon. She listened to Sophie's concerns and fears about the impact of the heart attack on her life. The chaplain assessed Sophie as an emotionally healthy, intelligent, capable, and caring woman whose recent experience would be life-changing. Her role as spiritual counselor in Sophie's life while at the hospital was very important.

First and foremost, Chaplain Amy was a caring and supportive listener. Their conversations indicated to the chaplain that Sophie had many concerns about the impact of her heart attack on the quality of her life. She had been working at a job that was important to her and she believed to those she served. She wondered if she would be able to continue to work. Though her greatest concerns related to her relationship with Mario and her ability to be a healthy and productive partner in their marriage, she worried that this unexpected and frightening medical condition might prevent her from resuming her active social life, her sexual relationship with her husband, and their plans for having a baby.

Relevant History

Though Sophie grew up in a close Italian American family in the same small town in which Mario grew up as part of a large family, they knew each other only as acquaintances in high school. Sophie was married briefly after college but divorced at the age of 24. She was not seriously involved with another man until she ran into Mario at their 15th high school reunion. Their immediate attraction to each other led to two years of long-distance dating before Mario took a job in the city where she lived. To the delight of their families, when both were 36, they married. They decided to settle into their married life together, do some traveling, and buy a house prior to starting a family. Despite pressure from both families to have children, they stayed with their plan of waiting a while. They enjoyed their jobs, had an active social life, a satisfying sex life, and had only discontinued their birth control method three months before Sophie's heart attack.

Though Sophie was somewhat overweight, she had a healthy lifestyle and swam and biked on the weekends. She was a nonsmoker and had no prior history of symptoms of cardiovascular problems.

Diagnostic Criteria

Forty-five percent of coronary heart disease (CHD) occurs in people under age 65. Health problems are most often due to atherosclerosis (deposits of fat/cholesterol plaques in the lining of coronary arteries). This condition results from factors that are sometimes modifiable and sometimes not (Allan, 1996). Risk factors that can be changed or treated include smoking, hypertension, high cholesterol, sedentary lifestyle, stress, excess weight, and diabetes. Other risk factors (heredity, family medical history, age, race, gender) are out of an individual's control (Allan, 1996; Lancaster, 2001). When cardiac arrest (stopping of the heartbeat) occurs, death can result within minutes. Approximately 250,000 people die each year from CHD *without* the person being hospitalized. This is about one-half of all CHD deaths (American Heart Association, 2003) and highlights the importance of knowledge and prevention. Knowledge about risk reduction, CHD, and heart attack warning signs can help people to make choices and lifestyle modifications and can lead to earlier treatment and more positive outcomes.

Warning signs of heart attack include pressure, fullness, squeezing, or pain in the chest lasting more than a few minutes; discomfort in other areas of the body (for example, arms, neck, back, jaw); shortness of breath; lightheadedness; fainting; or cold sweats (American Heart Association, 2003; Lancaster, 2001). Though many people fear resuming sexual relations after a heart attack, most people are able to gradually begin sexual activity within one month after being discharged from the hospital. While decreased libido can be a side effect of some medications or of depression, this is often successfully addressed by changing or adjusting medications. If a depressed mood persists, mental health counseling is indicated. Pregnancy can be complicated by a woman's heart problems, but is by no means ruled out. Close medical monitoring, special tests, and an experienced medical staff can help ensure a safe pregnancy and delivery even for women whose heart problems place them in the category of high-risk pregnancy (Pashkow and Libov, 2001).

Cardiovascular disease (CVD) is the number-one cause of death in the United States, accounting for more than 39 percent of all deaths. Nearly 62 million people in the United Stated have CVD, and the risk increases with age, with about 84 percent of CVD deaths occurring in those over age 65 (American Heart Association, 2003). Pastoral counselors in almost any setting are likely to face CVD-related situations; therefore, it is important for them to know the CVD risk factors and general information. Having basic knowledge provides a firm foundation for offering support, guidance, and comfort. The pastoral counselor who recognizes environmental situations involving stressors and stress-related behaviors (for example, divorce, deaths, or job problems leading to increased eating or smoking, poor sleep, excessive anger) and who recognizes related psychological conditions (for example, depression, anxiety) can offer or refer for treatment as indicated.

Response to Vignette

For many years Chaplain Amy had been at the hospital through a nondenominational medical chaplaincy group. Because of her extensive experience in working with a wide variety of people with medical and life-threatening issues, she possessed a significant wealth of medical knowledge. She was used to crises of faith precipitated by serious illnesses, as well as to patients being catapulted into faith by a medical wake-up call. She was knowledgeable about and comfortable working with people of various religious and spiritual traditions. Because the chaplain was female, Sophie was comfortable talking with her about personal matters. This was a fortuitous match for Sophie.

She initially talked about her fear of living a severely limited life. The chaplain was knowledgeable about the services for cardiac patients, and so was able to assure Sophie that cardiac rehabilitation services would be readily available. She talked about diet and exercise, and personally introduced Sophie to a hospital dietitian and to a therapist from the rehabilitation program. The chaplain encouraged Sophie to include Mario in the initiation of an open and frank discussion with her cardiologist about sex and future pregnancy if her physician did not do so. This guidance and the introductions to professionals who answered her questions and would be involved in her posthospital treatment reassured Sophie and helped to dispel some of her fears.

Treatment within the Faith Community

Though few studies have addressed the impact of spirituality on CVD, recent findings suggest that some aspects of religious involvement serve as a protective factor (Powell et al., 2003). Many people turn to religious practices for comfort and help in coping with physical and mental health problems — even those with no previous affiliation (Ferraro and Kelley-Moore, 2000).

A study by Oxman and colleagues in 1995 examined the relationship between postoperative mortality and religion and social support in older patients who had elective open-heart surgery. Of the 232 patients included in the study, 21 died within 6 months of surgery. When the interaction between social support and comfort from religion was examined along with biomedical predictors of mortality, the risk of mortality for those patients who were both low on group participation and low on strength and comfort from religion was over 14 times greater than in those with high group participation and high comfort from religion. The results strongly suggest that participation in social or community groups and feeling a sense of strength or comfort from religion are related to a lower risk of death during the 6-month period after cardiac surgery.

Sophie looked forward to the chaplain's visits. She appreciated her calmness and ability to listen and reassure without minimizing or discounting Sophie's fears. She felt a personal connection that was missing from her interactions with the medical staff. Though she was not totally comfortable about it, Sophie asked Chaplain Amy to say a prayer with her. This spiritual act resulted in an emotional release for Sophie; through her tears she admitted that she was afraid of dying. She was not only questioning why she had the heart attack, but was also questioning why she had lived. She felt a renewed gratitude for her life, but was uncertain as to what this experience meant for her life's direction. She expressed sadness that her time with Chaplain Amy would be over once she was discharged from the hospital and came to realize that she craved a deeper spiritual connection and presence in her life, though she did not know where to turn for it.

Chaplain Amy realized that Sophie's beliefs precluded a good fit with many of the nearby churches. She was politically liberal, intellectual, pragmatic, open to both Eastern and Western religious and philosophical traditions, and not much interested in ritual or structure. Because of this Sophie had not ever attempted to find a compatible faith community. Chaplain Amy's knowledge of and connections with local churches enabled her to steer Sophie to one she believed would match her spiritual needs without alienating her with incompatible doctrine. The chaplain called the minister and introduced him to Sophie over the telephone, facilitating Sophie's transition from individual spiritual seeker to eventual membership in a supportive faith community of relatively like-minded people.

Indications for Referral

Adjusting to a life-threatening condition, experiencing a medical emergency, or coping with a chronic illness or disability can result in psychological complications. Depressive symptoms (for example, sad mood, sustained loss of interest or pleasure in usual activities, appetite or sleep disturbances, fatigue, feelings of worthlessness, concentration difficulties, and impairment in social or occupational functioning) warrant a referral of the individual to a mental health professional (American Psychiatric Association, 2000). A study by Frasure-Smith (cited in Clay, 2001) found patients who had heart attacks and who were depressed were three times more likely to die in the year afterward than those who were not depressed — regardless of the severity of their initial heart disease. The same researcher reported that one's social support seems to lessen the impact of depression. A study of Swedish women found that family stress, particularly marital stress, increased CHD risk and that social isolation and depressive symptoms predicted poor prognosis for women with CHD (Orth-Gomer, 2001).

A referral for mental health counseling would also be indicated if the person was experiencing significant anxiety. Panic attacks are a type of anxiety disorder involving relatively short periods of intense fear or discomfort with symptoms such as increased heart rate or palpitations, sweating, shaking, shortness of breath, choking sensations, feelings of unreality, tingling sensation, chills or hot flashes, and fear of losing control or of dying. Additional symptoms often include chest pain or discomfort, nausea, dizziness, or light-headedness; panic attacks can look and feel much like a heart attack and can lead to ER visits, medical tests, and frightening experiences for individuals and those around them. Agoraphobia, another anxiety disorder, can develop as the result of a person experiencing a medical emergency, having a chronic or life-threatening condition, or having panic attacks. This is a disorder in which persons have such extreme anxiety related to certain places or situations and intense fear that escape is impossible or that help will be unavailable that they avoid the situations or places or are afraid to even leave their homes. Other anxiety disorders can also develop related to the medical event: symptoms of recurrent distressing recollections of the event, ongoing distressing dreams, reliving the event as if it were happening again, persistent avoidance of associated stimuli, excessive worrying, excessive irritability, and/or muscle tension (APA, 2000) are possible indications for a referral to a mental health professional.

Similar but less severe symptoms of depression or anxiety might occur and are reason enough to refer an individual for follow-up mental health counseling when one is unable to provide it due to circumstances or lack of knowledge, time, or training.

In recent years, the medical community has begun to recognize the relationship of psychological factors to heart disease (Clay, 2001). Anger (Williams et al., 2000), hostility (Iribarren et al., 2000), and stress (Krantz et al., 2000) have been found to negatively affect cardiac health. When these are noted to be significant in a parishioner's life, whether or not the person has already been diagnosed with CVD or has had a heart attack, this is a "red flag" for referral for mental health treatment.

Professional counseling can treat depression and anxiety (Pashkow and Libov, 2001); address issues of anger, hostility, and stress; and support people in making lifestyle changes that will decrease their risk factors for CVD (Cooley, 1996). Ideally psychological symptoms and traits are addressed prior to any serious cardiac event, and thus mental health counseling serves as a preventive and protective intervention. When CHD is already present, counseling can focus on cognitive behavioral therapies to decrease or eliminate depression and/or anxiety, relaxation and stress management, education, anger management, and lowering risk factors through lifestyle modifications.

Treatment by Mental Health Specialist

Once a person has a heart attack and has been hospitalized, psychological services should begin in the hospital to help the patient cope with the trauma and fear associated with the event — with being treated in a high-tech and often impersonal medical environment, with the transfer from the perceived safety of the well-monitored and well-staffed CCU to a regular room, and then with the transition from the hospital to life at home (Fisher, 1996).

Medical services, dietary counseling, exercise/physical rehabilitation, education, and social support are all important components of holistic treatment of potential or actual cardiac patients. Mental health services are a vital element of this comprehensive treatment.

Sophie was continuing to experience anxiety two months after her discharge from the hospital. She often lay awake at night worrying about the possibility of having another heart attack. Although there is no added danger of physical complications, she was concerned that resuming sexual relations with Mario might precipitate another coronary event and so was avoiding intimacy of any kind with him. Their relationship was suffering as a result, at a time when she needed Mario most.

Sophie called the one person she could talk to about these problems. When Chaplain Amy heard about Sophie's difficulty sleeping, excessive worrying, and fears related to resuming her sex life, she referred her to a mental health professional for counseling. Through her therapy, Sophie learned cognitive and behavioral coping techniques that were effective in decreasing her anxiety symptoms. With encouragement and guidance from her therapist, Sophie scheduled an appointment with her cardiologist and went with a list of specific questions. The physician answered them and reassured her she could safely resume having sex. He asked Sophie if she wanted to include Mario, who was in the waiting room, in their discussion. She asked him to come into the office, and the frank and open talk with the doctor not only answered their questions, but allowed the beginning of a dialogue between the partners about this important matter they had been avoiding.

The work Sophie did in therapy enabled her to address the sexual concerns directly with her physician and with her husband. She and Mario continued to openly communicate about sexual issues and about their feelings; these discussions fostered greater emotional intimacy, more demonstrated affection and increased physical closeness. This eventually resulted in not only a resumption of sexual activity, but in sexual relations enhanced by their strengthened emotional bond.

Cross-Cultural Issues   CVD (all diseases of the heart and arteries) is the leading cause of death for African American, American Indian/Alaska Native, Asian/Pacific Islander, European American, and Hispanic women and men in the United States (American Heart Association, 2003). CHD has generally been considered by the media, the public, and those in the medical profession to be a disease that affects only men. However, those in the United States who die each year from CVD number nearly 1 million, and women account for over half of these deaths (American Heart Association, 2003; Lancaster, 2001). Still, most heart research has been focused on men (Pashkow and Libov, 2001). Fortunately, in 1992, the National Institutes of Health mandated the inclusion of women in clinical studies when appropriate, and as a result, gender-balanced research results have become increasingly available (Legato and Colman, 2000). Despite the still widely held belief that mostly men are at risk for CHD, it is the number-one cause of death for American women (American Heart Association, 2003; Pashkow and Libov, 2001). Gender-biased beliefs have also been the norm in the United Kingdom where CHD has been seen as a man's disease, though it is the leading cause of death of women there (Emslie et al., 2001). CVD accounts for approximately 500,000 female deaths in the United States each year, and almost half of these are due to heart attacks. While polls show that even women consistently rank breast cancer as their biggest health concern (Pashkow and Libov, 2001), for every woman who dies from breast cancer, 12 others die from CVD (American Heart Association, 2003; Lancaster, 2001). The gender bias in research has carried over into a treatment bias. Physicians have been less likely to suspect heart problems in women, and so fewer preventative cardiac treatments have been given to females.

Bias in research has also occurred along racial lines, with most studies being conducted using European American men. Studies in the late 1990s found lower numbers of coronary procedures were done on African American hospitalized patients, and fewer referrals of African Americans were made for cardiac testing and treatment (cited in Pashkow and Libov, 2001). However, African Americans between the high-risk ages of 35 and 74 are more likely to die of heart disease than European American women overall. This is likely due to African American women being more at risk than European American women to develop the cardiac risk factors of hypertension, diabetes, and obesity at younger ages. By age 75, African American and European American women die of heart disease at about the same rate (Pashkow and Libov, 2001).

Both men's and women's risk of CVD increases as they age (Pashkow and Libov, 2001), with more than 84 percent of those who die of CVD being aged 65 or older (American Heart Association, 2003). Women's risk increases significantly postmenopause (American Heart Association, 2003; Lancaster, 2001). Men aged 55 and under have heart attacks or die from CHD two to three times more often than women, but gender differences in death rates decrease with age, with more cardiovascular-related deaths among elderly women than elderly men (Jacobs and Sherwood, 1996).

Resources

American Heart Association; 7272 Greenville Avenue, Dallas, TX 75231; (800)242-8721; *www.americanheart.org*; a nationwide resource with a national center and 12 affiliate offices around the United States. The Web site provides information on cardiovascular diseases, statistics by population group and state-by-state, risk factors, warning signs, information about healthy lifestyles, news, and links to other related Web sites. It publishes brochures and books (including heart-healthy cookbooks) which can be ordered online; the organization also publishes five related journals.

Centers for Disease Control and Prevention; 1600 Clifton Road, Atlanta, GA 30333; *www.cdc.gov/health/cardiov.htm*; an agency of the U.S. Department of Health and Human Services; provides cardiovascular disease statistics, risk factors, information about prevention, and links to other related Web sites.

Health Heart Program; St. Paul's Hospital and the University of British Columbia, B180–1081 Burrard Street, Vancouver, V62

1Y6, BC; (604)806-8591; *www.healthyheart.org* is a hospital- and university-based Web site that has information on heart disease risk factors, exercise, nutrition and research, and provides Internet resources links to related journals, smoking cessation, and nutrition information.

Helpful Books   *American Heart Association Low-Salt Cookbook* (New York: Clarkson Potter, 2003).

American Heart Association Low-Fat, Low-Cholesterol Cookbook (3rd ed.) (New York: Random House, 2004).

Cleveland Clinic Heart Book: The Definitive Guide for the Entire Family from the Nation's Leading Heart Center (Eric Topol, Editor, New York: Hyperion, 2000).

Female Heart (Marianne Legato and Carol Colman, New York: Quill, 2000).

Mayo Clinic Heart Book (2nd ed.) (Bernard Gersh, New York: William Morrow, 2000).

One-Dish Meals (American Heart Association, New York: Clarkson Potter, 2003).

To Your Health: A Guide to Heart-Smart Living (American Heart Association, New York: Clarkson Potter, 2001).

Women's Heart Book: The Complete Guide to Keeping Your Heart Healthy (Fredric Pashkow and Charlotte Libov, New York: Hyperion, 2001).

References   Allan, R. (1996). Introduction: The emergence of cardiac psychology. In R. Allan and S. Scheidt (eds.), *Heart and Mind: The Practice of Cardiac Psychology* (pp. 3–13). Washington, DC: American Psychological Association.

American Heart Association. (2003). *American Heart Association.* Retrieved June 7, 2003, from *www.americanheart.org.*

American Psychiatric Association. (2000). *Diagnostic and Statistical Manual of Mental Disorders* (4th ed., text revision) (Washington, DC: American Psychiatric Association.

Clay, R. A. (2001). Research to the heart of the matter. *Monitor on Psychology*, 32(1), 42–45.

Cooley, D. A. (1996). [Foreword]. In R. Allan and S. Scheidt (eds.), *Heart and Mind: The Practice of Cardiac Psychology* (pp. 1–2). Washington, DC: American Psychological Association.

Emslie, C., Hunt, K., and Watt, G. (2001). Invisible women? The importance of gender in lay beliefs about heart problems. *Sociology of Health and Illness*, 23, 203–233.

Ferraro, K. F., and Kelley-Moore, J. A. (2000). Religious consolation among men and women: Do health problems spur seeking? *Journal for the Scientific Study of Religion*, 39, 220–235.

Fisher, J. (1996). Is there a need for cardiac psychology? The view of a practicing cardiologist. In R. Allan and S. Scheidt (eds.), *Heart and Mind: The Practice of Cardiac Psychology* (pp. 125–145). Washington, DC: American Psychological Association.

Iribarren, C., Sidney, S., Bild, D. E., Liu, K., Markovitz, J. H., Roseman, J. M., and Matthews, K. (2000). Association of hostility with coronary artery calcification in young adults: The CARDIA study. *Journal of the American Medical Association*, 283, 2546–2551.

Jacobs, S. C., and Sherwood, J. B. (1996). The cardiac psychology of women and coronary heart disease. In R. Allan and S. Scheidt (eds.), *Heart and Mind: The Practice of Cardiac Psychology* (pp. 125–145). Washington, DC: American Psychological Association.

Krantz, D. S., Sheps, D. S., Carney, R. M., and Natelson, B. H. (2000). Effects of mental stress in patients with coronary artery disease: Evidence and clinical implications. *Journal of the American Medical Association*, 283, 1800–1802.

Lancaster, M. (2001). *Women and Heart Disease*. Walla Walla, WA: Coffey Communications.

Legato, M., and Colman, C. (2000). *Female Heart*. New York: Quill, 2000.

Orth-Gomer, K. (2001). Women and heart disease: New evidence for psychosocial, behavioral, and biological mediators of risk and prognosis. *International Journal of Behavioral Medicine*, 8, 251–270.

Oxman, T. E., Freeman, D. H., and Manheimer, E. D. (1995). Lack of social participation or religious strength and comfort as risk factors for death after cardiac surgery in the elderly. *Psychosomatic Medicine*, 57, 5–15.

Pashkow, F. J., and Libov, C. (2001). *The Women's Heart Book*. New York: Hyperion.

Powell, L. H., Shahabi, L., and Thoresen, C. E. (2003). Religion and spirituality: Linkages to physical health. *American Psychologist*, 58, 36–52.

Williams, J. E., Paton, C. C., Siegler, I. C., Eigenbrodt, M. L., Nieto, J., and Tyroler, H. A. (2000). Anger proneness predicts coronary heart disease risk: Prospective analysis from the atherosclerosis risk in communities (ARIC) study. *Circulation*, 101, 2034–2039.

Sexual Harassment

"Her boss questioned her about her sex life"

Joanne asked to see her pastor, Rev. Barbara White. She was clearly upset and began to tell her story. Within the second year of her employment, Joanne Kim began to experience behavior from her male supervisor that made her dread going to work. He asked her about her sex life and made comments about how bad his was. He complimented her on her good looks and made sexual comments to her about other female employees. Recently, he asked her for a date — which she rejected. He commented that going out with him could be a good career move. All of this unwanted, unsolicited behavior caused significant stress. She began to have problems sleeping, eating, and concentrating. Soon she was calling in sick to avoid seeing her supervisor.

Pastoral Care Assessment   Sexual harassment is a significant social problem because of its frequency and its negative consequences for victims. Being sexually harassed can have serious effects on psychological well-being and vocational development (Barling et al., 1996). Those who have experienced such behavior often change their jobs, career goals, work assignments, educational programs, or academic majors. Women report psychological reactions to harassment that are similar to symptoms of other serious forms of stress (Claudia and O'Donohue, 2002). Among women who have been sexually harassed, at least 75 percent said that they had felt one or more symptoms of emotional or physical distress due to their harassment (Loy and Stewart, 1984). Research shows that the range of symptoms and effects of sexual harassment reported by victims includes anger, fear, depression, anxiety, irritability, shame, self-blame, loss of self-esteem, and a sense of helplessness and vulnerability (Schneider et al., 1997). Physical effects reported included headaches, loss of appetite, inability to sleep, weight loss, headaches, gastrointestinal distress, sleep disturbances, panic reactions, and sexual problems (Piotrkowski, 1998).

In part, as a consequence of women's growing presence in the work- **Relevant**
force, sexual harassment has been recognized as a widespread and **History**
serious form of sexual discrimination. In the late 1970s and early
1980s, a series of legal rulings established that sexual harassment was a
form of sexual discrimination in employment prohibited by Title VII of
the Civil Rights Act of 1964 and Title IX of the Education Amendment.
The U.S. Equal Employment Opportunity Commission states that "un-
welcome sexual advances, requests for sexual favors, and other verbal
or physical conduct of a sexual nature constitute sexual harassment"
(Equal Employment Opportunity Commission, 1980). "Quid pro quo"
sexual harassment occurs when advances involve threat or bribery and
conditions of employment. When harassment affects a victim's ability
to perform his or her job, or creates an "intimidating, hostile or offensive working environment," that is also sexual harassment (Equal
Employment Opportunity Commission, 1980).

Any unwanted sexual comment, advance, or demand, either verbal **Diagnostic**
or physical, that is reasonably perceived by the recipient as demeaning, **Criteria**
intimidating, or coercive is sexual harassment. It is best understood as
exploitation of a power relationship rather than simply a sexual issue.
It includes the creation of a hostile or abusive working environment
resulting in discrimination on the basis of gender. Sexual harassment
undermines the climate of mutual respect between men and women.

Sexual harassment is widespread. It touches the lives of 40 to 70 percent of working women in many different settings (Piotrkowski, 1998;
Pryor, 1995; Vukovich, 1996) and similar proportions of female students in colleges and universities (Fitzgerald et al., 1988). In a 1994
survey of federal employees, 44 percent of women and 19 percent
of men reported that they had experienced some form of unwanted
sexual attention during the 2 years preceding the survey (U.S. Merit
Systems Protection Board, 1994). Research has confirmed that sexual harassment also has negative consequences on employees' health
and psychological well-being (Schneider et al., 1997). Moreover, sexual harassment has been found to increase absenteeism and turnover
in organizations as well as to decrease job satisfaction, organizational
commitment, and productivity (Glomb et al., 1999).

Most harassment has nothing to do with flirtation or sincere sexual
or social interest. Rather, it is offensive, often frightening and insulting
to women. Research shows that women are often forced to leave school
or jobs to avoid harassment (Glomb et al., 1999). Individuals rarely file
complaints that are false and infrequently file complaints even when
they are justified.

Data shows that only 13 percent of female and 8 percent of male federal employees reported harassing behaviors to a supervisor or other official, while 45 percent of female and 44 percent of male federal employees ignored the behaviors or took no action (U.S. Merit Systems Protection Board, 1994). Reilly, Lott, and Gallogly (1986) found that 61 percent of sexually harassed college students ignored the behaviors or took no action, and only 16 percent told the perpetrator to stop.

Harassment does not occur because women dress provocatively or initiate sexual activity in the hope of getting promoted and advancing their careers. Studies have found that victims of sexual harassment vary in physical appearance, type of dress, age, and behavior. The only thing they have in common is that the great majority are women. If harassment is ignored, it is very unlikely that it will go away. Simply ignoring the behavior is ineffective; harassers generally will not stop on their own. Ignoring such behavior may even be seen as agreement or encouragement.

Response to Vignette

Pastor White told Joanne about an experience she had in college with a professor. A married male instructor had been friendly with her from the beginning of the semester. He went out of his way to talk to her about personal things that did not pertain to class. One day, she went to the instructor's office to talk about a class assignment. To her utter surprise, he offered her a better grade in the class if she would go on a date with him. She told him in no uncertain terms that she was a Christian woman and she expected him to act in a professional manner. She dropped the class and never had contact with the instructor again. Years later, while in therapy, her anger about the event came to the surface.

Rev. White shared with Joanne that women she had counseled over the years who had been sexually harassed most often were completely surprised by the harasser's behavior. They usually try to ignore the harassment, joke about the conduct, or politely refuse advances. Women often describe feeling humiliated, embarrassed, and guilty that they might have somehow caused or encouraged the harasser's behavior. It is common that after each incident, victims of the harassment imagined that it would stop. When the harassment escalates, the victim begins to feel powerless. The pastor said she has found that until victims labeled the behavior as harassment and decided that they were not responsible for it, the self-blame and harassment continued. Women also indicate that if the harassment persists, their concentration, motivation, and work performance are diminished. As work achievement and pleasure erode, victims' self-esteem becomes negatively affected.

After her conversation with Rev. White, Joanne felt empowered to speak with her union representative at work to see what information and guidance she could obtain. She found out that according to the National Labor Relations Act, unions are required to represent and aid their members in stopping sexual harassment. Her union assured her that it was committed to eliminating sexual harassment in her workplace and that it was willing to aggressively help her resolve the problem. The union representative informed her of her rights and educated her about the corporation's policies and procedures regarding harassment. The union told her that employers are responsible for the conduct of supervisors and managers, and they have a responsibility to protect their employees. Managers are also liable for sexual harassment between coworkers if they know about it and take no steps to stop it. The union representative accompanied her while she told her story to the person in the corporation who administers the harassment policies. After a brief investigation, it was discovered that her supervisor had a chronic problem involving several women. He was reassigned and later terminated.

Treatment within the Faith Community

Sexual harassment is a barrier to hospitality. This alienating behavior causes brokenness in relationships — the opposite of God's intention for us in human community. Educating faith communities on the issue of sexual harassment is important. Information in newsletters, sermons, and classes on the topic is useful, giving a victim the signal that her congregation takes harassment seriously and that she can find help among people who care. The church and synagogue should educate members that sexual harassment is not a private problem but a community concern to be addressed by all responsible people.

The value of church-based support for persons experiencing difficult situations is well documented (Weaver et al., 2003). People at church can provide emotional support (for example, express interest and concern in the well-being of a victim), tangible assistance (for example, help with forming support groups), or spiritual support, such as sharing of experiences and feelings as well as helping others use religious teachings in daily life (Krause, 2002). Support from church members and religious participation have been found to buffer psychological distress (Kim and McKenry, 1998).

Indications for Referral

A person who is experiencing significant psychological distress resulting from harassment should be referred to a mental health professional who understands the difficulties caused by such a problem.

Joanne told her pastor that she has problems sleeping, eating, and concentrating. Joanne also indicated that there have been days she called in sick to avoid facing her supervisor. These could be signs of depression, and they need to be evaluated. How much difficulty is she having sleeping and eating? Are these minor problems or major difficulties that are markedly interfering with her ability to live her life?

Other signs of a persistent depression include sadness and the inability to experience pleasure with no signs of improvement after several weeks; a significant weight loss or weight gain; severe fatigue or complaint of slowed movement (psychomotor retardation); intense helpless or hopeless feelings, very pessimistic thinking; difficulty remembering or making decisions; or marked irritability, agitation, restlessness, or suicidal thoughts. At any point that a person's difficulties are beyond a pastor's level of training or experience, a referral should be made.

Treatment by Mental Health Specialist

Mental health professionals treating women or men who have experienced sexual harassment have several issues to address. Survivors may experience confusion, fear, self-blame, anxiety, depression, and anger. The stress of sexual harassment can also be complicated by a history of prior victimization.

Individual therapy may begin by validating a victim's experience and sorting through immediate practical issues related to employment and legal decisions. It is important to focus on the ways that sexual harassment can affect an individual's self-image, as well as to assess her or his overall coping. The therapist can best serve the person by providing emotional support and understanding that can reduce negative feelings and physical symptoms. Persons who rely on avoidance or substance use to reduce the stress of harassment will need help to address these issues. Community resources like assertiveness training and alcohol treatment centers can be helpful along with therapy. Strong feelings of helplessness can be related to unresolved experiences of abuse, sexual assault, or dysfunctional family patterns. The extent to which a victim's feelings (for example, depression, anxiety, and fear) continue past the harassment is one indication that such past experiences are contributing to the distress. It is equally important that practitioners explore work-related issues as potential sources of distress.

Sexual harassment counseling groups can be useful. Such settings can help persons to understand their experiences, sort through legal and employment decisions, and learn new coping skills, as well as providing personal support. Once sexual harassment victims acknowledge that they have been harassed, frustration and anger often emerge. Women who have been sexually harassed, like victims of crime, have a need to understand why this happened to them and how they can avoid future occurrences.

A questionnaire was administered to nurses and nursing students in Israel (80 percent women) from five medical centers (Bronner et al., 2003). Seven types of sexual harassment behavior patterns were evaluated. Ninety percent of subjects reported experiencing at least one type of sexual harassment and 30 percent described at least four types. Severe types of harassment were experienced by a third of the nurses, in comparison to a quarter of the nursing students. Women were significantly more exposed than men to "mild" and "moderate" types of sexual harassment, while 35 percent of men compared to 26 percent of women were exposed to "severe" types of harassment. Interestingly, women in this study responded significantly more assertively than men to severe sexual harassment. The authors recommended that greater attention be given to sexual harassment among male students and nurses because they may be subjected to the more offensive sexual behaviors and at the same time may lack the ability to respond assertively (Bronner et al., 2003).

Facts About Sexual Harassment; U.S. Equal Employment Opportunity Commission, *www.eeoc.gov/facts/fs-sex.html*, gives definitions of terms and policies for the workplace, as well as other information and resources for victims of sexual harassment.

Feminist Majority, *www.feminist.org*, provides information on a variety of women's issues, as well as useful links.

Information on Sexual Harassment, *www.de.psu.edu/harassment*, provides useful facts about sexual harassment.

LawGuru Sexual Harassment Law FAQs, *www.lawguru.com/faq/16 .html*, provides a wealth of information about the legal policies concerning sexual harassment, as well as links to resources.

National Organization for Women: NOW and Sexual Harassment, *www.now.org/issues/harass*, information about policy, action, and referrals to lawyers.

Nine to Five, National Association of Working Women; 152 West Wisconsin Avenue, Suite 408, Milwaukee, WI 53203; (414)274-0925, (800)522-0925; *www.9to5.org*; is a national membership organization that strengthens women's ability to work for economic justice. It has activists in more than 200 cities and members in every state.

Sexual Harassment — Fact vs. Myth, *www.menweb.org/throop/harass/ myth.html*, provides useful facts about sexual harassment.

Sexual Harassment Resources, *library.uncg.edu/depts/docs/us/harass .html*, has useful links on all issues concerning sexual harassment.

Shevolution, *www.feminist.org-911-harass.html1.htm*, develops systems, services, and media for women and men to work together as equals in work, life, and politics.

Women's Rights at Work; (888)979-7765, ext. 42; *www.citizenactionny .org/wrw_dir/index.htm*, a sexual harassment and gender discrimination outreach and education project that provides support, information, and resources to women who have experienced sexual harassment in the workplace.

Women's Studies Database: Gender Issues, *www.de.psu.edu/harassment*, is a Web site with links to many useful facts about all aspects of sexual harassment.

Helpful Books   *Sexual Harassment: A Practical Guide to the Law, Your Rights, and Your Options for Taking Action* (Tracy O'Shea and Jane LaLonde, New York: St. Martin's Press, 1998).

Sexual Harassment on Campus: A Guide for Administrators, Faculty, and Students (Bernice R. Sandler and Robert J. Shoop [Eds.], Needham Heights, MA: Allyn and Bacon, 1997).

Sexual Harassment: Theory, Research, and Treatment (William O'Donohue [Ed.], Boston: Allyn and Bacon, 1997).

Sexual Harassment: What Teens Should Know (Carol Rust Nash, Berkeley Heights, NJ: Enslow Publishers, 1996).

Workplace Sexual Harassment (Anne C. Levy and Michele Antoinette Paludi, Upper Saddle River, NJ: Pearson Education, 2001).

References   Barling, J., Dekker, I., Loughli, C. A., Kelloway, E. K., Fullagar, C., and Johnson, D. (1996). Prediction and replication of the organizational and personal consequences of workplace sexual harassment. *Journal of Managerial Psychology*, 11(5), 4–25.

Bronner, G., Peretz, C., and Ehrenfeld, M. (2003). Sexual harassment of nurses and nursing students. *Journal of Advanced Nursing*, 42(6), 637–644.

Claudia, A., and O'Donohue, W. (2002). Sexual Harassment and PTSD: Is sexual harassment diagnosable trauma? *Journal of Traumatic Stress*, 15(1), 69–75.

Equal Employment Opportunity Commission. (1980). Guidelines on discrimination because of sex, 29 C.F.R., 1604(11).

Fitzgerald, L. F., Shulman, S. L., Bailey, N., Richards, M., Swecker, J., Gold, Y., et al. (1988). The incidence and dimensions of sexual harassment in academia and the workplace. *Journal of Vocational Behavior*, 32(2), 152–175.

Glomb, T. M., Munson, L. J., Hunlin, C. L., Bergman, M. E., and Drangow, F. (1999). Structural equation models of sexual harassment: Longitudinal explorations and cross-sectional generalizations. *Journal of Applied Psychology*, 84, 14–28.

Kim, H., and McKenry, P. C. (1998). Social networks and support: A comparison of African Americans, Asian Americans, Caucasians, and Hispanics. *Journal of Comparative Family Studies*, 29(2), 313–334.

Krause, N. (2002). Exploring race differences in a comprehensive battery of church-based social support measures. *Review of Religious Research* 44, 126–149.

Loy, P. H., and Stewart, L. P. (1984). The extent and effects of the sexual harassment of working women. *Sociological Focus*, 17(1), 31–43.

Piotrkowski, C. S. (1998). Gender harassment, job satisfaction, and distress among employed White and minority women. *Journal of Occupational Health Psychology*, 3(1), 33–43.

Pryor, J. B. (1995). The psychosocial impact of sexual harassment on women in the U.S. military. *Basic and Applied Social Psychology*, 17, 581–603.

Reilly, M. E., Lott, B., and Gallogly, S. M. (1986). Sexual harassment of university students. *Sex Roles*, 15, 333–358.

Richman, J. A., Rospenda, K. M., Flaherty, J. A., and Freels, S. (2001). Workplace harassment, active coping, and alcohol-related outcomes. *Journal of Substance Abuse*, 13, 347–366.

Schneider, K. T., Swan, S., and Fitzgerald, L. F. (1997). Job related and psychological effects of sexual harassment in the workplace: Empirical evidence from two organizations. *Journal of Applied Psychology*, 82, 401–415.

U.S. Merit Systems Protection Board. (1994). *Sexual Harassment in the Federal Workplace: Trends, Progress and Continuing Challenges.* Washington, DC: U.S. Government Printing Office.

Vukovich, M. C. (1996). The prevalence of sexual harassment among female family practice residents in the United States. *Violence and Victims*, 11, 175–180.

Weaver, A. J., Flannelly, L. T., and Preston, J. D. (2003). *Counseling Survivors of Traumatic Events: A Handbook for Pastors and Other Helping Professionals.* Nashville: Abingdon Press.

Sexual Orientation

"He came home with the news that he was gay"

After rescheduling their appointment twice, Gary and Joyce Moore appeared at Rev. Mark Stone's office. They looked sad, distraught, and tired. They had slept very little in the past week. Their only son, Brad, had come back from his second year in college with the news that he was gay. A very bright young man, he is attending a prestigious college on a full academic scholarship. Brad had been the captain of his high school basketball team and president of his senior class. The Moores were a devout couple who had been active members of their church for 20 years. They came from a long line of Methodists, including several prominent clergy. They asked themselves how this could be happening. Mr. Moore said, "The news felt like a blow to the stomach from a mallet." He asked his pastor, Rev. Mark Stone, "What have I done as a father to make this happen? Good kids raised in a Christian home don't become gay overnight. I must have failed Brad—his homosexuality must be my fault, but how?"

Pastoral Care Assessment   This is a pastoral care situation that requires a loving, sensitive, and knowledgeable pastor. All the members of the Moore family will need a compassionate and healing reminder of the presence of God, who loves them. An able clergyperson can be of great assistance in helping a family deal with their emotional reactions, facilitate good communication, work at problem solving, and patiently lead them toward reconciliation.

The Moores are being faced with the painful fact that their long-held dreams (expectations of heterosexual marriage, children, and grandchildren) have been dramatically altered with Brad's announcement. The parents are grieving and blaming themselves in ways similar to a loss by death. The difference here is that Brad is alive and the Moore family needs their pastor to help them find Christian reconciliation.

Persons like Brad are caught in a trap. Gays and lesbians almost always have a deep desire to have an open relationship with their parents, siblings, and other family members, yet they are often afraid of how their families will react. It is their desire for an honest relationship where they are accepted and loved that leads to their "coming out."

In 2002, there were about 200 million Americans who were 20 years old or older (United States Department of Commerce, 2002). Using a conservative estimate of 4 percent of the population being gay or lesbian, there are approximately 8 million adults whose sexual orientation is exclusively homosexual (Fay et al., 1989). Therefore, there are tens of millions of parents, grandparents, aunts, uncles, cousins, and siblings of gays and lesbians who care about their welfare and are negatively affected by the bias against homosexuals in our society. **Relevant History**

All mainstream mental health organizations, including the American Psychological Association and the American Psychiatric Association, have taken the position that homosexuality is not a mental disorder (American Psychiatric Association, 2003). In 1973 the American Psychiatric Association's Board of Trustees removed homosexuality from its official diagnostic manual, *The Diagnostic and Statistical Manual of Mental Disorders, Second Edition,* following a review of the scientific literature by experts in the field (American Psychiatric Association, 2003). Scientists have found that homosexuality does not meet the criteria for a mental illness, nor is there scientific evidence that homosexuality results from arrested development or from pathological attachment patterns in early life — theories that were posited in the early history of psychiatry (Haldeman, 1994). **Diagnostic Criteria**

Fears and misunderstandings about homosexuality abound. Belief that erotic attraction to persons of the same sex is a choice is fairly widespread in American society. However, scientific studies of genetics, brain physiology, and hormones increasingly suggest that for many (if not most) gay and lesbian persons, sexual attraction is not a choice, but an inborn trait (Bailey and Pillard, 1991; Bailey et al., 2000; Blanchard and Klassen, 1997; Hu et al., 1995).

A second widespread assumption is that the environment in which a child is raised has a strong effect on sexual orientation. This is not supported by scientific evidence (Bailey et al., 1995; Golombok et al., 2003; Golombok and Tasker, 1996). For example, a longitudinal study of 27 lesbian mothers and their 39 children, with a control group of the same number of heterosexual mothers and their children, was conducted by a group of researchers in London (Golombok and Tasker,

1996). In both groups the children were raised without the fathers being in the home. The youngsters and the mothers were interviewed extensively when the children were at an average age of 9.5 years. They were all interviewed again when the children were an average age of 23.5. The results showed that there were no statistically significant differences in the sexual orientation of the offspring of the two groups of mothers. There was no difference between the two sets of children in their experience of love in the family and of their sense of well-being. The conclusion was that "the commonly held assumption that children brought up by lesbian mothers will themselves grow up lesbian or gay is not supported by the findings of this study" (Golombok and Tasker, 1996).

Response to Vignette

Rev. Stone spent many hours listening to Gary and Joyce. A lot of tears were shed. The Moores loved their son, but their disappointment was severe. The pastor let them talk and share their feelings without judgment. He knew that it was necessary for them to go through disbelief, confusion, and sorrow in order to get their necessary grief work done. It was clear as they talked that they loved Brad deeply and that they were concerned for his welfare, not just about their personal needs and wishes. Rev. Stone reminded them that their grief was a sign of deep love for their son and the means by which healing could take place in their relationship with him.

Gary and Joyce were worried about Brad, who was unhappy and disturbed by their negative reaction to his news. Gary also felt guilty. He confessed that one of his relatives was probably homosexual. His Uncle Earl had never married, and it had been an unspoken assumption in the family that he was gay. He thought that maybe Brad had his uncle's gay gene.

With Rev. Stone, the Moores prayerfully examined what the Bible says about homosexuality. Gary and Joyce had a great deal of confidence in their pastor's judgment as a scholar of the scriptures. He pointed out that bias against gay and lesbian persons is partly rooted in an inaccurate interpretation of a few selected biblical texts (Williams, 1989). The well-known Old Testament passages are: Genesis 19:1–29, the Sodom and Gomorrah story that actually is an indictment of inhospitality and social injustice, and the Holiness Code in Leviticus 18:22 and 20:13 that is a condemnation of the sacred prostitution and sexual orgies in Canaanite fertility rites, both of which were a part of the idolatrous worship of other gods (Nelson, 1978; Switzer, 1999).

The New Testament records no words of Jesus about same-sex relationships. The only explicit references in the New Testament appear in

Romans 1:26–27, 1 Corinthians 6:9, and 1 Timothy 1:10. In 1 Corinthians, Paul is condemning male prostitution, and this may also be the target in 1 Timothy. The condemnation is broader in Romans, where female relationships are mentioned as well as male. Paul's characterization of these as "unnatural" and expressive of "degrading passions" is based on the presupposition that all same-sex relationships arise from the unrestrained lust of heterosexual persons. Scholars have documented that none of these texts refer to what we today would call a gay orientation or the committed expression of intimacy between two adults of the same sex. At the time the scriptures were written, people did not conceive of such behavior as an expression of a sexual orientation. There is nothing in Holy Scripture to warrant the condemnation of persons who are gay and lesbian simply because of their orientation (Furnish, 1994; Switzer, 1999).

Over time, Gary and Joyce were able to come to accept Brad's decision to come out as a gay man. A critical part of the reconciliation came when Gary talked to his favorite uncle, Earl, whom he suspected was gay. Earl was an active member of the Episcopal Church and a very caring Christian person. His uncle confessed to him that he was gay and that he had lived in a time and part of the country that made him fear for his life if he came out. Earl said that he thought what Brad had done was very brave and healthy for him and that Gary should support his son and love him as God made him.

Treatment within the Faith Community

Bias-related incidents arising from racism, intolerance based on religion, ethnicity, and anti-gay and anti-lesbian prejudices are all too common and continue to be a source of social disruption and individual psychological trauma. According to the *Summary of Hate Crime Statistics,* in 2000 there were 8,063 hate crimes reported to the Federal Bureau of Investigation. Of the incidents, 4,337 were motivated by racial bias; 1,472 by religious bias; and 1,299 by sexual-orientation bias (Summary of Hate Crime Statistics, 2000).

These actions occurred in both urban and rural areas. Such hate-based attacks consisted of acts of violence or harassment, which resulted in emotional and physical trauma for individuals, as well as stigmatization of affected groups. Hatred, vividly manifest in bias-related incidents, wounds the basic human need for dignity, often resulting in despair and hopelessness among the survivors. It is important that survivors do not fall into the common trap of self-blame but instead recognize that their individual identity did not lead to the attack, which was an act aimed at a group.

People of faith can stand together and speak out against those who try to use hate and violence to divide persons. A religious presence can act as a deterrent to hate violence toward gays and lesbians. Faith communities can develop educational efforts aimed at dispelling sexual-minority stereotypes, reducing hostility between groups, and encouraging broader understanding. Hate groups seek to exploit diversity as an evil and to pit various groups against one another. Diverse persons of faith working together exert a moral force that can resist hate.

Indications for Referral

When a person comes out to his or her family, it can be emotionally difficult for all involved. Most parents, like Gary and Joyce Moore, are concerned for the welfare of their children and recognize the difficulties posed by being a member of a stigmatized group. Often parents also fear rejection by their own family, friends, religion, or social affiliations. Fortunately, support exists for those who are struggling to come to terms with their child's homosexuality. Parents and Friends of Lesbians and Gays (PFLAG) is an organization that provides information and assistance to parents and friends of gay men, lesbians, and bisexuals. If a family does not have a caring, experienced, and knowledgeable pastor like Rev. Stone, it needs to be referred to an experienced pastoral counselor or mental health professional who is informed regarding religious considerations. That person can be helpful in dealing with questions and concerns about a gay child, including whether or not a person can receive treatment that will change his or her sexual orientation.

Treatment by Mental Health Specialist

While talking with Rev. Stone, Gary and Joyce asked about possible counseling to help Brad get over his homosexual feelings. Rev. Stone suggested that they talk to Dr. Thomas Handford, an experienced psychiatrist whom he knew. Dr. Handford was a devout Lutheran with whom Rev. Stone had consulted on several complicated pastoral care cases over the years.

The psychiatrist explained to Gary and Joyce that numerous individuals and family members had come to him in his 25 years of practice requesting counseling or some other form of treatment to change his or her sexual orientation or that of a family member. Most individuals came to him seeking conversion to heterosexuality because of the difficulties that they encountered as a member of a stigmatized group.

Dr. Handford told Gary and Joyce that there is no credible scientific evidence supporting the efficacy of "conversion therapy" or "reparative therapy" as a treatment to change one's sexual orientation (Shidlo and Schroeder, 2002). Moreover, mental health experts are not convinced that such therapy is an appropriate goal of mental health treatment (American Psychological Association, 1998). Several major professional organizations (including the American Psychological Association, the American Psychiatric Association, the National Association of Social Workers, and the American Academy of Pediatrics) have made statements against conversion therapy because of concerns for the harm caused to patients (American Psychiatric Association, 2003).

The potential risks of conversion therapy are considerable. They include depression, anxiety, and self-destructive behavior, since a therapist's alignment with societal prejudices against homosexuality can reinforce self-hatred already experienced by a person (Haldeman, 2002b). Many patients who have undergone conversion therapy relate that they were inaccurately told that homosexuals are lonely, unhappy individuals who never achieve acceptance or satisfaction, which is not based upon scientific facts or helpful to the well-being of an individual (Haldeman, 2002b). Dr. Handford told the Moores that his professional experience had taught him that those who integrate their sexual orientation into a positive sense of self are psychologically healthier than those who do not, and that family members are very important in that process.

Cross-Cultural Issues

In Southern California researchers examined the attitudes of a group of European American, Hispanic American, and Asian American female undergraduates regarding homosexuality (Span and Vidal, 2003). Overall, the number of homosexual friends the student had was inversely related to negative attitudes toward gays and lesbians. Asian American students scored significantly higher on their negative views of gays and lesbians than European American students. Both Asian American and Hispanic American students were more likely than European American students to indicate that the university would be better if only heterosexuals attended. No significant differences were found regarding attitudes toward lesbians versus gay men (Span and Vidal, 2003).

Resources

The Coming Out of a Lesbian's Mother, *www.angelfire.com/co/lesmom/index.html*, is the story of a mother's acceptance of her daughter as a lesbian.

Dignity USA: Gay, Lesbian, Bisexual, and Transgender Catholics; 1500 Massachusetts Avenue, NW, Suite 11, Washington, DC 20005-1894; (800)877-8797, (202)861-0017; *www.dignityusa.org/index.html*; is the largest national lay movement of gay, lesbian, bisexual, and transgender Catholics and their families and friends.

Gay and Lesbian Family Resources, online at *http://www.geocities.com/ WestHollywood/1769/family.html*, provides information and resources for families with gay or lesbian members.

Gay/Lesbian Politics and Law: World Wide Web and Internet Resources, *www.gaypoliticsandlaw.com*, is a selective, annotated guide to resources on politics, law, and policy about homosexuality for students, scholars, teachers, journalists, activists, and others.

Gay and Lesbian Resources; 1625 North Schrader Boulevard, Los Angeles, CA 90028; (323)806-5806; provides resources and information for gays and lesbians.

Health Care Information Resources: Gay, Lesbian and Bisexual Health Links; McMaster University Health Sciences Library, 1200 Main Street West, Hamilton, Ontario, Canada L8N 3Z5; *hsl.mcmaster .ca/tomflem/gay.html*; provides information about health and diseases.

My Child Is GAY! Now what do I do? *www.bidstrup.com/parents.htm*, provides support, information, guidance, and resources for the parents of gay, lesbian, bisexual, and transgender youth.

National Gay and Lesbian Task Force; 1325 Massachusetts Avenue, NW, Suite 600, Washington, DC 20005; (202)393-5177; *www.ngltf.org*; is an organization working for the civil rights of gay, lesbian, bisexual, and transgender people.

Ontario Consultants on Religious Tolerance; Box 27026, Kingston, Ontario, Canada K7M 8W5; *www.religioustolerance.org/homosexu .htm*; attempts to explain both sides of the issue of homosexuality: the positions taken by those in favor of and opposed to equal rights for persons of all sexual orientations. It includes a collection of essays, news, information, and commentary.

Our Family Coalition; 870 Market Street, Suite 724, San Francisco, CA 94102; (415)981-1960; *www.ourfamily.org*; protects the civil rights and well-being of families with lesbian, gay, bisexual, and transgender members through education, advocacy, social networking, and grassroots community organizing. It serves as a clearinghouse for information, resources, medical and legal referrals, and family events.

OutProud: The National Coalition for Gay, Lesbian, Bisexual, and Transgender Youth; 369 Third Street, Suite B-362, San Rafael, CA 94901-3581; *www.outproud.org*; provides a wide range of resources for youth and educators.

Parents, Families, and Friends of Lesbians and Gays (PFLAG); 1726 M Street, NW, Suite 400, Washington, DC 20036; (202)467-8180; *www.pflag.org*; is a national nonprofit organization with over

200,000 members and supporters and almost 5C0 affiliates in the United States. This vast grassroots network is cultivated, resourced, and serviced by the PFLAG national office, located in Washington, DC, the national board of directors, and 14 regional directors.

Planet Out; P.O. Box 500, San Francisco, CA 94104-0500; (415)834-6500, (415)834-6502; *www.planetout.com/pno/splash.html*; news, resources, information, and chat rooms for gays, lesbians, and bisexuals.

Read This before Coming Out to Your Parents, *www.qrd.org/qrd/youth/read.this.before.coming.out.to.your.parents*, a guide to coming out as a homosexual, including stories, information, support, and resources.

Spirituality for Lesbian, Gay, Bisexual, Transgender and Intersex People, *cwpp.slq.qld.gov.au/spirit/index.html*, seeks to give homosexuals the opportunity to explore and discover the reciprocal influences of religion and spirituality upon sexual and gender identity and to provide information about and links to lesbian, gay, transgender, and intersex religious and spiritual groups.

World Congress of Gay, Lesbian, Bisexual, and Transgender Jews: Keshet Ga'avah; P.O. Box 23379, Washington, DC 20026-3379; (202)452-7424; *glbtjews.org*; holds conferences and workshops representing the interests of lesbian, gay, bisexual, and transgender Jews around the world. The focus of these sessions varies from regional to global.

Helpful Books

Beyond Acceptance (Carolyn Welch Griffin, Marian J. Wirth, and Arthur G. Wirth, Englewood Cliffs, NJ: Prentice Hall, 1986).

Coming Out as Parents: You and Your Homosexual Child (David K. Switzer, Louisville: Westminster John Knox, 1996).

Homosexuality: Catholic Teaching and Pastoral Practice (Gerald D. Coleman, Mahwah, NJ: Paulist, 1995).

Homosexuality in the Church: Both Sides of the Debate (Jeffery S. Siker, Louisville: Westminster John Knox, 1994).

Now That You Know: What Every Parent Should Know About Homosexuality (Betty Fairchild and Nancy Hayward, San Diego: Harcourt Brace Jovanovich, 1986).

Pastoral Care of Gays, Lesbians, and Their Families (David K. Switzer, Minneapolis: Augsburg Fortress, 1999).

Reconciling Journey: A Devotional Workbook for Lesbian and Gay Christians (Michal Anne Pepper, Cleveland: The Pilgrim Press, 2003).

We Were Baptized Too: Claiming God's Grace for Lesbians and Gays (Marilyn Bennett Alexander and James Preston, Louisville: Westminster John Knox, 1996).

References   American Psychological Association. (1998). Resolution on the appropriate therapeutic responses to sexual orientation. In Proceedings of the American Psychological Association, Incorporated, for the legislative year 1997. *American Psychologist*, 53, 882–935.

American Psychiatric Association. (2003). *Fact sheet: Gay, lesbian and bisexual issues.* Retrieved July 31, 2003, from the Web site at *www.psych.org/public_info/gaylesbianbisexualissues22701.pdf.*

Bailey, J. M., Bobrow, D., Wolfe, M., and Mikach, S. (1995). Sexual orientation of adult sons of gay fathers. *Developmental Psychology*, 31(1), 124–129.

Bailey, J. M., Dunne, M. P., and Martin, N. G. (2000). Genetic and environmental influences on sexual orientation and its correlates in an Australian twin sample. *Journal of Personality and Social Psychology*, 78(3), 524–536.

Bailey, M., and Pillard, R. C. (1991). A genetic study of male sexual orientation. *Archives of General Psychiatry*, 48, 1089–1096.

Blanchard, R., and Klassen, P. (1997). H-Y antigen and homosexuality in men. *Journal of Theoretical Biology*, 185, 373–378.

Fay, R. E., Turner, C. F., Klassen, A. D., and Gagnon, J. H. (1989). Prevalence and patterns of same-gender sexual contact among men. *Science*, 243(4889), 338–348.

Furnish, V. P. (1994). *The Moral Teaching of Paul: Selected Issues.* Nashville: Abingdon Press.

Golombok, S., Perry, B., Burston, A., Murray, C., Mooney-Somers, J., Stevens, M., and Golding, J. (2003). Children with lesbian parents: A community study. *Developmental Psychology*, 39(1), 20–33.

Golombok, S., and Tasker, F. (1996). Do parents influence the sexual orientation of their children? Findings from a longitudinal study of lesbian families. *Developmental Psychology*, 32(1), 3–11.

Haldeman, D. (1994). The practice and ethics of sexual orientation conversion therapy. *Journal of Consulting and Clinical Psychology*, 62, 221–227.

Haldeman, D. (2002a). Gay rights, patient rights: The implications of sexual orientation conversion therapy. *Professional Psychology: Research & Practice*, 33(3), 260–264.

Haldeman, D. (2002b). Therapeutic antidotes: Helping gay and bisexual men recover from conversion therapies. *Journal of Gay and Lesbian Psychotherapy*, 5, 119–132.

Hu, S., Pattatucci, A. M. L., Patterson, C., Lin, L., Fulker, D. W., Cherny, S. S., Kruglyak, L., and Hamer, D. H. (1995). Linkage between sexual orientation and chromosome Xq28 in males but not in females. *Nature Genetics*, 11, 248–256.

Nelson, J. B. (1978). *Embodiment: An Approach to Sexuality and Christian Theology*. Cleveland: Pilgrim Press.

Shidlo, A., and Schroeder, M. (2002). Changing sexual orientation: A consumers' report. *Professional Psychology: Research & Practice*, 33(3), 249–259.

Span, S. A., and Vidal, L. A. (2003). Cross-cultural differences in female university students' attitudes toward homosexuals: A preliminary study. *Psychology Report*, 92(2), 565–572.

Summary of Hate Crime Statistics 2000. Retrieved March 29, 2002 from *www.infoplease.com/ipa/A0004885.html*.

Switzer, D. K. (1999). *Pastoral Care of Gays, Lesbians, and Their Families*. Minneapolis: Augsburg Fortress.

United States Department of Commerce. (2002). *U.S. Census Bureau: Statistical abstract of the United States, 2002*. Retrieved on August 11, 2003, from *www.census.gov/prod/2003pubs/02statab/pop.pdf*.

Williams, R. (1989). *The Body's Grace*. London: The Institute for the Study of Christianity and Sexuality and the Lesbian and Gay Christian Movement.

BISEXUALITY

Bisexuality is sexual attraction to or involvement with members of both sexes. A comprehensive study, *Sex in America*, conducted in 1992 by the University of Chicago, found that less than 1 percent of either males (0.7 percent) or females (0.3 percent) had engaged in sexual activity with both males and females within the previous year. While no statistics exist on the numbers of Americans who fit the definition of bisexuality, estimates range from the millions to tens of millions (Michael et al., 1994). Many bisexuals hide their identity from others. Some lead dual lives, expressing their homosexual sides with one group, while reserving their heterosexual identity for a separate social circle.

TRANSSEXUALITY

Transsexuality, also termed Gender Identity Disorder or (GID), is defined by persistent feelings of gender discomfort and incongruity of anatomic sex. People with GID desire to live as members of the opposite sex and often dress and use mannerisms associated with the other gender. A transsexual is a person in which the sex-related structures of the brain that define gender identity are exactly opposite the physical sex organs of the body. It was not until the 1950s that clinicians recognized that there were individuals who felt intensely uncomfortable with their biological sex. It is a rare disorder affecting about 3 of every 100,000 males and 1 of every 100,000 females (APA, 2000).

References

American Psychiatric Association. (2000). *Diagnostic and Statistical Manual of Mental Disorders* (4th ed., text revision). Washington, DC: American Psychiatric Association.

Michael, R. T., Gagnon, J. H., Laumann, E. O., and Kolata, G. (1994). *Sex in America*. New York: Little, Brown.

PART THREE

Summary

Summary and Conclusions

Religion plays an essential role in the lives of individuals and their families, especially when facing difficult matters. Given that clergy are often the first professionals sought for help with personal problems including sexual issues, those in ministry need to understand the key concerns to be addressed. Information is needed about how to diagnose and assess problems, types of treatment that can be initiated in the faith community, when referral is required, and to whom to refer. This volume identifies 17 sexual and related issues, provides illustrative cases, lists resources available, and suggests when and from whom to seek additional professional assistance. There is an emphasis on self-help resources available on the Internet, an increasing source of information today.

Because of the valued role that religion plays in the lives of many, it is essential that pastors, chaplains, parish nurses, and others in ministry be knowledgeable about the sexual issues that affect individuals and families they serve. Religious faith is a primary, positive coping strategy for many persons who address sexual questions and related psychological issues. Faith communities can have a positive role by providing accurate information for individuals regarding these matters. Congregations often have long-established communication networks that allow them to stay in touch with members in need of education and support on this subject and other health concerns. Accurate information about sexual and related issues can be disseminated through these networks.

Pastoral care is a responsibility of the whole religious community. Clergy can offer guidance and direction, but the task of caring for those suffering from psychological trauma requires a larger group of helpers. Much emphasis is given to prevention through education within the community of faith. The book offers concrete suggestions about how the issues addressed can be understood as forms of ministry for the entire congregation.

Making Effective Referrals

A clergyperson is more likely than a mental health specialist to have an individual who is emotionally distressed seek her or him for assistance. Most of those who consult clergy do not subsequently contact a mental health professional (Hohmann and Larson, 1993). At the same time, clergy indicate that they believe seminary training does not adequately prepare them to respond to the emotional and family problems encountered in ministry (Orthner, 1986). Seventy to 90 percent of pastors surveyed recognized a need and indicated a desire to have additional training in mental health issues (Weaver et al., 1997).

It is essential for the responsible practice of ministry that clergy and other religious professionals be prepared to identify the emotional needs of persons in distress and make effective referrals. The fundamental task of a pastor in relation to a mental health network is to identify the needs of individuals who seek assistance and to connect them to a larger circle of specialized helpers. This section makes several suggestions as to how clergy can become more effective in a mental health network.

1. Develop a working relationship with at least one, preferably several, mental health professionals who have a comprehensive knowledge of the services available in your community and are willing to work with you as a colleague. Some psychologists, psychiatrists, social workers, pastoral counselors, and other mental health professionals have specialized training in treating persons with sexual issues. Seek out mental health professionals who are open to persons of faith and have some appreciation of the scientific research showing that religious commitment can be a positive coping resource in difficult times (Koenig et al., 2001). Interview a mental health professional on the telephone before you refer someone who trusts you to make an educated referral. Keep a record of available providers to whom you can refer in an emergency. Ask the specialists direct questions to assess their skill level, expertise, and fee schedule. Inquire in detail about their experience, training, and education. For example:

- What sorts of cases have they worked with in the past? What are their specialties?

- Have they worked with individuals and families suffering from sexual issues?

- How do they develop treatment plans for various issues related to human sexuality?

- How easily can they be located in an emergency?

- Are they willing to do some low-fee work?

2. It is important to create a list of professional and community resources before you are faced with a mental health emergency. Equip yourself with such knowledge as the location of the nearest hospital emergency room, in case a person becomes suicidal or psychotic; the location of the closest outpatient mental health center; and which social services (such as Planned Parenthood) are available and how they can be accessed in a crisis. Most regions publish lists of resources available in case of an emergency. These should be used to develop appropriate plans of action with your mental health colleagues.

3. Self-care is essential. Clergy have many responsibilities and require good self-care practices to keep them emotionally healthy and effective. Pastors are required to fulfill many responsibilities to parishioners and the community that place extensive requirements on their time and energy. There are few occasions when clergy are not on call, and they are often sought out to help persons who are troubled (Weaver, 1995). Pastors in emotional turmoil are limited in their ability to help those in need of assistance. Research indicates that numbers of clergy and their spouses need counseling (Orthner, 1986; Weaver et al., 2002).

Here are a few practical suggestions supported by psychological research:

- Talk about how you are feeling. Human feelings are powerful. Venting is cathartic; it is a helpful process by which people use words and nonverbal communication to let go of distressing emotions.

- Spend time with others. Coping with stressful events is easier when people help each other. Ask for support and assistance from your family, friends, colleagues, or community resources. Join or create support groups.

- Take time to grieve and cry, if needed. To feel better in the long run, you must let these feelings out instead of pushing them away or hiding them.

- Set small goals to tackle big problems. Approach one thing at a time instead of trying to do everything at once. If you are attempting to do too much, eliminate or delay the things that are not absolutely necessary.

- Eat healthfully and take time to walk, stretch, exercise, and relax, even if just for a few minutes at a time. Make sure you get enough rest. You may need more sleep than usual when you are under high stress.

- Do something that just feels good, like taking a warm bath, sitting in the sun, or spending time with a pet.

- Celebrate your sense of humor. Laughing, being playful, telling jokes, and being humorous are particularly positive activities for those whose environment is filled with difficult human problems.

- Receive spiritual direction from a trusted pastor, or, if needed, treatment by a mental health professional who appreciates the value of faith for Christians coping with stress.

- Make your spiritual health a priority. One way millions of Christians have found useful is called Centering Prayer. It is a method of contemplative prayer that can help a person deal with stress as well as seek a deeper relationship with God. This type of praying is rooted in silence. It is a receptive mode of prayer, seeking a personal relationship with God — like two friends sitting in silence, just being in each other's presence. Centering Prayer is drawn from the ancient practices of the Christian contemplative heritage, notably the desert fathers and mothers, the Cloud of Unknowing, St. John of the Cross, St. Teresa of Avila, and *lectio divina* (praying the scriptures).

"Lectio divina" literally means divine reading. It is a monastic term for the meditative reading of scripture. It is a discipline of dwelling on a biblical text as the means of seeking communion with Christ. *Lectio divina* has four elements: *lectio* (reading), the slow reading of a short passage of scripture; *meditatio* (meditation), an effort to understand the meaning of the text and make it personally relevant to oneself in Christ; *oratio* (prayer), a personal response to the text, moving over it toward union with God; and *contemplatio* (contemplation), sitting quietly and giving God a chance to be with you in whatever way God chooses. It is an exposure to the divine presence, truth, and compassion.

The Roman Catholic monk Thomas Merton found that contemplation can bring a sense of oneness with life itself, with other people, and with God. These are moments when we can experience a deep peace and harmony. Such times can help renew us when stress is draining our spirit. Merton spoke of the joy that brings renewal of the spirit through prayer and contemplation. In *Seeds of Contemplation*, he wrote, "The only true joy is to escape from the prison of our own selfhood...and enter by love into union with the Life Who dwells and sings within the essence of every creature and in the core of our minds."

May God bring you joy and song.

4. Continuing education is a necessity. Unlike growth in other areas of pastoral ministry (such as administration, preaching, teaching), pastors report that no matter how long they serve, they believe that their counseling skills do not improve without continuing education (Orthner, 1986). Referral skills are closely related to evaluative skills, since clinical evaluation usually guides the course of action, particularly the treatment goals and objectives. Research has demonstrated that training clergy in diagnostic skills enhances their ability as pastoral counselors as well as their effectiveness in making referrals (Clemens et al., 1978). Pastors must understand that a timely referral is an act of responsible pastoral care. Clergy can serve most effectively in the mental health network as skilled facilitators who identify the needs of persons and then connect them to a larger circle of specialized helpers.

Resources

American Association for Marriage and Family Therapy; 1133 Fifteenth Street, NW, Suite 300, Washington, DC 20005; (800)374-2638; *www.aamft.org*; offers continuing education programs for those who work with families.

American Association of Pastoral Counselors; 9504A Lee Highway, Fairfax, VA 22031; (703)385-6967; *www.metanoia.org/aapc*; provides information on qualified pastoral counselors and church-related counseling centers.

American Association of Sex Educators, Counselors, and Therapists; P.O. Box 5488, Richmond, VA 23220-0488; (212)819-9770; *www.aasect.org*; promotes understanding of human sexuality and healthy sexual behavior.

American College of Obstetricians and Gynecologists; 409 Twelfth Street, SW, P.O. Box 96920, Washington, DC 20090; (202)683-5577; (800)762-2264; *www.acog.org*; an organization of obstetricians and gynecologists dedicated to the advancement of women's health through education, advocacy, practice, and research.

American Psychiatric Association; 1400 K Street, NW, Washington, DC 20005; (202)682-6000; *www.psych.org*.

American Psychological Association; 750 First Street, NE, Washington, DC 20002; (202)336-5500; *www.apa.org*.

Association of Mental Health Clergy; 12320 River Oaks Point, Knoxville, TN 37922; (615)544-9704.

Canadian Association for Pastoral Practice and Education; 47 Queen's Park Crest, East, Toronto, Ontario M5S 2C3, Canada; (416)977-3700; *www.cappe.org*.

Interfaith Health Program, The Carter Center; One Copenhill, Atlanta, GA 30307; (404)420-3846; *www.interaccess.com/ihpnet*.

International Parish Nurse Resource Center; 205 West Touhy Avenue, Suite 104, Park Ridge, IL 60016; (800)556-5368; *www.ipnrc .parishnurses.org*.

National Alliance for the Mentally Ill: Religious Outreach Network; 1900 NW Eighty-ninth Street, Seattle, WA 98117; (206)784-3789; *www.nami.org*; provides educational materials to clergy and religious groups, enabling them to dispel myths about mental illness and to guide churches and synagogues to serve the mentally ill.

National Association of Social Workers; 750 First Street, NE, Suite 700, Washington, DC 20002; (202)408-8600; *www.socialworkers.org*.

National Organization for Continuing Education of Roman Catholic Clergy; 1337 West Ohio Street, Chicago, IL 60622; (312)226-1890; *www.nocercc.org*.

Samaritan Institute; 26965 South Colorado, Suite 380, Denver, CO 80222; (303)691-0144; *samaritan-institute.org*; helps communities develop interfaith counseling centers.

SIECUS: Religion and Sexuality, *www.siecus.org/toc.html#RELI*, provides a list of Web sites that deal with issues concerning religion and sexuality and a list of links to fact sheets, community resources, and policy issues related to sexuality and sex education.

Stephen Ministries; 2045 Innerbelt Business Center Drive, St. Louis, MO 63114; (314)428-2600; *www.stephenministries.org*; offers training in counseling skills for local church members for peer ministry.

References Clemens, N. A., Corradi, R. B., and Wasman, M. (1978). The parish clergy as a mental health resource. *Journal of Religion and Health*, 17(4), 227–232.

Hohmann, A. A., and Larson, D. B. (1993). Psychiatric factors predicting use of clergy. In E. L. Worthington, Jr. (ed.), *Psychotherapy and Religious Values* (pp. 71–84). Grand Rapids: Baker.

Koenig, H. G., McCulloch, M., and Larson, D. B. (2001). *Handbook on Religion and Health*. Oxford: Oxford University Press.

Orthner, D. K. (1986). *Pastoral Counseling: Caring and Caregivers in the United Methodist Church*. Nashville: General Board of Higher Education and Ministry of the United Methodist Church.

Summary of Hate Crime Statistics. (2002) Retrieved March 29, 2002, from *www.infoplease.com/ipa/A0004885.html*.

Weaver, A. J. (1995). Has there been a failure to prepare and support parish-based clergy in their role as front-line community mental health workers? A review. *Journal of Pastoral Care*, 49(2), 129–149.

Weaver A. J., Flannelly, K. J., Larson, D. B., Stapleton, C. L., and Koenig, H. G. (2002). Mental health issues among clergy and other religious professionals: A review of the research. *The Journal of Pastoral Care and Counseling*, 56(4), 393–403.

Weaver, A. J., Samford, J., Kline, A. E., Lucas, L. A., Larson, D. B., and Koenig, H. G. (1997). What do psychologists know about working with the clergy? An analysis of eight American Psychological Association journals: 1991–1994. *Professional Psychology: Research and Practice*, 28(5), 471–474.

Glossary

Abortion: The termination of a pregnancy before the fetus can survive on its own outside of the uterus. Induced abortions occur intentionally. Spontaneous abortions occur naturally and are often called miscarriages.

Abstinence: Voluntarily refraining from sexual intercourse.

Adultery: Sex between a married person and a person other than their spouse.

AIDS (Acquired Immune Deficiency Syndrome): Increased susceptibility to opportunistic infections as a result of a lowered immune system. Caused by the human immunodeficiency virus (HIV).

Anal sex: Also known as sodomy. Penetration of the anus with an object or penis.

Artificial insemination: Placing semen into a woman's vagina or uterus by a means other than intercourse, for the purpose of inducing pregnancy.

Asexual: Without sexual feelings, desires or qualities.

Behavior therapy: A school of psychological therapy based on learning theory that focuses on observable behavior and not the unconscious.

Birth control: The regulation of conception, pregnancy, and/or birth.

Birth control pills: A series of progesterone and/or estrogen hormone pills taken throughout the monthly cycle to prevent pregnancy by inhibiting the release of an egg from the ovaries.

Bisexual: Sexual attraction to both males and females.

Body fluids: Blood, semen, vaginal secretions, urine, feces, saliva, and/or tears.

Caesarean section: Delivery of a baby through a surgical incision in the abdominal wall. Also known as C-section.

Calendar method: A contraceptive method based on calculating "safe" days based on a formula involving a woman's longest and shortest periods. Also known as the "rhythm method."

Candidiasis: A yeast infection caused by the fungus candida albicans.

Castration: The removal of the testes or ovaries. In popular use, also refers to the amputation of the penis.

Celibacy: Abstinence from sexual activity.

Celibate: Unmarried, or as more popularly used, someone who does not engage in sexual activity.

Cervix: The cylindrical part of the uterus that protrudes into the vagina. The area where pap smear cell samples tend to be collected.

Chancre: A painless sore that appears during the first stage of syphilis.

Chastity: Sexual abstinence.

Chlamydia: A sexually transmitted infection that may or may not include symptoms. If symptoms occur they may include discharge and itching. Curable with antibiotics.

Chromosomes: The genetic material in the nucleus of every cell in the body. In most cases, human cells have 46, except for sperm and eggs, which each have 23. Humans with certain rare genetic conditions (for example, Down's syndrome and Turner's syndrome) may have more or fewer than 46 chromosomes.

Circumcision: The surgical removal of the foreskin of the penis, or, in some cultures, the clitoral hood, clitoris, and/or labia.

Climacteric: A syndrome that affects about 5 percent of men over the age of 60. Symptoms include decreased sexual interest, poor appetite, weakness, and fatigue.

Climax: Orgasm.

Clitoris: A small, highly sensitive sexual organ in the female, located above and in front of the vaginal entrance.

Coitus: Sexual intercourse.

Coming out: The process of acknowledging that one is gay, lesbian, bisexual, or transgender.

Condom: Latex or polyurethane membrane used to shield the penis against skin-to-skin contact and sharing of bodily fluics during penetrative and oral sex in order to guard against pregnancy and transmission of STDs, including HIV. Animal intestines have also been used as condoms; however, the membrane of this type of condom has not been shown to block the transmission of certain STDs, including HIV.

Contraception: The prevention of conception by the use of birth control devices or agents.

Copulation: Vaginal intercourse.

Corpora cavernosa: Two parallel bodies of erectile tissue, which form the largest part of the shaft of the penis. These become engorged with blood, leading to erection.

Covert sensitization: A form of aversion therapy in which negative thoughts are used to punish and therefore rid someone of unacceptable thoughts or behaviors.

Crabs: Also known as pubic lice. Parasites that can be transmitted to the pubic area through sexual and nonsexual contact (for example, use of contaminated towels and/or bedding).

Cross-dressing: Wearing the clothing of the opposite sex.

Cunnilingus: Oral sex performed on a woman.

Cybersex: Using a computer in some way to enhance sexual stimulation.

Delayed ejaculation: A sexual dysfunction characterized by the male's difficulties with ejaculating during intercourse.

DES: Diethylstilbestrol, a synthetic estrogen once used to prevent miscarriages, and which is now known to increase the risk of certain cancers not only in the women who were given the drug, but their offspring. It is still occasionally used as a form of "morning-after" birth control.

Desensitization: A sex therapy technique used to overcome fears and phobias.

Deviant sexual behavior: Sexual behavior that diverges from the norm.

Dilation and curettage (D&C): The process of dilating the cervix and then scraping the lining of the uterus. Used to remedy a variety of medical problems.

Dilation and evacuation (D&E): A combination of sucking and scraping the contents of the uterus through a dilated cervix. Can be used as a method of abortion.

Dominant: Also known as a "top." A person who prefers to assume the proactive role in sadomasochistic (SM) play.

Domination and submission (D&S): Sexual arousal derived from the acting out of sexual fantasies in which one person dominates while the other submits.

Drag queen: A gay man who dresses as a woman for comic effect.

Dysmenorrhea: Painful menstruation, which may include headaches, backaches, bloating, and cramping.

Dyspareunia: Painful intercourse.

Ectopic pregnancy: A pregnancy that occurs when a fertilized egg implants itself somewhere outside the uterus. In most cases, the site of implantation is a fallopian tube, in which case the condition is known as a tubal pregnancy.

Ejaculation: The expulsion of seminal fluid from the penis, usually during orgasm.

Endometriosis: The growth of endometrial tissue in areas outside of the uterus. Can lead to female infertility if untreated.

Endometrium: The inner lining of the uterus, part of which is shed during menstruation.

Erectile dysfunction: Also known as impotence. The inability to develop or maintain an erection for penetrative sex. Can be classified as primary (always existing), secondary (having functioned previously), or situational (occurring only in specific situations).

Erection: The enlargement and hardening of the penis due to vasocongestion that occurs during sexual arousal in the male.

Erogenous zone: Any area of the body that is especially sensitive to sexual stimulation and touching.

Erotica: Sexual material, writing, or art, whether the sexuality is explicit or implied.

Estrogen: The principal female hormone, secreted by the ovaries, testes, and placenta.

Exhibitionism: A paraphilia characterized by getting sexual gratification from exposing the genitals to an (often unwilling) observer.

Extramarital sex: Sexual activity by a married person with someone other than her or his spouse.

Fallopian tube: One of the two tubes extending from the ovary to the uterus through which eggs are transported.

Fellatio: Oral stimulation of the male genitals.

Fertilization: The union of sperm and egg, resulting in conception.

Fetishism: The use of an inanimate object for sexual arousal. A sexual preoccupation with a specific object or characteristic — for instance, feet or long hair.

Flaccid: Not erect.

Foreplay: A term used to refer to sexual activities other than intercourse. The term comes from the view that some individuals hold that all activities of a sexual nature are merely designed to lead up to intercourse.

Foreskin: Also referred to as the clitoral hood in women. The loose skin which covers the penis and clitoris.

Frenulum: A highly sensitive area of skin on the underside of the penis, where the glans meets the body of the penis.

Gamete intra-fallopian transfer (GIFT): A procedure for infertile couples in which sperm and eggs are collected and then inserted together into the woman's fallopian tube.

Gardnerella vaginalis: The bacterium that is the most common cause of bacterial vaginosis. It also refers to the infection itself, which causes a thin, smelly discharge in both men and women.

Gay-bashing: Violence against gay men or lesbians because of their orientation.

Gender: The characteristics associated with being a male or a female; as distinguished from the term "sex," which is more ambiguous. Also sometimes used to merely refer to the state of being either male or female.

Gender dysphoria: Dissatisfaction with one's gender. In extreme cases, this condition is known as transsexualism, in which a person desires to be the other gender.

Gender identity: The gender one feels himself or herself to be, whether physiologically male or female.

Genetic sex: The differentiation of males and females based upon chromosomal and hormonal differences.

Genitals: The sex organs of the pelvic region including the vulva, vagina, and clitoris in the female, and the penis, testes, and scrotum in the male.

Genital herpes: Also referred to as herpes simplex II. A viral infection that can cause painful blisters for which there is no cure. Symptoms may occur on a random basis. Outbreaks can be somewhat inhibited through medication.

Genital warts (human papilloma virus): Also known as HPV. A viral infection that causes dry, painless warts externally and internally that has been linked to cervical cancer. There is no cure and no diagnostic test. However, pap smears may at times reveal these warts on the cervix. Often, symptoms may not occur until several years after the virus has been contracted.

Glans: The head of the penis or clitoris.

Gonad: An organ that produces gametes; ovaries or testes.

Gonorrhea: A sexually transmitted bacterial infection causing genital discharge and itching. Curable with antibiotics.

Granuloma inguinale: A fairly rare STD that is characterized by nodules on the genitals that become lumpy, painless ulcers that bleed on contact.

Hard-core: Sexually explicit material that graphically depicts the genitals and sexual acts.

Hepatitis: A viral disease affecting the liver; two types of virus may be sexually transmitted: hepatitis A and hepatitis B.

Hermaphrodite: Also called intersexed. A person with some or all of the primary sex characteristics of both genders (for example, both a penis and a vulva).

Herpes simplex type II: An STD infection characterized by outbreaks of painful sores on the genitals. Infection occurs through physical contact with a person infected with the herpes simplex virus during an active outbreak of the sores.

Heterosexual: Also known as straight (adjective or noun). A person who is sexually and/or romantically attracted to the opposite sex but not to the same sex.

HIV (human immunodeficiency virus): The retrovirus that causes AIDS.

Homophobia: An irrational fear of and hostility toward homosexuals.

Homosexual: Also known as gay (male) or lesbian (female) or queer. A person who identifies as someone who is sexually and/or romantically attracted to a person of the same sex.

Hormone: The chemical messengers of the body, secreted by the endocrine glands, which regulate several functions including sexual development.

Hormone-replacement therapy (HRT): The administration of estrogen, progesterone, or a combination of the two to counteract the hormonal effects of the decrease in these hormones during menopause.

Hot flashes: A negative side effect of menopause reported by some women. Although typically only lasting a couple of minutes, it is accompanied by intense warmth, flushing, and perspiration.

Human immunodeficiency virus (HIV): The virus that causes AIDS.

Human papilloma virus (HPV): The virus that causes genital warts.

Hymen: A thin membrane that partially covers the vaginal entrance of most females at birth; although an intact hymen is sometimes erroneously thought to prove virginity, it can actually be broken by many activities besides intercourse.

Hypersexual: Also erroneously referred to as nymphomania or oversexed. Someone who has an enormous sex drive.

Hypoactive sexual desire: A sexual disorder characterized by low or absent sexual desire.

Hypothalamus: A part of the brain which is vital in regulating many body functions, including sex hormone production.

Hysterectomy: The surgical removal of the uterus, and also sometimes the fallopian tubes and ovaries.

Implantation: The embedding of the fertilized egg into the lining of the uterus.

Impotence: Inability to have an erection.

Incest: Sexual activity between relatives or family members.

Infertility: The inability to achieve pregnancy, usually after one year or more of active attempts.

Inhibited orgasm: Persistent difficulty in having orgasm or inability to have orgasm; in males, also called ejaculatory incompetence or retarded ejaculation.

Inhibited sexual desire: A sexual disorder characterized by low or absent sexual desire.

Intercourse: Sexual activity in which the penis is inserted into an orifice such as the vagina or anus; the term is often modified accordingly (e.g., anal intercourse).

Intrauterine device (IUD): A plastic or metal device that is inserted into the uterus by a physician for contraceptive purposes. The exact mechanism of contraceptive action is unknown.

In vitro fertilization (IVF): A technique in which sperm and egg are removed from the body, combined in the laboratory, then implanted as a fertilized egg in the woman's uterus. A means of treating infertility; the result is commonly referred to as a "test tube baby."

Lesbian: A female homosexual.

Libido: Term used by Sigmund Freud to refer to sexual energy; the driving force in humans according to him.

Limbic system: The set of structures around the midbrain involved in regulating sexual behaviors.

Lubricant: The slippery fluid secreted from the walls of the vagina during sexual arousal; also available in synthetic form to supplement or replace the natural version. The synthetic version is also used for activities that require lubrication such as anal intercourse.

Lumpectomy: A surgical procedure for breast cancer in which only the malignant tumor and surrounding tissue are removed while the rest of the breast is left intact.

Lust: A very strong sexual urge.

Masochism: A sexual variation in which the individual derives sexual pleasure from experiencing pain.

Mastectomy: The surgical removal of the breast; usually done as a treatment for breast cancer.

Masturbation: Self-stimulation of the genitals for sexual pleasure.

Menopause: The cessation of menstruation at the end of a woman's reproductive capacity, usually during late middle age.

Menses: The more or less monthly sloughing of the uterine lining which results in a bloody discharge from the vaginal opening.

Menstrual cycle: The more or less monthly process during which the uterus is readied for implantation of a fertilized ovum. If fertilization does not occur the uterine lining is then shed.

Menstrual extraction: The removal of the endometrial contents by suction; sometimes used as a form of abortion or postcoital birth control.

Menstruation: The sloughing off of the endometrial lining, usually occurring on a monthly basis from puberty until menopause.

Midwife: A person (often a nurse) who acts as a birth attendant.

Miscarriage: A spontaneous abortion; a pregnancy that terminates on its own prior to birth.

Modeling: The process of learning behavior through the observation of others.

Molluscum contagiosum: A viral STD characterized by smooth, round, shiny lesions, generally appearing on the trunk, on the genitals, or around the anus.

Monogamy: Sexual and romantic fidelity or exclusivity in relationships.

Nocturnal emissions: Also known as wet dreams. Involuntary orgasms experienced mostly by men (but also some women) during sleep.

Nonfetishistic transvestism: A nonparaphilic behavior by persons who cross-dress to relieve the tensions associated with having to maintain the sex role of their gender.

Nongonococcal urethritis (NGU): Urethral inflammation caused by something other than gonorrhea.

Obscenity: That which is legally deemed offensive to "accepted" standards of decency or morality.

Oral contraceptive: Pills that contain synthetic estrogen and/or progesterone that cause a "false pregnancy," thereby preventing ovulation. Used as a contraceptive, they are commonly referred to as "the pill."

Oral sex: Also referred to as fellatio (performed on a male) or cunnilingus (performed on a female). Oral stimulation of the genitals.

Orgasm: An intense sensation that occurs at the climax of sexual excitement that is accompanied by rhythmic muscle contractions and intense pleasure, followed by release of sexual tensions. In men, orgasm is usually accompanied by ejaculation.

Ovaries: The two small organs in the female that produce eggs and hormones; located above and to the sides of the uterus.

Ovulation: The release of an egg from the ovary.

Ovum: A fertilized, mature egg that has the potential to create a human life.

Pap smear: A test for cervical cancer done by examining cells scraped off the cervix during a pelvic examination.

Paraphilia: A sexual behavior characterized by intense recurrent sexual urges and sexually arousing fantasies lasting at least 6 months and involving nonhuman objects or parts of human objects, the suffering or humiliation of oneself or one's partner, or children or other nonconsenting individuals.

Pedophile: An individual who is sexually attracted to prepubescent children.

Pedophilia: A paraphilia characterized by intense, recurring sexual urges or fantasies involving sexual activities with a prepubescent child.

Pelvic inflammatory disease (PID): Infection of the pelvic organs such as the fallopian tubes that often causes scarring, which can then lead to infertility.

Penetration: The insertion of the penis or another object into the vagina or anus for sexual purposes.

Penis: The primary male sexual and reproductive organ through which both urine and semen pass.

Penis pump: A device used on the penis to create a vacuumlike suction in order to achieve the stimulation and temporary enlargement of the penis.

Perversion: An old-fashioned term for a sexual deviation.

Phallus: A penis or an object that is penis-like in shape or form.

Phobic: Irrationally fearful.

PID: Abbreviation for pelvic inflammatory disease.

Pimp: A prostitute's protector and manager.

Pituitary gland: A gland located on the lower surface of the brain that secretes several hormones important to sexual and reproductive functioning.

Plethysmograph: A device used to measure physiological sexual arousal in the male.

Pornography: Sexually oriented material that is not considered acceptable to the viewer; the same material when judged subjectively acceptable is often referred to as "erotica."

Postmenopause: The period of time after a woman's final menstruation.

Postpartum depression: Depression experienced by some women following childbirth.

Premarital sex: Sexual activities, especially sexual intercourse, prior to marriage.

Premature ejaculation: A sexual dysfunction characterized by the inability to control or delay ejaculation as long as desired.

Premenstrual syndrome (PMS): A combination of physical and psychological symptoms (such as depression and irritability) that occurs in some women just prior to menstruation.

Prenatal: Before birth.

Prognosis: A prediction made as to the potential outcome of a disease.

Prophylactic: A drug or device used to prevent disease; commonly used to refer to a condom.

Prostatectomy: The surgical removal of the prostate gland, usually due to prostate cancer.

Prostate gland: A muscular gland encircling the urethra in the male that produces much of the seminal fluid.

Prostatitis: An infection of the prostate that causes an inflammation.

Psychoanalysis: A psychological system developed by Sigmund Freud that traces behavior to unconscious motivations and drives, especially sexual.

Puberty: The stage of human development when the body becomes capable of reproduction.

Pubic hair: Hair on the lower abdomen and genital area that begins to appear at puberty.

Pubococcygeus (PC muscle): The muscle that encircles the vagina/base of the penis and the anus. This muscle can be strengthened with Kegel exercises to aid in childbirth and bladder control, and to increase orgasmic intensity.

Radical mastectomy: A surgical treatment for breast cancer in which the entire breast, as well as the underlying muscle and lymph nodes, are removed.

Radical prostatectomy: Surgical removal of the prostate and nearby areas like the seminal vesicles.

Rape: Forcible sexual intercourse with an individual without that person's consent under actual or threatened force.

Refractory period: The period of time in men immediately following ejaculation, during which further erection or orgasm is not possible; not present in the female's sexual response cycle.

Retarded ejaculation: A sexual dysfunction in which the male is unable to have an orgasm despite sufficient arousal and stimulation.

Retrograde ejaculation: Urine flowing backward into the bladder during orgasm. This may occur in men who have medical conditions such as diabetes, multiple sclerosis, and prostate surgery or may be voluntary as a part of spiritual practices or to achieve the erotic sensation of ejaculating into the bladder.

Retrovirus: A virus capable of altering the normal genetic writing process, causing the host cell to replicate the virus instead of itself. HIV is an example of such a virus.

Rubber: Slang term for condom.

RU-486: An oral, postcoital birth control method that works by causing expulsion of the conceptus.

Scabies: An contagious skin condition that is characterized by an intensely itchy rash and caused by a barely visible mite that burrows under the skin.

Scrotum: The loose sac of skin that contains the testes.

Secondary sex characteristics: The physical characteristics other than the sex organs that distinguish men from women (e.g., breasts, facial hair, etc.).

Semen: The alkaline fluid expelled from the penis during ejaculation, containing fluids combined from several glands as well as sperm.

Seminal fluid: The liquid portion of the male ejaculate.

Seminal vesicles: One of two glands lying on either side of the prostate which secrete much of the fluid in semen.

Sensate focus: An exercise prescribed by sex therapists that concentrates on touch and the giving and receiving of pleasure in a nondemand situation as opposed to focusing on intercourse and achieving orgasm.

Serial monogamy: An increasingly common form of dating and marriage in which a person mates with just one other person at a time but then ends that relationship and forms another.

Sex-change operation: The surgery done on transsexuals to change their anatomy to that of the other gender.

Sex flush: Also referred to as sex glow. A temporary reddening of the skin experienced during and after sexual excitement, caused by increased blood flow.

Sexologist: A certified and/or degreed professional who has been trained in a comprehensive manner in the scientific study of sex. Some may also receive additional training in sex therapy.

Sex therapist: A counselor who is trained in providing therapy to individuals and couples to overcome sexual problems or to enhance their sexuality.

Sexual arousal disorder: Failure to obtain or maintain erection or vaginal lubrication, despite adequate interest and stimulation.

Sexual aversion: Also known as erotophobia. An irrational fear of sexual activity that leads to an avoidance of sexual situations.

Sexual coercion: A broad term referring to any kind of sexual activity that is forced on another person through the use of force, pressure, alcohol and drugs, or authority.

Sexual dysfunction: A difficulty with sexual responding that causes a person subjective distress (e.g., anorgasmia).

Sexual enhancement: Improvement or enrichment of sexual relationships among otherwise healthy, well-functioning individuals.

Sexual harassment: The use of status and/or power for sexual ends.

Sexual identity: A person's sense of one's own sexual orientation, whether heterosexual, homosexual, or bisexual.

Sexually transmitted diseases (STDs): Those illnesses that are communicated to another person via sexual contact.

Sexual orientation: The preference for a sexual partner of a specific sex. For instance: same sex (homosexual), opposite sex (heterosexual), or both sexes (bisexual).

Sexual variation: Sexual behavior that is not part of the norms for a given culture; atypical sexuality.

Sodomy: An ambiguous legal term which, depending on the jurisdiction, refers to so-called unnatural acts such as anal intercourse, sexual relations with animals, or oral sex.

Soft-core: Nonexplicit sexually oriented material.

Sperm: The male reproductive cell.

Spermicide: A substance that acts to kill or immobilize sperm; usually used as a contraceptive.

Spontaneous abortion: The natural expulsion of the conceptus; commonly referred to as miscarriage.

Squeeze technique: A technique used by sex therapists for the treatment of premature ejaculation in which the man or his partner squeezes the erect penis below the glans when he feels the likelihood of ejaculating, thereby reducing the urge.

Start-Stop: A sex therapy technique in which a man learns to control ejaculation by repeatedly ceasing stimulation prior to orgasm.

Statutory rape: Sexual intercourse with a person who is under the legal age of consent.

STD: Acronym for sexually transmitted disease.

Sterilization: A surgical procedure performed to make an individual incapable of reproduction.

Straight: Heterosexual.

Suction abortion: An abortion technique in which the conceptus is removed from the uterus via a suction machine; also called vacuum aspiration.

Syphilis: A sexually transmitted bacterial infection. The primary stage is characterized by chancres; the secondary by rash, body aches, fever, and weight and hair loss; and the tertiary by heart, brain, and spinal cord damage. This disease can be cured with antibiotics.

Systematic desensitization: A behavior therapy technique often useful with sexual phobias in which deep muscle relaxation is used to reduce the anxiety associated with certain situations.

Testes: Two egg-shaped glands within the scrotum that produce sperm and secrete male hormones.

Testicles: The term "testicles" is used to describe the testes and its system of ducts that are within the scrotum.

Testosterone: The major natural androgen, it is secreted by the testes and serves to maintain secondary sex characteristics, sperm production, and sex drive.

Thrush: A yeast infection of the mouth/throat.

Toxic shock syndrome (TSS): A potentially life-threatening condition caused by the Staphylococcus aureus bacterium and linked to the use of superabsorbent tampons.

Transgendered: Someone who identifies as both genders, or is at some point on a continuum between genders, physically and/or psychologically.

Transsexual: An individual whose individual gender identity is different from his or her anatomical sex. They thus feel trapped in the body of the wrong gender.

Transsexualism: The desire to live as a member of a different gender than one's anatomical or genetic gender. Some transsexuals choose to reassign their physical sex through surgery and hormone therapy.

Transvestite: A person who receives sexual gratification and often a relief from anxiety by dressing in the clothing of the opposite sex. Unlike a transsexual, this person usually does not wish to live as a member of the opposite sex or change their gender. The term is usually applied to heterosexual men.

Transvestism: Dressing in the clothing of the other gender.

Trichomoniasis: An inflammation of the vagina characterized by a whitish discharge, caused by the Trichomonas vaginalis parasite. Often abbreviated as trich.

Tubal ligation: Sometimes referred to as sterilization. A medical procedure in which the fallopian tubes are cut, cauterized, and/or blocked to prevent pregnancy.

Tubal pregnancy: An ectopic pregnancy in which the embryo is implanted in the woman's fallopian tube.

Urethra: The tube through which urine passes out of the body; in males, it is also the tube through which semen is discharged.

Urologist: A doctor who specializes in diseases of the male sex organs and in diseases of the urinary organs in both men and women.

Uterine cycle: Another term for menstrual cycle.

Uterus: Also known as the womb. A hollow, muscular organ in women in which a fertilized egg can embed itself and develop into a fetus.

Vacuum aspiration: The preferred method of abortion during the first trimester. The cervix is dilated and the contents of the uterus are removed through a tubular suction device.

Vagina: The inner canal that has the potential to expand and contract during penetrative sex and childbirth.

Vaginismus: A sexual dysfunction characterized by strong, involuntary muscle spasms around the vaginal entrance, preventing the insertion of a penis.

Vaginitis: Inflammation, infection, or chemical irritation of the vagina.

Vas deferens: A pair of tubular structures that carry spermatozoa from the testes.

Vasectomy: Sometimes referred to as sterilization. Surgical procedure on men that consists of the cutting, tying, or cauterizing of the vas deferens in order to prevent transfer of sperm into seminal fluid, and therefore prevent pregnancy.

Vasocongestion: An accumulation of blood in the genital region (causing swelling or erection) due to sexual excitation.

Venereal disease: A disease transmitted primarily by sexual contact.

Virginity: The state of never having had sexual intercourse.

Voyeurism: A sexual variation in which a person derives sexual pleasure from watching others nude or having sexual intercourse (often without their knowledge).

Vulva: The external female sex organs, consisting of the mons, labia, and clitoris.

Wet dream: Slang term for nocturnal emission.

Withdrawal: A highly risky method of birth control in which the penis is removed from the vagina prior to ejaculation.

Yeast infection: A bacterial infection, usually of the vagina. Can be transmitted sexually.

Zygote: The single cell created by the penetration of the egg by the sperm.

Zygote intrafallopian transfer (ZIFT): A treatment for infertility by which a woman's eggs are fertilized in vitro, and then the zygote is placed directly into the fallopian tube.

Index

References in **bold face** can be found in resource or bibliography sections.